PRIVATE SCHOOLS IN TEN COUNTRIES

PRIVATE SCHOOLS IN TEN COUNTRIES

Policy and Practice

Edited by
GEOFFREY WALFORD

R
ROUTLEDGE
London and New York

First published 1989
by Routledge
11 New Fetter Lane, London EC4P 4EE
29 West 35th Street, New York, NY 10001

© 1989 Geoffrey Walford (in the editorial material and his own
contributions). Chapters 1, 3, 4, 5, 6, 7, and 9 © Routledge.
Chapter 8 © 1984 by Comparative and International Education Society.

Printed and bound in Great Britain by
Mackays of Chatham PLC, Chatham, Kent

British Library Cataloguing in Publication Data

Private Schools in ten countries: policy and practice.
  1. Independent schools
  I. Walford, Geoffrey
  371′.02

ISBN 0 415 03464 7

CONTENTS

vi

CONTRIBUTORS

John Bergen is Professor Emeritus of Educational Administration at the University of Alberta, Edmonton, Canada. Before joining the Faculty of Education in 1965, he had many years of experience as a teacher and school principal. He has published several papers on private school issues and on the governance of public education, with particular attention to councils of ministers of education in federal countries.

Peter W. Cookson Jr. teaches at the University of Massachusetts and Queens College. He has studied private education in the United States for more than a decade and has taught in both public and private schools. He is the joint author (with Caroline Hodges Persell) of Preparing for Power: America's Elite Boarding Schools (Basic Books, 1985) and has published widely in scholarly journals and popular magazines. He continues to be interested in the relationship between education and social stratification and is currently undertaking an international analysis of class background and educational mobility.

Janice Dudley is a post-graduate student and research assistant in the School of Education at Murdoch University, Western Australia.

Tony Edwards is Professor of Education and Head of Department at the University of Newcastle-upon-Tyne, UK. His books include Investigating Classroom Talk (Falmer, 1987) (with D.P.G. Westgate), The Language of Teaching (Heinemann, 1978) (with V. Furlong), and The State and Private Education: An Evaluation of the Assisted Places Scheme (Falmer, forthcoming) (with Geoff Whitty and John Fitz).

John Fitz is currently a lecturer at the Department of Education, Bristol Polytechnic, UK. Prior to this he had several years teaching at the Open University and worked with Tony Edwards and Geoff Whitty on an evaluation of the Assisted Places Scheme. He has written several articles and is co-author of The State and Private Education: An Evaluation of the Assisted Places Scheme (Falmer, forthcoming).

Contributors

Dr Brian Holmes is Emeritus Professor of Comparative Education at the University of London, UK. He has published several books on comparative education and numerous articles in journals all over the world. He has acted as a consultant to: UNESCO; the International Bureau of Education in Geneva; OECD; and several foreign ministries. He helped found the Comparative Education Society in Europe, the British International and Comparative Education Society, and the World Council of Comparative Education Societies. He first visited Japan some 20 years ago when he was invited to participate in a comparative research project on moral education. The chapter in this volume was prepared while he was in Japan as a Senior Visiting Fellow of the Japan Society for the Promotion of Science in 1987/88.

Estelle James is Professor of Economics at the State University of New York, Stony Brook. She previously held the Chair at the Economics Department and was Provost of Social and Behavioral Sciences at Stony Brook. She has co-authored three books: Hoffa and the Teamsters: A Study in Union Power, The Nonprofit Enterprise in Market Economies (Harwood Academic Publishers, 1986) and Public Policy and Private Education in Japan (Macmillan, 1988) and has edited a volume on The Nonprofit Sector in International Perspective. She has also written numerous articles on the economics of education, the economics of non-profit organizations, and other topics in applied welfare theory.

Dr Cornelia Mattern studied economics of education, pedagogics, and sociology at the Technical University of Berlin. She was Research Associate at the Institute of Educational Research in Berlin (1972-6), and Assistant at the College of Education in Berlin in the Faculty of Economics and Operations Research (1976-80). Since 1980, she has been a lecturer at the University of Distance Education in Hagen in the Faculty of Vocational and Economic Education. Her main research topics are: economics of education (cost and financing), educational planning, and private schools. Her books include: Bildungsfinananzierung (Diesterweg, 1979); Einführung in die ökonomische Theorie von Bildung, Arbeit und Produktion (with G. Weisshuhn) (Diesterweg, 1980); and Praktisches Lernen in Hiberniapädagogik (editor, with F. Edding and P. Schneider) (Klett, 1985).

Don Smart is Associate Professor in Politics of Education at Murdoch University, Western Australia. He has written widely on private education and his books include Federal Aid to Australian Schools (University of Queensland Press, 1978). Most recently he co-edited Educational Policy in Australia and America: Comparative Perspectivecs (Falmer, 1987).

Dr Richard Teese is a lecturer in education at the University of Melbourne, Australia. He has published papers on private schooling in Australia and France, and has written a statistical monograph on education and training in these two countries. His main research has been into long-term, regional and gender differences in school completion rates in Australia, and more recently into the origins and impact of private school success. He was a visiting scholar in the Centre de Sociologie Européenne in Paris in 1984, and returned there in 1987 to do comparative research.

Geoffrey Walford is a lecturer in sociology and education management at the Business School, Aston University, Birmingham, UK. He has researched and published widely on private education, higher education, and research methods. He is author of Life in Public Schools (Methuen, 1986) and Restructuring Universities: Politics and Power in the Management of Change (Croom Helm, 1987); and editor of British Public Schools: Policy and Practice (Falmer, 1984) and Doing Sociology of Education (Falmer, 1987). He was a visiting research fellow at the Centre for Educational Sociology, University of Edinburgh, in 1986.

Dr Manfred Weiss studied business administration and economics at the University of Frankfurt. He is a Research Associate in the Department of Economics of Education at the German Institute for International Educational Research and part-time lecturer in the Faculty of Educational Organization, Administration and Policy. Main research topics: economics of education (cost, financing, and efficiency), educational planning, research on school effectiveness, and private education. His books include: Effizienz im Bildungswesen (Beltz, 1975); Effizienzforschung im Bildungsbereich (Duncker and Humblot, 1982); Klassengrösse: Je kleiner desto besser? (with K. Ingenkamp) (Beltz, 1985); and Perspektiven des Bildungswesens in der Bundesrepublik Deutschland (with H Weishaupt, H. v. Recum

Contributors

and R. Haug) (Nomos, 1988).

Geoff Whitty is Professor and Head of the Department of Education, Bristol Polytechnic, UK. Prior to this, he was at the University of Bath, and King's College, University of London. He was co-editor (with Michael F.D. Young) of Society, State and Schooling (Falmer, 1977), and Explorations in the Politics of School Knowledge (Nafferton, 1976); author of Sociology and School Knowledge: Curriculum theory, research and politics (Methuen, 1985); and co-author (with Tony Edwards and John Fitz) of The State and Private Education: An Evaluation of the Assisted Places Scheme (Falmer, forthcoming).

TABLES

FIGURES

INTRODUCTION

PRIVATE SCHOOLS POLICY AND PRACTICE IN COMPARATIVE PERSPECTIVE

Geoffrey Walford

Politicians and policy-makers tend to hold very firm opinions about private schools. They are either 'for' or 'against' with little room for compromise, and political debate on the private schools has often been conducted in these simplistic terms. Polemic is more common than informed argument. On the one side are seen the strong supporters of private education, who believe that the freedom to be able to choose the kind of education that parents want for their children is one of the basic rights of a democratic society. They believe that the existence of the private sector encourages a healthy diversity of provision of education, and competition in the market-place will ensure that the quality of education provided remains high. They claim that parents should be able to spend their money on schooling for their children in exactly the same way that they spend money on holidays, homes or cars.

In contrast, there are those who are equally strongly 'against' private schools, arguing that they exacerbate inequalities of class, race and gender and lead to a more socially divided society. Education is seen not as a private consumer good, but as a public good, and as a means by which the society's social cohesion and social aims are achieved. It is believed that those parents who are wealthy should not be able to purchase an unfair advantage for their children, but that all children in the society should be given equality of opportunity to succeed.

These two diametrically opposite views may appear to be greatly over-simplified caricatures, but an analysis of government policy on private schools shows that the actions of political parties often seem to have been justified by such uncomplicated and uncritical understandings. Discussion about private schools has tended to be polarized, and at the

1

level of polemic and propaganda, leaving little room for rational analysis. Recent policy changes within the United Kingdom provide a good example of this. In 1979 in England and Wales, 6.1 per cent of all pupils were in private schools. The General Election of that year brought to power a Conservative government concerned to reduce public spending and encourage private enterprise in all spheres. In education, the government's desire to support the then somewhat ailing private school system was such that new public spending was allocated to an Assisted Places Scheme at a time when cuts were being made to the state-maintained sector. This scheme was designed to 'give able children a wider range of educational opportunity' by giving help with tuition fees at private schools to 'parents who could not otherwise afford them' (DES, 1985).

> The scheme was justified in terms of an extension of parental choice, a restoration of academic opportunities to children who would not be fully 'stretched' in schools coping with the full range of ability, and a protection for both those individuals and the nation's supply of talent against the levelling down effects attributed to comprehensive reorganisation.
>
> (Edwards et al., 1985)

In devising and financing the scheme, the government was thus advertising that it thought private sector schools were superior to, and more desirable than, many of those schools for which it was itself ultimately responsible (Walford, 1987).

The development of the Assisted Places Scheme is the clearest case, but it is only one example of the financial and ideological support for the private sector that has been evident since 1979. After the 1987 General Election, the degree of support has deepened, with a small extension to the Assisted Places Scheme and government proposals for new forms of private schooling. At the same time, the state-maintained sector has become increasingly under-funded in terms of its needs, and the morale of teachers in such schools is suffering, as they have had their negotiating rights removed at the end of a long and bitter dispute over pay and conditions of service. By 1988 some 7.0 per cent of pupils were in private schools.

As the British Conservative government has increased its commitment to private education, so the Labour Party in opposition has become more solidly opposed. When it was last in power, from 1974 to 1979, government funding to the semi-private direct-grant schools was gradually phased out, but there was a failure to remove any of the other government subsidies to the private schools derived from their charitable status. Now, however, if returned to power, the Labour Party is pledged to cut immediately the Assisted Places Scheme and to remove all government subsidies to private schools as quickly as is practical. The strength of feeling and depth of polarization on the issue is such that private schools are seen by the Labour Party as being almost inherently evil.

Many more details of the English and Welsh case are given in the first chapter of this book, but even the very brief outline given above makes it clear that discussion of private schools and related decision-making has often been conducted in very simple terms, with little consideration of the complexities involved. In Great Britain, private schools and privatization have become a major area of political conflict, as has also occured in several of the other major industrial nations, yet there has been little attempt to gather or analyse empirical data on private schools within Great Britain and even less attempt to examine the nature and role of private education in other countries. Debate has been characterized by subjective impressions, isolationism and insularity.

One of the major aims of this book is to provide information which will allow educationalists, politicians, policy-makers, and members of the public to look beyond the narrow confines of their own country and consider the variety of ways in which education can be provided and funded. The comparative study of education systems and education policy provides a 'check on parochialism in thinking about policy and theory' (Wirt, 1987), and is of vital importance in the search for general principles.

One of the most obvious aspects about the way in which educational systems differ is that there is a great diversity in the extent of private provision. Different countries have made very different choices about the way in which their governments control, provide, and finance education, so that the size of the private sector at primary and secondary levels varies from zero in some countries to 100 per cent in others. The range is somewhat smaller for the major industrial countries, but is still considerable. Within the ten countries considered in this book, for example, the range is from just 4 per cent of pupils in private schools in Scotland to over 70 per cent in The Netherlands. Both of these countries, incidentally, are ones which have extensive public welfare provision. Such a wide variation in the proportion of pupils in private schools should immediately cause us to question our assumptions about the inevitability of one particular way of funding and organizing educational services. But to make such simple statistical comparisons is just the start of a process of understanding. As the following chapters make clear, these figures have to be understood within a wider consideration of each society's political, social and economic history. Quite simply, the term 'private education' has a somewhat different meaning in each of the countries discussed.

This should not be seen as a problem for the comparative study of private schools, but as an important part of coming to an understanding of exactly how each educational system operates. The differences in meanings stem directly from the different assumptions about educational provision which are held in each country, and it is these assumptions which can be challenged and explored by way of a comparative perspective.

The relationship between ideology and terminology is well illustrated by the nomenclature used by various groups in Great Britain. The major private schools for many years were designated as 'public schools', which was a source of confusion to both the British and others, but a source of pride to the schools themselves and an indicator of their social exclusivity. However, during the late 1960s and early 1970s, when the schools felt under some attack, they succesfully attempted to rid themselves of the associations of elitism and privilege which had been linked with the term 'public school' and opted for the term 'independent' instead.

This new term was designed to suggest liberty and individual enterprise. The change of title was achieved through the establishment of the Independent Schools Information Service which brought together a wide range of private schools under the same umbrella. The full range of 'independent' schools were to be seen as providing a variety of different educational facilities according to academic, social and religious needs and, of course, according to ability to pay. However, while the schools themselves now wish to be considered as 'independent', their critics would prefer terms such as 'fee-paying' or 'commercial'. The term 'non-public' still has a strange ring to it in Britain, while 'private' and 'privatization' have very different associations depending on political orientations.

This variety of terms used to designate the private sector is in large part a reflection of differing ideologies, but is also a result of lack of homogeneity within the system. Within any country's private educational sector there is a considerable diversity of schools in terms of quality, exclusiveness, and degree of direct and indirect state support received. While some schools have excellent academic facilities and expect all pupils to enter higher education, others are more concerned with presenting one particular world view or religious belief system to pupils, and may be sub-standard in more usual terms.

Comparative study shows that the private sector cannot be considered in isolation from the state-maintained public system. In practice, even the line drawn between the two sectors is often permeable, as many private schools receive direct and/or indirect funding from the state. This is to be expected, as, in most countries, education was first provided by the churches and other philanthropic groups - the state only becoming involved much later in providing schools. The arrangements that were made to integrate these new state schools with those already existing, and the subsequent changes in the relationship between them, are of vital importance in understanding private schools now.

In Great Britain the majority of religious schools, both Church of England and Roman Catholic, were eventually incorporated within the state-maintained sector. Although they have a special status as voluntary-aided or voluntary-controlled schools, these religious schools are considered by all to be part of the maintained sector of schooling and the vast majority of the funding is provided by the state. This historical difference has meant that the debate about private education in Britain has usually been conducted in terms of elitism, whereas in most other countries, the majority of private schools have been usually associated with promoting or maintaining religious diversity, and the concern has been with the relationship between the state and denominational religious education. Elite schools have existed, but they have been in the minority.

Even this brief sketch makes it clear that the comparative study of private education is unlikely to lead to immediately transferable 'solutions' to perceived problems. But such a realization is itself important, and it does not mean that there are no lessons to be learnt. Careful study of the diversity of educational systems can provide a powerful challenge to our assumptions, and act as a cure for political and educational myopia.

The chapters

The countries considered in this volume have been selected to illustrate some of the diversity of ways in which school systems are funded and organized. However, in order to be able to make meaningful comparisons, all of the countries chosen are major western industrial societies. Great Britain consists of three separate countries. England and Wales, which are subject to the same legal and educational system, have been discussed together in one chapter, but Scotland, which has a different educational and legal system has been treated in a separate chapter. This means that the book considers ten countries in nine chapters.

The authors of each chapter are experts in their field who have previously conducted research and written about the country under study. They draw upon their own work and review the work of others to produce accounts which have three aspects. First, each chapter gives an outline of the nature and extent of private schooling in the country under discussion. This description is set in an historic, economic, and social context, and, where relevant, looks especially at the changes that have occurred in the last 5-10 years. Next, the chapters describe and discuss any recent changes in government policy towards the private sector. These policy changes may be directly aimed at the schools or be the indirect results of policies primarily aimed at other aspects of the government's responsibilities. The authors attempt to assess how these changes in policy have affected the schools. Finally, each chapter gathers together available evidence on the relationship between attendance at private schools and the maintenance or reproduction of inequalities in society. The evidence here is varied in nature, and it is clear that for most of the countries, more empirical data is necessary before definitive conclusions can be drawn.

There is considerable variety in the ways in which the authors have tackled their task, and a diversity in the style of argument and presentation of the data. Part of this is due to the fact that while most of the authors are writing about their own countries, and thus giving an insider's view, others are non-natives and are able to give the rather different insights available to the outsider. The authors also do not all hold to one particular ideological viewpoint on private schools. Readers should be aware of these differences in viewpoint, and take them into consideration in drawing their own conclusions and analyses. As a whole, the book presents a unique and up-to-date account of the nature and role of private education in modern industrial society.

References

Department of Education and Science (1985) Assisted Places at Independent schools: a brief guide for parents, London: DES.

Edwards, T., Fitz, J., and Whitty, G. (1985) 'Private schools and public funding: a comparison of recent policies in England and Australia', Comparative Education 21 (1), 29-45.

Walford, G. (1987) 'How dependent is the independent sector?', Oxford Review of Education 13 (3), 275-96.

Wirt, F.M. (1987) 'National Australia-United States education: a commentary', in W.L. Boyd and D. Smart (eds) Educational Policy in Australia and America: Comparative Perspectives, Lewes: Falmer.

CHAPTER 1

ENGLAND AND WALES: THE ROLE OF THE PRIVATE SECTOR

Geoff Whitty, Tony Edwards and John Fitz

Private education attracts about half a million children of school age in England and Wales, or about 6.4 per cent of the school population. The sector is much smaller than in most industrial countries, much more selective both academically and socially, and much more closely associated with recruitment to occupational elites. It is hardly associated at all with promoting or maintaining religious and cultural diversity, whereas the debate about private schooling in other countries is often dominated by relationships between church and state, and the defence of the private sector is largely a defence of the right of parents to educate their children within a particular religious tradition (Mason, 1983; Praetz, 1983). Although many English public schools were religious foundations and continue to include a strong Christian tradition among their qualities, most church schools have been incorporated within the state system as a result of the so-called 'historic compromises' of 1870, 1902, and 1944. These are the voluntary-aided and voluntary-controlled schools which contain about 17 per cent of secondary pupils. In Australia, on the other hand, all church schools are in a non-government sector which caters for just over a quarter of the school population - about the same proportion as are in English independent and voluntary schools taken together - and pluralist arguments are widely used in its defence. An alliance has developed there between a Catholic hierarchy, anxious to avoid state aid being debated as a sectarian issue, and representatives of elite independent schools (catering as in England for about 6 per cent of secondary pupils), anxious to avoid being isolated as 'bastions of privilege' (Edwards et al., 1985). It is exactly that kind of isolation of an 'elite sector' which has dominated debate about the private sector in England, both politically and sociologically.

In this chapter, we describe the structure of the private sector and its social selectiveness. We then describe recent changes in government policy towards it, in the context of increasingly powerful support for the privatizing of educational provision. Before proceeding, we need to clarify how these schools are to be labelled. We have used 'private' initially because it is the term included in the title of this collection. The private sector itself prefers the term 'independent'. Bodies like the Independent Schools' Information Service (ISIS) consciously strove for a change of name in the 1970s because 'independence' had more positive connotations, and made it easier to advance the political arguments against state monopoly and in favour of parental freedom (Howarth, 1972; ISIS, 1974). It is arguable that the Thatcher government has since rehabilitated the term 'private' by associating it not with privilege but with greater choice, efficiency, and innovation - although 'independence' is also used to contrast favourably with faceless, state-run bureaucratic institutions (Seldon, 1981). Critics wanting to emphasize fee-controlled access prefer such terms as 'fee-paying' or 'commercial' as well as 'private' (Halsey, 1981; Halsey et al., 1984), and may well argue the illogicality of applying 'independent' to schools (especially those with charitable status) which are substantially subsidized both directly and indirectly from public funds to the tune of at least £500m per year (Edwards et al., 1985; Pring, 1986, 1987; Walford, 1987). From this ideologically-loaded list of terms, we shall describe the schools as 'independent' and the sector as 'private' - a compromise which draws attention both to the organizational autonomy of the schools and the financially-selective character of most of their intake. Though it is less used today than in the past, we shall also continue to use the traditional but rather confusing term 'public schools' to describe those independent schools which comprise the elite segment of the private sector and which, as we shall see later, were the object of the Public Schools Commission's first inquiry in 1965-8.

The scope and function of the private sector

The proportion of children attending independent schools increases markedly in the later stages of schooling. Just over 6 per cent of 9-year-olds and about 8 per cent of 14-year-olds are privately educated, compared with 18 per cent of sixth formers in school, while more than a quarter of school leavers with the three passes at GCE Advanced-level (which constitute the main passport to higher education and to high-status occupations) come from the private sector (Halsey et al., 1984; DES 1987a; Welsh Office, 1986). These figures are slightly lower than in the immediate post-war period, but noticeably higher than when the Wilson government established the Public Schools Commission in 1965. At that time, the sector accounted for only 5 per cent of 14-year-olds and 14 per cent of 17-year-olds (compared with 8 per cent and 22 per cent in 1946), and there were still those in the Labour Party who were hopeful that it might in time conveniently wither away. Its declining share of the market, a consequence of minor schools closing rather than of falling rolls in the market-leaders, was attributed to the success of maintained grammar schools in preparing their pupils to compete for university places (including those at Oxford and Cambridge) and for high-status jobs. The increase over the past 20 years partly reflects a middle-class flight from a public sector which had lost the 'attractions' of academically-selective schools, as virtually all local education aurhorities (LEAs) reorganized their secondary schools on comprehensive lines. However, it was reinforced by the Labour government's decision in the mid-1970s to end the direct-grant arrangements which had hitherto allowed some schools to be directly funded by central government and thus independent of LEAs - a decision which led most of those 'semi-independent' schools to enter the 'fully independent' sector. In the 1980s the trend has been for independent schools to experience a small increase in their actual intakes, but a larger increase in their share of the market as a result of falling rolls in state secondary schools. Thus the 1988 ISIS census showed the fifth successive rise in pupil numbers and the second largest increase.

Within England and Wales, the overall figures hide some important variations. There is an uneven distribution of independent schools as a consequence of decisions made long ago by philanthropic individuals and merchant companies to found 'free' grammar schools, and of more recent (mainly Victorian) decisions to transform some of them into boarding schools with national appeal or to found new schools to socialize the children of the new industrial ruling class. The outcome is a concentration of independent grammar schools in some of the great trading cities (London, Bristol, Liverpool, and Manchester), and of boarding schools in the affluent and densely populated south-east of England (Bamford, 1974).

Furthermore, it is important to emphasize how internally differentiated the private sector is, especially as discussion of it has been so largely dominated by the 'public schools'. As we stated earlier, the term 'public schools' is reserved for the elite segment of the private sector. Originally applied to old foundations endowed to provide for 'poor scholars', they had become the preserve of the ruling elite by the mid-nineteenth century, offering boarding education and providing the context within which the sons of the new industrial ruling class were socialized into the professions and the style and manners of the gentry. The core of the elite segment identified by the Taunton Commission in 1867, comprised Eton, Harrow, Westminster, Winchester, Charterhouse, Rugby, and Shrewsbury. Even these schools were very differently ranked in their late Victorian 'golden age' (Honey, 1977), and the 'Eton' and 'Rugby' groups, (which Walford, 1986, still identifies as the core of the segment) contain only some 0.5 per cent of the 13-16 age group. However, the term 'public schools' has subsequently become more loosely applied to all fee-paying schools in membership of the Headmasters' Conference (HMC) or the Governing Bodies of Public Schools Association (GBA) and, in the case of girls schools, the Girls' Schools Association (GSA) and the Governing Bodies of Girls' Schools Association (GBGSA). This definition now includes virtually all the ex-direct-grant schools, thus making this segment (which altogether attracts 3 per cent of the total school population) highly selective academically as well as socially.

We noted earlier the clustering of boarding schools in the southern counties, and the day-school members of the Headmasters' Conference at times still see the 'Thames Valley' boarding schools as representing the centre of gravity within that prestigious organization, and constituting a power bloc from which most Conference chairmen have been drawn (although, for example, the chairman for 1987-8 was the headmaster of Bradford Grammar School - a day school formerly on the direct-grant list). Traditionally, the 'public schools' have been boys' schools, the few girls' boarding schools being markedly less prestigious. While there are almost as many girls in the private sector as a

11

whole, about 20 per cent of privately-educated pupils have boarding places and 65 per cent of these are for boys. A declining demand for boarding education has brought a decided shift towards co-education in these schools, something which previously was confined largely to the sector's 'progressive' wing (to schools like Dartington Hall and Bedales). It is an accelerating trend in boys' public schools, especially at the sixth-form stage (Walford, 1986: 150-4), and some schools like Clifton are now admitting girls at the 'common entrance' age of 13. These developments have not been welcomed by headmistresses, who feel that, by 'poaching' able girls, the boys' schools are both filling their own places and enhancing their academic reputation (GSA, 1987). More generally, the ISIS surveys show a significant shift from boarding places to day places, and from full to weekly boarding. Recruiting pupils from overseas countries has helped to fill some otherwise vacant places, but the overall decline has also enhanced the importance to this part of the private sector of government-financed places available to military personnel and to civil servants of certain grades on overseas postings (Walford, 1987).

The academic distinctiveness of the private sector owes most to such leading day schools as St. Paul's and Dulwich College, and to those former direct-grant grammar schools which have chosen to become 'fully' independent. The 176 English direct-grant schools which had to choose in the mid-1970s between receiving continued support from public funds and remaining academically selective were a mixed category. Some of them - like Manchester Grammar School, North London Collegiate School, and the King Edward Schools in Birmingham - were the most academically selective grammar schools in the country, drawing their pupils from a wide geographical area and regularly renewing their reputation for academic excellence. There were also many much smaller, predominantly boarding schools with relatively high proportions of fee-payers (e.g. Oakham and Stamford Schools), local grammar schools (e.g. Bromley Grammar and Kingston Grammar) differentiated only by historical accident from their maintained-sector equivalents, and Catholic schools which might recruit widely for sectarian reasons, but which also had a very high proportion of free places and were usually among the least selective grammar schools both academically and socially. In the main, it was the more academic schools which chose 'full' independence in 1976. The trend towards co-education has been less apparent here, and there are as many girls' as boys' schools in this part of the private sector. Some former voluntary grammar schools have also joined the private sector since the early 1970s, relinquishing LEA support and control in order to resist becoming academically comprehensive. Indeed, as we found from many parental interviews during our investigation of the assisted-places scheme, many former direct-grant schools are seen primarily as the only surviving grammar schools, their 'independence' being hardly noted at all as a strong attraction (Fitz et al., 1986).

Nevertheless, almost half the pupils being privately educated are in more obviously independent secondary schools (often called 'colleges' when not claiming to be 'grammar schools') with at best a local reputation and often offering the social protection of fee-paying without much academic quality, or in independent primary schools dominated by the preparatory schools which prepare pupils at age 13 for the Common Entrance Examination to 'public schools', or at 11-13 for entry to the leading independent grammar schools (Leinster-Mackay, 1984). Preoccupation with 'elite formation' has usually drawn attention away from these other parts of the private sector - especially from the 20 per cent of ISIS members and the 44 per cent of all independent schools which did not have charitable status in 1985, most of them being privately owned and run for profit, many of them benefiting unjustifiably from the 'halo effects' thrown over the whole private sector by its market leaders.

Sociologically and politically, debate about the private sector in England has centred on those 'leading schools' because of their apparent importance in what is described from different perspectives as elite recruitment or class reproduction. It has therefore focused largely on the 'remarkable social homogeneity' which many of those schools have displayed and retained. Looking only at the boys' schools which have dominated the political debate, Halsey et al. (1980: 53) demonstrated an increasing social selectiveness as one moved up the hierarchy of types of school, using their own categorization of occupations - as 'service class' (professionals, administrators, managers, and substantial proprietors), 'intermediate class' (clerical, sales and other rank-and-file service workers, self-employed, and the 'artistocracy' of labour), or 'working-class'.

It can be seen from Table 1.1 that there is a virtual absence of children from manual backgrounds in Headmasters' Conference schools, and that their significant

13

Table 1.1   School composition by social class

Fathers' class	Comprehensive	Grammar	Non-HMC Independent	Direct-grant	HMC Independent
Service	13.6	27.7	47.7	50.4	66.7
Intermediate	26.3	35.7	41.1	33.6	27.0
Working	60.2	36.5	11.2	16.0	6.3

Source: Halsey et al., 1980: 53.

under-representation throughout the private sector included the direct-grant schools which claimed to be a significant route of social mobility for bright children from working class backgrounds. The Public Schools Commission, using a rather different system of classifying both schools and occupations, produced figures suggesting that over 90 per cent of children in non-direct-grant public schools had fathers in professional and managerial jobs and only 1 per cent in semi-skilled or unskilled manual occupations (PSC, 1968: vol. 2, table 10). In the direct grant schools, the figures were 60 per cent and 7 per cent respectively (PSC, 1970: vol. 1, 51-2). A study of HMC schools commissioned by the Conference itself showed the leading direct-grant schools to be as socially selective as the 'public' boarding schools (Kalton, 1966: 35). Nearly two decades later, a study of the 'public schools' by Irene Fox (1985) reported very little change, with 69 per cent of her sample in Class 1 and children of manual workers almost entirely absent.

As in other studies concerned with elite recruitment, Fox's investigation was limited to boys' schools. Girls' independent schools are seen as having a much weaker influence on their pupils' 'life-chances'. They have consistently claimed to recruit more widely, and to be less educationally insulated because a much higher proportion of their teachers and pupils have some experience of maintained schools (Kamm, 1971; Howarth, 1985). Whether this view can be sustained today is at least questionable. Overall, however, it is evident that the freedom of choice regularly cited in defence of independent schools is a freedom largely reserved for those with well above average incomes, the main surviving modification of the cash-nexus being the Assisted Places Scheme which we refer to later. In 1982-3, for example, when average annual earnings for adult males were £7,878, average boarding fees in HMC schools were £3,675 (Griggs, 1985: 29-31). Nor, in such a labour-intensive industry, is the social hierarchy of schools reflected in difference in fees. In 1983, tuition fees at Clifton, Malvern, Repton, Wellington, and Stowe were all around £3,000, as they also were at Carmel College, Canford, Denstone and the Leys School. They were approximately half that figure at most of the leading independent day schools, including all the Girls' Public Day School Trust (GPDST) schools for girls. But fees have been rising much faster than the general rate of inflation: in 1987-8 they rose by 11 per cent, some 4 per cent above the rise in average earnings (ISIS, 1988).

It is not merely the social selectiveness of independent schools that is interesting sociologically and politically, though this clearly has consequences for the character of the education they offer. There is also the extent to which they have been regarded, in the words of Tony Crosland, as 'the greatest single cause of stratification and class consciousness in Britain' and 'the strongest remaining bastion of class privilege' (Crosland, 1956: 191 and 1962). That view was repeated in the Labour Party's (1980) discussion document on 'private schools', in which they were described as the main means of transmitting economic status and social position because recruitment to them was so strongly class-based, and because attendance at them was 'almost a basic requirement for entry to the ruling elite'. While complex questions arise about how far they confer elite status or merely confirm it, study after study has demonstrated what a stranglehold the 'leading' schools have on recruitment to elite occupations and provided evidence suggesting a significant role in social and cultural reproduction. Boyd's study of Elites and their Education (1973) showed that, although the significance of a public school background had declined in some prestigious occupations since the Second World War, it actually seemed to have increased in others (see Table 1.2).

Table 1.2 Public school attendance of six elite groups (in percentages)

	1939	1950	1960	1971
Civil Service (Under-secretaries and above)	85	59	65	62
Judiciary (High Court judges and above)	80	85	83	80
Ambassadors (Heads of embassies and legations)	74	73	83	83
Army (Major-Generals and above)	64	71	83	86
Clearing Banks (Directors)	68	76	73	80
Church of England Clergy (Bishops and above)	71	75	69	67

Source: Boyd, D. (1973) Elites and their Education, Slough: NFER.

More recent figures complied by Reid (1986) (see Table 1.3) for the 1980s, do not show the substantial downward trend that many would have predicted. As Reid observes, the continuing high percentages are staggering if one bears in mind the very small percentage of the whole population that attended these schools.

Table 1.3   Public school and Oxbridge holders of elite positions in the 1980s (in percentages)

	Public School	Oxbridge
The establishment		
Civil Service (under-secretaries and above)	50	61
High Court and appeal judges	83	83
Law lords	89	89
Church of England bishops	59	71
Ambassadors	69	82
Commerce and industry		
Directors of major life insurance companies	92	50
Directors of clearing banks	70	47
Chairmen of clearing banks	83	67
Directors of the Bank of England	78	89
Chairmen of merchant banks	88	59
Directors of 40 major industrial firms	66	40

Source: Reid, I. (1986) The Sociology of the School and Education, London: Fontana.

The other thing that is evident from the figures in Table 1.3 is the continuing close and disproportionate link with Oxbridge, which is itself a major route into these elite occupations. As can be seen from Table 1.4 the public schools are significantly more highly represented at Oxbridge than in universities as a whole:

Table 1.4 Entrants to Oxbridge and to all universities (in percentages)

	From LEA schools	From independent schools
Oxbridge	48	52
Other universities	75	25

Source: Reid, I. (1986) The Sociology of the School and Education, London: Fontana

    The general conclusion to be drawn from this evidence is that although state grammar schools may have contributed to an increase in mobility into what the Scottish Mobility Survey (Payne, 1977) calls the 'lieutenant class', a contribution difficult to assess because changes in the labour market have multiplied such 'junior officer' positions, the highly socially-selective public schools have remained effective gatekeepers for entry into the really top jobs in English society. It has also been argued that the character of the education traditionally offered, with its arts-slant and rigid hierarchies, has biased its recipients against leadership roles in industry and powerfully reinforces an 'anti-industrial spirit' which has contributed to Britain's economic decline (Wiener, 1981; Barnett, 1986).

    Traditionally, the 'public schools question' has been defined in the terms outlined in the previous section - the disproportionate hold of some schools over recruitment to elite positions and the social exclusiveness of many more. Until the 1960s, public debate focused mainly on whether that social exclusiveness could be ameliorated. As long as the debate was muted and the schools were in no immediate danger, they received somewhat lukewarm and inconsistent support from the Conservative Party. Nor is it accurate to claim that the Labour Party 'consistently objected to their presence' (Labour Party, 1980: 5). Throughout the period 1945-60, their presence was more of a background irritation, as is evident in the absence of any explicit policy statements on public schools in six successive election manifestos 1945-64 (Craig, 1982). The most sustained attempt to translate educational and political objections into public policy was embodied in the proceedings of the

Public Schools Commission, and it is to the context and nature of its deliberations that we now turn.

The Public Schools Commission (PSC) 1965-70

When the Labour Government appointed this Commission in 1965 to 'advise on the best way' of integrating the 'public' boarding schools 'with the state system', difficult questions about the co-existence of public and private sectors were brought to the surface. Did the independent schools provide necessary alternatives to public provision, complement it, compete with it, or undermine it? To their defenders, institutional independence was an essential defence against state monopoly, and for that reason alone was not to be tampered with. To some of their critics, abolition was the only effective remedy for the privileges they perpetuated. However, the dominant view, held by some within the private sector was well as by outsiders (e.g. Dancy, 1963: 13-14, 35-6), was that, while their abolition was neither fair nor feasible, the schools were too socially exclusive for their own or the country's good; they should broaden their intakes by broadening their purposes. Tony Crosland was appointed as Minister responsible for the Commission, and had previously made explicit his view that the 'public schools' were a far more 'flagrant' source of inequalities of opportunity than the grammar schools with which (as he saw it) so many socialists seemed obsessed (Crosland, 1956: 261-5). But he also dismissed the abolitionist solution as being both unacceptable on libertarian principles and unenforceable in practice, while discounting as excessively optimistic any hope that schools which conferred such 'real advantages' on their pupils would conveniently wither away as standards in the public sector improved. He later described the Commission's creation as both a political response to strong pressure from within the Labour Party for something to be done about the public schools, and as an attempt 'once and for all' to establish whether any compromise was possible between the 'nihilist' solution of abolition and the 'fig-leaf' solution of admitting a 'handful of state pupils' to schools which would remain essentially unchanged by their presence (Kogan, 1971: 196-7; Susan Crosland, 1983: 149-50).

After two years' work, the Commission produced positive proposals for 'integrating' the schools which its

19

second chairman (David Donnison) described as having created 'a record in the history of committees of inquiry' in being 'totally rejected' from all sides (Times Educational Supplement, 13 September 1968: 453). Although seven forms of integration were set out, appropriate to different kinds of school, it was hardly surprising that the main proposal was the one summarized caustically by one of its own members (John Vaizey) as changing half the bodies in the beds (PSC, 1968: 221-4). The Commission's original chairman, Sir John Newsom, had long argued the case for more boarding education for socially disadvantaged children, and most of his fellow members were impressed by Royston Lambert's (1966) evidence of a large gap between supply and demand. They accepted both his estimate that 80,000 boarding places would be needed by 1980, compared with the 35,000 available in 1965, and his argument that more than half that larger number should be assisted from public funds according to nationally defined criteria of need. Meeting that need would provide 'a humanely acceptable and administratively feasible' basis for integrating the public schools, because they would then be seen to be complementing public provision rather than competing with it.

In the light of the Commission's own diagnosis that the schools' social exclusiveness certainly intensified social divisions even if it had not created them, it had to reject any notion of scattering assisted places around 'like confetti' because this would leave unscathed the schools' close association with 'particular classes'. In every integrated school, the proportion of assisted pupils was to be at least 50 per cent of its annual intake by the end of a 7-year transitional period, because so high a number of non-traditional entrants could not be assimilated without radical changes in the schools themselves (PSC, 1968: 21-43). They would certainly have to change academically, because there was no convenient coincidence between boarding need and high ability. It would have been illogical anyway for a government now committed to comprehensive secondary education in the public sector to have 'integrated' public schools which were allowed to remain academically selective. For both reasons, the academic scope of schools accepting (and acceptable for) integration had to extend as far as the entire CSE-band, and 'preferably beyond' that 60 per cent of the ability range (PSC, 1968: 129).

As far as HMC and many other representatives of the independent sector were concerned, the 'price' demanded for integration had been set absurdly high. Implicit in HMC discussion of the proposals was a double fear. If the schools lost their social exclusiveness, they risked losing fee-paying parents for whom it was a salient attraction. If they simultaneously lost their academic exclusiveness, they would lose their strongest appeal to many potential refugees from an increasingly non-selective public sector, and their distinctive function in the training of elites. The Commission's proposals for the public schools were therefore flatly rejected.

Given a new chairman and some new members, the Commission's terms of reference were now extended to include the direct-grant schools. Their initial exclusion, against which the schools themselves complained, was justified by Crosland on the grounds that their future had already been provided for in Circular 10/65. Either they found ways of co-operating with the local LEA's plans for comprehensive reorganization, or their whole future would come into question. Even by 1968, however, there was little sign of serious negotiation, let alone of integration. They had long claimed to provide a 'bridge' between the public and private sectors, but they were now becoming unacceptably distinctive, since it was clearly 'indefensible' to transform maintained grammar schools into comprehensive schools while 'preserving other grammar schools with similar aims and functions' supported from public funds (PSC, 1970: 113-204). Against the familiar argument that schools recruiting only 2 per cent of secondary-age pupils could surely be accommodated within an otherwise comprehensive system, the Commission noted that, in the LEAs surveyed on its behalf, the direct-grant schools contained almost all pupils with verbal-reasoning scores above 140 and 62 per cent of those with scores above 130 (PSC, 1970: 118, volume 2, appendix 8). In her more detailed evidence to the Commission, Renee Saran described how one LEA's arrangements for the 2 per cent of pupils it supported at direct-grant schools shaped its whole policy for secondary education, and how the outflow of free-place pupils depressed the intakes and the status of its maintained schools (see Saran, 1973). Such evidence of 'creaming' convinced the majority of the Commission that 'grammar schools of the traditional kind cannot be combined with a comprehensive system of education; we must choose which we want' (PSC, 1970: 4). It was also unimpressed by the two main arguments used in these schools' defence - that they obtained exceptionally good academic results from a 'unique social mix' (e.g. Cobban, 1969). Any apparent academic superiority was attributed to the social and academic selectiveness of schools, many of which were able to take their pick of pupils from at least three LEAs and recruit a majority of new pupils from the top 2.5 per cent of the ability range (PSC, 1970: 51 and 155). Socially, the leading direct-grant schools were described as 'predominantly middle-class institutions', able to reap the simultaneous benefits of attracting academic high-fliers by their social prestige, and fee-payers by their academic reputation. The majority of the Commission therefore recommended that, whether they became fully integrated into the LEA-maintained system or retained a special relationship with central government, continued support from public funds should depend on their transformation into comprehensive secondary schools.

Predictably, it was the leading academic schools which rejected these recommendations outright. They could see only the extinction of their particular qualities in any of the forms of participation in the public sector which they were being offered. They would lose the protection afforded by fees against dictation from LEAs or from central government. They would also lose the academic selectiveness which was both the foundation of their appeal to parents, and of their invaluable contribution to creating the country's future leaders. Certainly, their immediate re-action to the PSC's second report would have justified Donnison repeating his comment on the public schools' rejection of its first - that, in the context of public sector secondary education being reorganized on comprehensive lines, there was no consensus about any kind of integration and 'no politically viable way forward'.

The issue was deferred, however, because the Labour government went out of office just as the PSC was producing this second report. While safe for the time being under the Heath government, the direct-grant schools were acutely aware that they would face the same issue again if the Labour Party returned to office. The failure of the PSC proposals not only to be implemented but even to be acceptable in principle began a period of increasingly sharp polarization of policy towards private education in the two main parties, and of more energetic and systematic self-defence by the independent schools. In this final section of the chapter, we consider the extent to which the schools have changed educationally, their emergence as a more robustly political formation, and the transformation in the political climate which has brought them increasingly strong ideological support.

From 'public school revolution' to privatization

The Oxford study of the relationship between education and social mobility reported that at the time the parents of today's school pupils were at school, there was marked out-flow from the private to the state sector (Halsey et al., 1980). The ability of the maintained and direct-grant grammar schools to provide the credentials necessary for upward social mobility posed questions about the kind of tangible advantages that the public schools offered to middle-class (and especially 'new middle-class') parents. While it was always likely that the elite schools would retain their status appeal, and while their boarding facilities provided something not available widely in the state sector, it was also the case that the public schools faced a considerable problem of 'modernization'. In the 1950s, the £3 million Industrial Fund from the private industry to build and equip science laboratories had contributed to the beginnings of the so-called 'academic revolution' (Gathorne-Hardy, 1977: 368-92; Rae, 1981: 154-59; Salter and Tapper, 1981: 157-88). This brought moves towards a more 'modern' curriculum, and a markedly greater emphasis on the academic credentials required for entry to higher education and the occupations which depended on it. While maintaining their traditional claims to develop character and leadership, and to uphold Christian values, the schools' publicity increasingly highlighted examination results (especially at Advanced level), and high rates of entry to the universities, especially to Oxford and Cambridge.

As well as enhancing the schools' market-appeal, the 'public school revolution' (Rae, 1981) has made it much easier to defend the private sector as having defensible and distinctive functions (ISIS, 1974; 1981). Especially after the academically prestigious direct-grant schools became 'fully' independent, the sector could be presented as maintaining 'real' academic education amid the alleged collapse of standards attributed to comprehensive reorganization. The success of this defensive strategy is evident in several recent studies of parental perceptions of private education.

23

For example, over half the couples interviewed by Irene Fox (1985) gave 'better academic results' as their main reason for choosing independent schools, with 12 per cent giving it as their only reason. There are similar findings in Walford's detailed study of two 'public schools', and from our own interviews with parents of fee-paying and assisted place pupils (Edwards et al., forthcoming; Walford, 1986). At the level of popular consciousness, the sector has succeeded in fostering an image of itself as being the 'last best hope' for parents wanting a traditional academic education and good examination results - a view which was announced and institutionalized by the Conservative Government through the Assisted Places Scheme (Fitz et al., 1986; Tapper and Salter, 1986).

As Labour policy towards the private sector became more consistently and specifically hostile, so the sector had to organize its defences more coherently. Circular 10/65's 'request' to LEAs to abandon selection at 11 years of age, had threatened the demise of maintained grammar schools and local authorities' take-up places in direct-grant schools, and it had prompted the formation in 1966 of a notably effective pressure group, the Direct Grant Joint Committee (DGJC), whose initial activities included advice on sustaining LEA links, presenting evidence to the Public Schools Commission, and canvassing political support. The DGJC also drafted an early 'Scheme for Assisted Places', which would both extend the scope of the direct-grant arrangements and avoid its greatest weakness - that of financing pupils without regard to parental income. More generally, and in response to explicit Labour proposals for 'reducing and eventually abolishing' private education (ending direct-grant and the benefits of charitable status, and eventually making the charging of fees illegal), the whole sector professionalized itself as a pressure group and established an effective public-relations unit. Developing out of the HMC's Public Relations Committee, the Independent Schools Information Service (ISIS) was founded in 1972 to provide facts and advice to member schools, and to publicize their 'value to the nation' and the dangers of a state monopoly in education. A key part of its rhetoric was its appeal for parents in a free society to have the right to choose 'efficient schools alongside the maintained system', especially where those schools were preserving the kind of education for which academic selection was necessary (ISIS, 1972; 1973; 1974; 1976). Then, in 1974, the Independent

Schools Joint Council (ISJC) was established to provide a discussion forum, co-ordination agency and, where appropriate, a common voice for the various bodies that represented the different segments of the private sector.

The establishment of these bodies was particularly timely, given the unexpected return of a Labour government in 1974 and its re-election later the same year. It was at this time that the form and the force of Labour's attack on both independence and selectiveness began to arouse a strong response from a Conservative Party which had previously shown only an intermittant enthusiasm for educational issues. Although the 1974-9 Labour Government failed to fulfil a manifesto promise to reform charitable status, its withdrawal of the direct grant and its instructions to LEAs to cease buying 'free places' wherever possible provided an issue from which an alliance could develop between the private sector and the only political party with which it seemed safe. The Conservatives returned to power in 1979 with a general commitment to the 'cause' of private education, and a specific commitment to providing means-tested assisted places in 'academically excellent' independent schools for 'bright children from modest backgrounds' who would not otherwise be able to attend them.

That scheme was denounced by its critics as an unjustified declaration of no confidence in the capacity of the public sector to cater for really able children. Its main defenders, including the minister responsible for its implementation (Mark Carlisle), saw it in strictly meritocratic terms as restoring a scholarship 'ladder' for able working-class children. Yet the evidence so far (as shown in Table 1.5) suggests that very few of the places have gone to this target-group and that, although some of the beneficiaries are 'non-traditional' users of independent schools, they provide another example of the middle classes taking advantage of a reform ostensibly introduced for the benefit of more socially disadvantaged groups (Douse, 1985; Fitz et al., 1986; Tapper and Salter, 1986). Table 5.1 summarizes evidence from our own study of the scheme's implementation.

However, even if the scheme had been more successful in these terms, its deliberately limited scope has little relevance to the 'New Right's' advocacy of a wholesale intrusion of consumer choice and market forces into education. In 1981, for example, Max Beloff urged the Annual Conference of Preparatory Schools to present the case for private education more boldly, not as a desirable

Table 1.5 Occupational status of parents (in percentages, using a classification derived from the Oxford Mobility Study)

	Service Class		Intermediate Class			Working Class		Not in paid employment
	I	II	III	IV	V	VI	VII	
Fathers								
Full feepayers	65.3	20.7	0	12.0	0	0	0	2.0
Assisted-places holders	11.9	38.1	10.2	15.3	8.5	6.8	2.5	6.8
Upper-band comprehensive	24.5	34.0	7.5	11.2	6.6	6.6	6.2	3.3
LEA grammar	54.3	34.7	0	6.5	0	0	2.2	2.2
Mothers								
Full feepayers	7.6	30.5	16.6	5.6	0	0	0	39.6
Assisted-places holders	0	22.2	36.8	2.8	1.4	1.4	2.8	32.6
Upper-band comprehensive	1.2	29.0	32.8	2.3	1.5	0	6.2	27.0
LEA grammar	2.0	46.0	28.0	4.0	0	0	0	20.0

Source: Fitz, J. et al. (1986) 'Beneficiaries, benefits and costs', Research Papers in Education 1 (3), 169-93.

alternative to state schools or as a useful yardstick againt which to measure those schools' presumably inferior performance, but as the proper way to organize educational provision (Times Educational Supplement, 4 September 1981). An Assisted Places Scheme limited to 5,000 places a year can only function as a slight meritocratic extension of a private sector which remains highly selective and does nothing for the 'choice' available to parents at large.

Some of the scheme's advocates therefore valued it mainly as the harbinger of a fully-fledged voucher system, some version of which would allow parents to 'cash' vouchers in independent schools by adding from their own resources whatever additional money was required. Despite concerted efforts to win his full support, Keith Joseph (the Secretary of State for Education) persisted in finding the idea intellectually attractive but, following his Civil Servants' advice, we also found it impractical (Seldon, 1986). In the last two years, however, a climate already favourable to other forms of privatization has become markedly more so in education (Pring, 1986 and 1987). While the Labour Party is committed to the abolition of the Assisted Places Scheme and (in theory at least) to squeezing the independent sector out of existence (Labour Party, 1980), a Conservative government increasingly explicit in its preference for private over public provision is actively promoting a much greater variety of schools outside LEA control. For supporters of state education, the new initiatives proposed in current legislation are seen as eroding the notion of 'state' and 'comprehensive' secondary schooling. At the time of writing, the Education Reform Bill before parliament (DES, 1987b) includes provision for the establishment of 'city technology colleges' and 'grant-maintained schools'. The former are to be an English equivalent of 'magnet schools', new schools run by independent charitable trusts receiving some capital funding from industrial sponsors and a recurrent expenditure budget from central government. Grant-maintained schools will be created by allowing existing schools to 'opt out' of LEA control on a simple majority vote of parents and receive their funding direct from central government.

Whether it is a result of conscious policy or merely the outcome of a series of apparently unrelated decisions, critics of current government proposals have discerned a possible future scenario in which a clear hierarchy of schools will re-emerge (Campbell et al., 1987; Cordingley and Wilby, 1987). This might place well-resourced

27

independent schools at the pinnacle, with the new centrally-funded schools in the middle, leaving LEA-maintained schools only as a safety-net for socially disadvantaged areas. The danger of this would be increased if those schools opting out of the LEA system exercised their right to apply to the Secretary of State to change their status and then became overtly academically selective. However, the more extreme privatizers on the New Right argue that such a development would only be a logical extension of the market principle and that anyway the government's reforms have not yet gone far enough. In their view, only a further curbing of LEA influence and the introduction of educational vouchers or 'pupil entitlements' will ultimately 'empower' all parents with rights of choice, including the critical right to 'discipline' unsatisfactory schools by withdrawing their custom (Sexton, 1987; Hillgate Group, 1987). The emphasis on parental choice in the 1988 Education Act, and the fact that independent schools need not adhere to the national curriculum, indicates that the present government favours the market as the best arbiter of educational standards.

It is difficult to predict the degree to which the fears of state comprehensive supporters and the hopes of the New Right will be realized in the aftermath of the Education Reform Act. It seems doubtful whether the traditionally elitist private sector would itself welcome a transformation of its relationships with the state sector on anything like the scale envisaged by the New Right. However, in the immediate future, the independent schools will have to face up to the threat posed by the new 'half-way houses' which may well be able to offer their traditional clients a selective education without the burden of fees. In that situation, it is possible that they will come to favour the more radical solution. What is already certain is the sharp contrast between today's climate and the period 20 years ago when it still seemed possible to envisage that the private sector might eventually wither away. For the moment, it is the public sector, certainly as conventionally conceived, that is decidedly on the defensive.

References

Bamford, T. (1974) _Public School Data_, Hull: University of Hull Institute of Education.

Barnett, C. (1986) The Audit of War, London: Macmillan.

Boyd, D. (1973) Elites and their Education, Slough: NFER.

Campbell, J., Little, V., and Tomlinson, J. (1987) 'Multiplying the divisions?', Journal of Educational Policy 2 (4), 369-78.

Cobban, J. (1969) 'The direct grant school', in C.B. Cox and A.E. Dyson (eds), Fight for Education: a black paper, Critical Quarterly Society.

Cordingley, P. and Wilby, P. (1987) Opting out of Mr Baker's Proposals, London: Education Reform Group.

Craig, F.W. (1982) Conservative and Labour Party Conference Decisions, 1945-1981, London: Parliamentary Research Services.

Crosland, C.A.R. (1956) The Future of Socialism, London: Jonathan Cape.

—— (1962) The Conservative Enemy, London: Jonathan Cape.

Crosland, S. (1983) Tony Crosland, London: Coronet.

Dancy, J. (1963) The Public Schools and the Future, London: Faber.

Department of Education and Science (1987a) Education Statistics for the United Kingdom, 1987 edn, London: DES.

—— (1987b) Education Bill, London: HMSO.

Douse, M. (1985) 'The background of assisted places scheme students', Educational Studies 11 (3), 211-17.

Edwards, A., Fitz, J., and Whitty, G. (1985) 'Private schools and public funding: a comparison of policies and arguments in England and Australia', Comparative Education 21, 29-45.

—— (forthcoming) The State and Private Education: An Evaluation of the Assisted Places Scheme, Lewes: Falmer Press.

Fitz, J., Edwards, A., and Whitty, G. (1986) 'Beneficiaries, benefits and costs: an investigation of the assisted places scheme', Research Papers in Education 1 (3), 169-93.

Fox, I. (1985) Private Schools and Public Issues: the Parents' View, London: Macmillan.

Gathorne-Hardy, J. (1977) The Public School Phenomenon, London: Hodder & Stoughton.

Girls' Schools Association (1987) Girls First, London: Girls' Schools Association.

Griggs, C. (1985) Private Education in Britain, Lewes: Falmer Press.

Halsey, A. (1981) Democracy and education, New Society, May 25.

Halsey, A., Heath, A., and Ridge, J. (1980) Origins and Destinations, Oxford: Clarendon Press.

―――― (1984) 'The political arithmetic of public schools', in G. Walford (ed.) British Public Schools: Policy and Practice, Lewes: Falmer Press.

Hillgate Group (1987) The Reform of British Education, London: Claridge Press.

Honey, J. (1977) Tom Brown's Universe, London: Millington.

Howarth, J. (1985) 'Public schools, safety nets and educational ladders: the classification of girls' secondary schools', Oxford Review of Education 11 (1), 59-69.

Howarth, T.E. (1972) 'The case for independent schools', in R. Boyson (ed.), Education: Threatened Standards, London: Churchill.

Independent Schools' Information Service (1973), What is a Direct Grant School?, London: ISIS.

―――― (1974) The Case for Independence, London: ISIS.

―――― (1976) Selection: Modern Education's Dirty Word, London: ISIS.

―――― (1981) The Case for Collaboration: the Independent Schools and the Maintained System, London, ISIS.

―――― (1988) Annual Census, London: ISIS.

Kalton, G. (1966) The Public Schools: a Factual Survey, London: Longman.

Kamm, J. (1971) Indicative Past: A Hundred Years of the Girls' Public Day School Trust, London: Allen & Unwin.

Kogan, M. (1971) The Politics of Education, Harmondsworth: Penguin Books.

Labour Party (1980) Private Schools: a Discussion Document, London.

Lambert, R. (1966) The State and Boarding Education, London: Methuen.

Leinster-Mackay, D. (1984) 'Old school ties; some 19th and early 20th century links between public and preparatory schools', British Journal of Educational Studies 32 (1), 78-83.

Mason, P. (1983) Private Education in the EEC, London: ISIS.

Payne, G. (1977) 'The lieutenant class', New Society, July 21.

Praetz, H. (1983) 'The non-government schools', in R. Browne and L. Foster (eds) Sociology of Education, (3rd edn), Melbourne: Macmillan.

Pring, R. (1986) 'Privatization of education', in R. Rogers (ed.) Education and Social Class, Lewes: Falmer Press.

—— (1987) 'Privatizing education', Journal of Educational Policy 2 (4), 288-99.

Public Schools Commission (1968) First Report, London: HMSO.

—— (1970) Second Report, London: HMSO.

Rae, J. (1981) The Public School Revolution: Britain's Independent Schools 1964-1979, London: Faber.

—— (1982) 'What future for the private sector?', Times Educational Supplement, September 17.

Reid, I. (1986) The Sociology of the School and Education, London: Fontana.

Salter, B. and Tapper, T. (1981) Education, Politics and the State: the Theory and Practice of Educational Change, London: Routledge & Kegan Paul.

—— (1985) Power and Policy in Education: the Case of Independent Schooling, Lewes: Falmer Press.

Saran, R. (1973) Policy Making in Education, a Case Study, London: Oxford University Press.

Seldon, A. (1981) Whither the Welfare State?, London: Institute of Economic Affairs.

—— (1986) The Riddle of the Voucher: an Enquiry into the Obstacles to Introducing Choice and Competition in State Schools, London: Institute of Economic Affairs.

Sexton, S. (1987) Our Schools: a Radical Policy, London: Institute of Economic Affairs.

Tapper, T. and Salter, B. (1986) 'The Assisted Places Scheme; a policy evaluation', Journal of Education Policy 1, 315-30.

Walford, G. (ed.) (1984) British Public Schools: Policy and Practice, Lewes: Falmer Press.

—— (1986) Life in Public Schools, London: Methuen.

—— (1987) 'How dependent is the independent sector?', Oxford Review of Education 13 (3), 275-96.

Wiener, M. (1981) English Culture and the Decline of the Industrial Spirit, Cambridge: Cambridge University Press.

CHAPTER 2

SCOTLAND: CHANGES IN GOVERNMENT POLICY TOWARDS PRIVATE SCHOOLS

Geoffrey Walford

Introduction

Scotland is a country within a larger state. Along with England and Wales it forms Great Britain, which is itself the major part of the United Kingdom of Great Britain and Northern Ireland. In terms of numbers, just over five million Scottish people form less than one tenth of the entire population of Great Britain, but this minority position does not mean that the distinctiveness of Scotland has been submerged by the larger partner. Partner is the appropriate description, as, unlike Wales, Scotland was never conquered by the English. The two crowns were united in 1603 when King James VI of Scotland also became King James I of England, but it was not until 1707 that the Scots actually united with the English in a voluntary Act of Union. Part of the bargain struck at the time was that Scotland should retain its own social institutions and not have those of England thrust upon it.

The result is that this small country has been able to preserve and develop its own independence while still being a part of a larger state. The degree of difference often shocks English or Welsh visitors, for their assumptions about everyday activities are frequently challenged. Scotland has its own newspapers and television channels, its football teams play in the Scottish Football League, it prints its own banknotes, there is a Scottish National Trust, a Scottish Arts Council and so on. At a far deeper level, however, Scotland has its own judicial and legal system which requires separate Acts of Parliament. The churches have a much higher membership and degree of influence than in England and Wales, with the established religion being Presbyterian rather than Episcopalian. The administration of Scotland is concentrated in Edinburgh, where some 55,000 civil servants deal with health, transport, police, prisons, taxation, and other services. One of the largest departments is the Scottish Education Department, which has overall responsibility for the Scottish local authority maintained sector, which is distinctively different from that in England and Wales.

The educational system in Scotland

The Scottish local authority maintained educational system has numerous differences from the system in operation south of the border. As these differences may not be widely known, it is necessary to give an outline of the system before considering the position of the private schools in Scotland.

Primary schooling is compulsory from the age of 5 until 12. Pupils have to attend secondary schooling until 16, by which point academically able pupils will have taken Standard Grade examinations, which broadly correspond to GCSE taken south of the border. Pupils who continue with their academic education in Scottish schools take four or five Highers rather than the two or three A levels which are common in England and Wales. The Highers-level curriculum is thus wider, and the narrow specialization characteristic of the English sixth form has never existed in Scotland. A futher major difference is that Highers may be obtained in just one year rather than two, which has major implications for entry into universities and higher education. Whilst most Scottish direct-entry university students are now 18, a large minority are only 17 (MacPherson, 1984), and honours degrees usually take four years rather than three. These differences between the educational structures of Scotland and of England and Wales underline the difficulties inherent in any comparative work. Even basic statistical comparisons of the proportions of pupils in private schools are thus not straightforward. In Scotland and in England and Wales a larger proportion of parents choose private schools for their children at secondary rather than primary level, but the difference is greater in Scotland. Thus any comparison has to take into account whether it is more appropriate to take 11 or 12 as the norm for transfer.

Within Scotland the official term used for a private school is 'independent'. An independent school is defined as one at which full-time education is provided for five or more pupils of school age or over (whether or not such education is also provided for pupils under or over that age), and not being a publicly funded school. All such schools are required by law to register with the Scottish Education Department and are listed in List F (SED, 1987), which in October 1987 contained 115 named schools. The exact number changes as various schools open, close, or merge. Not all these schools have the high status which is usually accorded to independent schools in most discussion or debate. For example, included within this total of 115 are 27 independent schools catering for special educational needs of one sort or another. These are schools for children with learning difficulties, autistic children, children with social and emotional difficulties, spastic children, and so on. All but one of these schools are very small, with about 38 pupils on average. More than 85 per cent of these children are boarding pupils.

Apart from these special schools, it would seem that there were 88 registered independent schools in Scotland in 1987. Whilst being technically correct in terms of registration, however, it is somewhat perverse for there are four preparatory schools which are run separately from the parent senior schools under a separate headmaster which are not included. Thus 92 schools need to be considered apart from the special schools.

The range of different types of school within these 92 schools is considerable. At one end of the spectrum, if it may be considered as such, are the major senior schools such as Loretto, Glenalmond, St Leonards, or Fettes, which were established in the nineteenth century and where the majority of pupils are boarders and fees were around £2,000 per term in 1987. A second group contains the independent secondary day schools, such as Edinburgh Academy or Glasgow Academy, which have long histories, and to which group the majority of former grant-aided schools have recently been joined. These ex-grant-aided schools will be discussed in more detail in the next section. The range of independent secondary schools then widens to include schools catering for particular and unusual client groups such as Total Oil Marine's French school and the American School in Aberdeen, both mainly serving those involved in the oil exploration industry. Another unusual independent school is Queen Victoria School in Dunblane which is a residential school for 250 sons of Scottish sailors, soldiers and airmen/airwomen, all of whom receive free board and tuition paid by the Ministry of Defence.

Of the 92 independent schools in Scotland in 1987, 39 taught children only up to an age which was 14 or less. As the age of transfer in Scotland is 12 in local authority schools, and some independent schools have their main intake at 13, while others accept pupils at 11, the age of transfer is not clear cut. The junior or preparatory schools have variable age ranges, some being 3 or 4 up to 9 or 10, others taking pupils from 8 to 13 or 14, and some taking the full range from 3 to 14. However, 19 of the 39 schools are members of the Incorporated Assocation of Preparatory Schools, a fairly exclusive organization which contains schools which prepare children for entry to the major academic independent secondary schools. Such schools as Fettes Junior School and the Combined Junior School of Mary Erskine School and Daniel Stewart's and Melville College are included in this group. Nevertheless, at the primary level, the range of provision is varied and includes schools such as the Living Waters Christian School in Paisley with about twelve pupils and the Torass Emess Jewish Day School in Glasgow.

At the secondary level, one way of categorizing schools is by looking at the associations of which the school is a member. With regard to boys' schools, the fact that the headmaster is a member of the Headmasters' Conference is generally taken to be significant (Walford, 1986: 8). There are some 230 headmasters in membership of the HMC in Great Britain, including 18 from Scotland. For girls' independent schools, the organization which is usually taken to be somewhat analogous to the HMC is the Girls' Schools Association (GSA) and the related Governing Bodies of Girls' Schools Association (GBGSA). Of the 92 Scottish schools, 14 are members of the GSA, including one school which is also in HMC. It is suprisingly difficult to categorize these secondary schools into boys', girls' or mixed schools. Some of the mixed secondary schools which started life as single-sex schools, still have only low numbers of the opposite sex, while some of those classified as single-sex schools may have the opposite sex in junior classrooms or as occasional day pupils in the senior school, especially in the sixth form. However, it would appear that, in 1987, there were 9 exclusively boys' schools, 14 exclusively girls' schools, 4 boys' schools with some girls in the sixth form only, and 26 mixed schools; 29 of the schools had some boarding accommodation and 4 were Roman Catholic.

Having given a general description of the schools it is necessary to consider the size of the independent sector in terms of pupil numbers. The official figures have changed dramatically in the last few years. In 1984 the total number of pupils aged 5 and over in all Scottish schools was 846,042 of which 14,585 were in officially classified independent schools (1.74 per cent). This figure includes pupils in independent special schools. In 1985 the numbers of pupils aged 5 and above in independent schools jumped to 30,808 (3.64 per cent). The difference, as will be discussed in the next section, was mainly due to the final phasing out of government grant-aid to the former grant-aided schools. In 1985 the grant-aided classification (which had accounted for 2.07 per cent of all pupils in 1984) was finally abolished and the remaining schools which had not become local authority maintained schools by this time were deemed to be fully independent. It is worth noting that the total figure for grant-aided plus independent sector pupils had remained virtually static over the preceding decade or so. In 1971, for example, the independent schools had 1.7 per cent of the population while the grant-aided schools had 2.5 per cent. In 1987, however, in spite of a decline in the number of school-age children as a whole in Scotland, there was an increase in the number in the enlarged independent sector - from 30,808 in 1985, to 31,062 in 1986 and to 31,377 in 1987. This might seem to indicate a considerable increase in the number of children in these schools but, in fact, it is mainly related to a further change in classification practice. In the last two years, ten special schools which were formerly classified separately under List 'D' and usually financed through the social services departments, have been transferred to independent status and funded by the regional councils. This has resulted in a small growth in pupil numbers of about 440. The number of children in non-special independent schools has risen only slightly in the last few years but, as the total number of school-age children has declined dramatically during this time, this has meant that an increasing proportion of children are now privately educated. By 1987 over 4 per cent of all pupils were in independent schools, as were more than 6 per cent of secondary pupils.

Tempting though it is to quote national figures, their use confuses as much as it reveals, for the provision of independent education in Scotland is far from homogeneous in terms of region and age group. The first column of Table

2.1 shows the overall percentage of pupils being educated in each region in independent schools in 1986. It is immediately obvious that the regional distribution of pupils in independent schools is of major significance. The three island districts, for example, have no independent provision of their own. Even considering the regions which do have independent schools, the diversity is considerable. There is a great concentration of private schooling in Edinburgh, which shows itself in the figures for Lothian Region as a whole, where more than one in nine pupils are educated privately. Further, it is evident that there are also major concentrations in both Grampian and Tayside.

Table 2.1 Percentage of pupils aged 5 and above in independent schools in each Region in 1987.

	Total	Primary	Secondary
Borders	0.94	1.11	0.72
Central	3.50	1.98	5.51
Dumfries and Galloway	0.85	0.65	1.11
Fife	1.31	0.67	2.18
Grampian	4.77	3.10	7.06
Highlands	0.35	0.04	0.76
Lothian	11.45	7.16	17.18
Strathclyde	2.90	1.99	4.11
Tayside	7.05	3.55	11.64
Orkney	0	0	0
Shetland	0	0	0
Western Isles	0	0	0
Scotland	4.13	2.60	6.18

Source: Scottish Education Department.

A further element to note is that the provision of independent schooling in Scotland has the nature of an inverted pyramid according to age. Table 2.1 shows that for Scotland as a whole there are more than twice as many pupils in private secondary education than in primary education. Much of the debate about private education is really about secondary schooling, and its possible role in facilitating entry into higher education and prestigious occupations. Thus, in most contexts, the figure of 6.18 per cent has greater utility in describing the size of the independent sector in Scotland. It is also worth noting that some regions have very high percentages in private schooling at the secondary level. In Lothian it reaches 17 per cent, while in Tayside it is over 11 per cent. As explained elsewhere (Walford, 1987b), for those staying on after the school leaving age, the proportions are even higher.

Changes in government policy - grant-aided schools

To many readers it will appear very strange that a virtual doubling of the size of the independent sector in Scotland occured as a result of a Labour government's policy decision. In 1975 the Labour government announced that it would phase out government support for the grant-aided schools in Scotland and the direct grant schools in England and Wales and that the schools would be given the chance to become fully independent or join the local authority sector (see Chapter 1). As explained more fully elsewhere (Walford, 1988) and in the next section, this Labour policy indirectly gave rise to the Assisted Places Scheme which was introduced in 1980 by the new Conservative government, so it is important to consider what occurred in detail.

In 1968 there were 29 grant-aided secondary schools in Scotland which received grant directly from the Scottish Education Department. They educated some 12,000 secondary level pupils - about 2.2 per cent of the relevant age group. These secondary schools were 'conducted by managers other than the education authorities' and received grant under the terms of the Grant-Aided Secondary Schools (Scotland) Grant Regulations of 1959. All but two of the schools charged fees, but most had provision for some remission of fees for a limited number of pupils who were successful in competitive scholarships and exhibitions, and some had special places for pupils who were able to satisfy the terms of the school's original foundation. The two schools which did not charge fees were Marr College, Troon (which acted more or less as the comprehensive school for the local area) and St Mary's Cathedral Choir School, Edinburgh (which was, and still is, a small, unique, music school for Scotland). The schools are well described in the report on Scotland by the Public Schools Commission (1970) and by Highet (1969), while the financial aspects are surveyed by MacLennan (1967).

The grant-aided schools were a diverse group. Some, like George Heriot's, were started as charitable 'hospital' schools, while others were originally independent schools, and one was even started by a town council. Eleven of the schools were for boys, fourteen for girls and four for mixed pupils. Thirteen of the schools had boarding places, but less than 10 per cent of all pupils boarded. All but one of the schools had a primary as well as a secondary department. Four were Roman Catholic.

The regulations under which the grant-aided schools worked were different in several significant ways from those for the direct grant schools of England and Wales. For example, they were not required to set aside any free places as a requirement of receiving the grant. In 1968, only six of the grant-aided schools had local authorities which had undertaken to support pupils, and a total of only 1,600 pupils were sponsored in this way, with 800 of these being at Marr College, Troon. In 1968 there were also some 1,000 pupils in the schools on scholarships which reduced the fees. However, this meant that about 80 per cent of the pupils paid full fees and a further 13 per cent paid part fees due to having scholarships.

The grant aid to the schools was not directly calculated on a per capita basis, but was related to non-capital expenditure. The total amount of grant aid available each year varied somewhat according to the political and economic climate, but could not exceed 60 per cent of approved expenditure. It was paid in respect of primary and secondary departments of the schools. The balance of expenditure was met by fees, income from foundation endowments where there were any, and other odd sources of income. Instead of using the bulk of the grant to support selected pupils, most of the grant-aided schools used the grant to substantially reduce fees for all of the fee payers well below the level at which they otherwise would have been set. There was no provision for a means-tested fee as there was with direct grant schools. The result was that parents obtained what amounted to an independent day-school education for their children, but at much reduced prices. Most of the grant-aided schools were highly selective academically, and to pay fees at these schools was seen as a sign of success, even if it was success only from within those families able and willing to pay the fees.

In practice, selection by ability to pay fees had also been a recent feature of the maintained sector in Scotland for, as late as the early 1970s, there were still a few fee-paying maintained schools which, in 1968, educated about the same number of pupils as did the grant-aided schools. At this date, the entire fee-paying sector educated about 5.4 per cent of the school population (Walford, 1987b), and provided a continuum of provision, according to ability to pay and social status, from the selective fee-paying maintained schools and grant-aided schools to the 'public' boarding schools on the English model.

As the majority of pupils paid fees in the grant-aided schools, these schools must be seen as having had a greater degree of continuity with the independent sector than did the direct grant schools in England and Wales. Indeed, in many ways they could be said to be central to the independent sector. Scotland has never had the strong tradition of boarding that has been such a feature of private education in England. There are a few schools, such as Loretto, Glenalmond, Fettes, and St Leonards, that are predominantly boarding and offer a 'public school' education on the English model, but most of the prestigious schools such as Edinburgh Academy or Glasgow Academy shared a day-pupil market with the grant-aided schools. The former charitable 'hospital' schools, such as George Heriot's, Mary Erskine and George Watson's, were converted into large day schools following the Argyle Committee's condemnation of the system in the 1860s, and eventually became full members of the grant-aided schools group.

The health of both the direct grant schools in England and Wales and the grant-aided schools in Scotland was closely related to the political and educational policies of successive governments. However, the funding system for the grant-aided schools (where the proportion of costs covered by the grant aid could be varied at will by government year by year) was inherently less stable than the funding system for the direct-grant schools (which was related to individual nominated pupils). In 1959/60, for example, 51 per cent of the grant-aided schools' costs were covered by the grant. In 1960/61 the figure was 53 per cent, while it had drifted down to 45 per cent by 1963/64.

After two general elections in 1974, Labour returned to power with a policy of phasing out both the direct grant and the grant-aided schools, and this measure was announced in March 1975. In England and Wales the decision related directly to the government's advocacy of comprehensive education rather than being a direct attack on the direct grant schools. As explained in Chapter 1, they were closed because they were seen as selective grammar schools working against the comprehensive ideal. In Scotland, however, where most of the pupils at grant-aided schools paid fees, the decision to close the schools was based upon the government's desire to cut support for what it saw as socially selective fee-paying schools.

For grant-aided schools, the way in which the grant aid was to be phased out was somewhat arbitary and open to crude political decisions. In 1974/75 the grant-aided schools received a total of £4.1 million. This same figure was provided in 1975/76 with no allowance for inflation. In early 1976 the government announced the rapid reductions indicated in the second column of Table 2.2.

Table 2.2 Government support for grant-aided schools and Assisted Places in Scotland (in millions of pounds)

	Planned grant aid (at 1976 prices)	Actual grant aid (at actual prices)	Assisted Places Scheme (at actual prices)	Total
1976/77	1.87			
1977/78	1.56			
1978/79	1.25			
1979/80	0.94	(2.30)		
1980/81	0.62	3.39		3.39
1981/82	0.31	2.82	+ 0.80	3.62
1982/83		2.22	+ 1.72	3.94
1983/84		1.52	+ 2.45	3.98
1984/85		0.80	+ 3.33	4.13
1985/86			4.26	4.26
1986/87			4.43	4.43

Source: Statutory Instruments, 1976/475; 1979/766; 1980/799; 1981/626; 1982/965; 1983/908; 1984/381 and SED Press Releases.

As there were high levels of inflation from the point at which the ceiling was first imposed and throughout the phased reduction, the drop in finance in real terms was very rapid. The schools were also caused additional problems by the Houghton Committee, which had awarded substantial salary increases to teachers in the maintained sector which had to be matched for teachers elsewhere. By 1978/79 the grant was only meeting about 8 per cent of expenditure (Bain, 1979). The reduction was thus considerably faster than that experienced by the direct-grant schools, and several of the grant-aided schools were experiencing substantial problems by the time of the return of a Conservative government in 1979. Had they been left to survive in the market place with no further government support, many of the schools would have been forced either to close or become local authority maintained schools in line with the Labour government's original plans.

Fitz et al. (1986) and Salter and Tapper (1985) have described in detail the ways in which pressure groups from within the independent sector and the Conservative Party worked together during the 1970s to construct the Assisted Places Scheme (to support selected pupils in independent schools) as an alternative to the direct grant. Similar processes were occurring in Scotland and, while the Scottish negotiations were clearly dependent on those of England and Wales in terms of the acceptance of any overall scheme, the details of the Scottish scheme were the subject of local political activity. The small size of Scotland and its educational system meant that these negotiations could be conducted at a much more personal level than in England and Wales.

In the early 1970s it was widely recognized that the grant-aided system of financial support was politically difficult to defend as it reduced fees payable at the schools, irrespective of parents' ability to pay. In addition, only those who happened to be living near a school could benefit, as the schools were unevenly distributed geographically.

As in England and Wales, behind-the-scenes negotiations for APS started in Scotland well before the 1979 election, but it was still not until 1981 that a detailed scheme could be put through Parliament and the first intake made. This 2-year gap in financial support could have caused some of the grant-aided schools considerable difficulties. Table 2.2 indicates the extent of the decrease in funding that had occured by 1979. Whereas in 1973 the grant aid had supported more than 40 per cent of expenditure, by 1978/79 this figure was down to less than 10 per cent. The high rates of inflation during the period had made the transition to independent status even sharper than had been planned.

It is an indication of the extent of the problem

experienced by some schools at this time that in July 1979 it was announced that the phasing-out scheme of 1976 would no longer be followed and that a sum of £2.30 million was to be made available for the financial year ending 1980. The intention at this stage was that the grant would cover about 20 per cent of the grant-aided schools' running costs (Bain, 1979). This figure is shown in the third column of Table 2.2, where it is also shown that the figure was raised to £3.39 million for the full year 1980/81. No such remission was made in England and Wales with respect to the direct grant schools, which had to wait until 1981/82 before any further grant was forthcoming, which by then was in the form of the Assisted Places Scheme. This substantial increase for the grant-aided schools must be seen as a considerable success for the independent schools, and it suggests that there were major fears that the finances for a number of the schools were so insecure that they would have been likely to have closed without this extra funding. The level of support negotiated for the grant-aided schools was, of course, to some extent arbitrary, but was set at 20 per cent of approved expenditure (corresponding to the degree of support given immediately prior to the start of the phasing-out process). However, once it had been set at this value, from 1981/82, it was reduced in line with the increased funding given to APS. Table 2.2 shows that the total support given to the independent sector, once inflation is taken into account, was relatively constant after 1980/81. Again, this second phasing out period for the grant-aided schools must be seen as a major success for the schools, but it might be argued that it could be fully justified in terms of recompense for the harshness of the original phasing out announced in 1976.

Change in government policy - the Assisted Places Scheme

Following the election of a Conservative government in 1979, the schools wished to formulate an Assisted Places Scheme which was 'right for Scotland'. There were two main elements to the Scottish case that needed to be taken into consideration. First, while the Conservative Party had swept to overwhelming victory in the United Kingdom as a whole, this was not true for Scotland where Conservative MPs were in a minority. Scottish MPs would be reluctant to be seen to back a scheme which was likely to antagonize too many potential future voters. Second, account had to be taken of the ways in which the maintained sector in Scotland differed from that in England and Wales in terms of the age of transfer to secondary school, the lower emphasis on sixth-form studies, and the lower age of entry to higher education. Further details of the political processes are available elsewhere (Walford, 1988).

Aims for the scheme

In England and Wales, the Assisted Places Scheme was centrally concerned with the selection of able children from maintained schools and the provision of a strongly academic education for them, which it was suggested was not available in maintained schools (Griggs, 1985: 89). The impression throughout was that selected independent schools were 'better' than LEA-maintained schools and that APS was a way of 'plucking embers from the ashes' (Edwards et al., forthcoming). While there were still many people in England and Wales who were believed to support the re-establishment of selective education, the Scottish tradition was quite different. Comprehensive education in Scotland had advanced far faster and further than in England and Wales, and the idea of egalitarianism in education was strong and deep (even if there was an element of myth in this belief (McPherson, 1983)). The idea of basing APS on academic selection would have been politically suicidal for the Scottish Conservative MPs. In consequence, the APS in Scotland was presented in terms of parental choice, and the legislation which introduced APS in Scotland was part of the same legislation which introduced greater parental choice in maintained schools (Education (Scotland) Act 1981). In terms of the Scottish Education Department's leaflets, the scheme is 'designed to widen the range of educational opportunity in Scotland and to give parents a greater choice of school' (SED, 1985).

It is clear that such an emphasis was desired by the MPs involved and by the independent schools themselves. Its major consequences are the greater range of schools involved and in the increased flexibility that it offers the schools in selecting pupils for assistance. In 1986/87 there were forty-one APS schools (the forty-second, St Margaret's Convent School, having closed in 1986). Eighteen of these schools had headmasters in membership of the Headmasters Conference, twelve were members of the Governing Bodies of Girls' Schools Association and the Girls' Schools Association, three were members of GSA only, and the remaining nine were not in membership of any of these bodies. The last nine are varied in nature and even include Kilquhanity House School, which is a small school with only about fifty pupils run on lines similar to that of A.S. Neill's Summerhill (Aitkenhead, 1986). In practice there are only twelve registered independent schools in Scotland, which offer schooling for the full secondary age range, which are not APS schools, and there are clear reasons for the exclusion of most of these. In consequence, APS in Scotland covers practically all of the secondary independent sector. The coverage extends from Fettes and Gordonstoun, through George Heriot's and Merchiston Castle, to the Edinburgh Rudolf Steiner School and Fort Augustus Abbey School.

The emphasis on parental choice also enables schools greater flexibility in the children they select. Clearly, the inclusion of Kilquhanity House, which is officially classified as a school for children with social and emotional difficulties (but has not been counted as such in this chapter), means that a wider range of children are involved, but the flexibility extends to individual schools. George Watson's, for example, has a special unit for dyslexic children, and thus has the freedom to accept children into this unit if it wishes. The schools are also able, with a clear conscience, to accept pupils with a brother or sister already in the school in preference to other applicants, or to accept children with special artistic, musical or sporting talents.

Age range of pupils

The scheme in England and Wales is restricted to pupils over the age of 11, which is the official age for entry into secondary education, even if this means that pupils on APS sometimes enter the preparatory schools of schools where the main entry is at 13. By comparison, in Scotland, secondary schooling is truncated at both ends, as it starts a year later and entry to higher education can be a year earlier. Clearly, it was open to the schools to argue that fairness between the two schemes demanded that a 7-year period was seen as the norm for both schemes. This was accepted, and APS in Scotland starts at 10 rather than 11, and thus covers the last two years of primary, on the condition that the pupil is already committed to follow a full course of secondary education. Additionally, in England

and Wales the scheme has fixed entry points at 11+, 12+, 13+ and 16+. In Scotland the scheme is open to any child who has reached the age of 10 by 31 July of the year in question, and schools can accept new pupils into the scheme at any age after that. As will be shown under the section on admission quotas (see p.47), the schools managed to achieve considerably increased flexibility by arguing for there being no fixed entry ages, and for the right to admit pupils to the scheme at any point.

Method of funding

In the official announcement, the funding of the scheme was outlined as follows:
> The whole of the resources at present available in the form of block grant to 21 schools (for which it represents 20% of their maintenance expenditure) will be converted over a period of five years into fee remission grant to be used to enable them to offer assistance with fees in accord with a statutory income scale. In the first year of the scheme - 1981/82 - one fifth of the available resources will be devoted to fee remission and this proportion will increase by equal steps during the phase over period.
> (Scottish Office Press Release, July, 1980)

Finance for APS in Scotland was to be seen as merely being 'phased over' from grant-aid, so that officially no new money was being found. Indeed, APS in Scotland was presented as being in accordance with the egalitarianism of that country's educational system - where grant aid had been available to support all pupils regardless of need, APS concentrated assistance on pupils from less affluent families. Independent schools were to be invited to join the scheme because 'not all of the existing grant-aided schools will be in a position to take up the whole of the grant available for fee remission'.

Columns three and four of Table 2.2 indicate this 'phasing over' of the grant, but the table also illustrates what was not made clear in the announcement - that the finance made available to the grant-aided schools had been sharply increased in 1979. The rapid raising of the grant in 1979, which was done with little fanfare, not only helped the grant-aided schools during what otherwise would have been very lean years, but also enabled APS to be presented as a direct replacement of grant aid in financial terms. No mention was made of the inherent arbitrariness of the level at which grant aid had been set in 1979.

Admissions quotas

In Scotland, unlike in England and Wales, there is no requirement that a proportion of the places be allocated to pupils from the maintained sector. The schools emphasized that quotas were not a part of the old grant-aided system, and that there was a need, especially in the early years, to allow fee remission to be available to children already in the participating schools whose families qualified under the income scale. Several schools had directed a proportion of their grant aid towards pupils from families in financial need. To have not allowed these pupils to have benefitted from APS, at the same time as phasing over the grant aid money to APS, would have meant these schools might not have been able to continue supporting those pupils in need whom they already supported.

In the first year of operation, 1981/82, 73 per cent of pupils on the scheme had previously attended an independent school. The figure had decreased to 60 per cent by 1983/84, and 57 per cent by 1984/85 (Government Statistical Service, 1985). At the beginning of the 1986/87 year it was down to 46 per cent, but was likely to rise as the year progressed, as further pupils were admitted to the scheme (Scottish Office, 1987).

Level of support

The total amount of funding given by government to support the Scottish Assisted Places Scheme is roughly the same as that given to the scheme in England and Wales in proportion to the total number of school-age children in the countries. However, this rough equivalence of treatment has interesting implications, for while England had some 309,000 pupils aged 11 and over in independent schools in 1985, Scotland only had 22,318 (or 24,197 aged 10+). Thus, in 1985, some 7 per cent of pupils aged 11+ in independent schools in England were being helped by APS, while in Scotland 11.6 per cent of pupils aged 11+ were on APS (10.7 per cent aged 10+). APS thus gives a higher level of support to the independent sector in Scotland than it does in England - simply because the sector is smaller.

Finally, it is worth briefly considering the level of

47

support given to individual schools. There is considerable variation between the APS schools in Scotland in the proportion of pupils supported by the scheme. In 1985/86, the three Merchant Company schools in Edinburgh - Daniel Stewart's and Melville College, George Watson's College and Mary Erskine School - had over 550 pupils on APS, which was about 16 per cent of the relevant schools' rolls, and some 21 per cent of the total number of pupils in Scotland on APS. The Merchant Company's former importance within the grant-aided sector has been maintained within APS. Similarly, George Heriot's had over 200 pupils on APS out of a total school roll (from age 3+) of 1,400. As might be expected, the former independent schools usually had a lower number of pupils on APS than did the former grant-aided schools. Loretto, for example, only had 22 pupils on APS, but the total school roll was less than 400. Fettes had 26, while St Georges School for Girls had only minimal involvement with 13. At the other extreme, some schools seem to have a rather high proportion of pupils on APS. Fort Augustus Abbey School, for example, has 39 of its (approximately) 90 pupils on APS, which is of special interest as the school only has one non-boarder. Boarding fees must be being found from other sources. In a similar way, Kilquhanity House School has 17 of its approximately 50 pupils on APS. In all, while for most independent schools in Scotland APS has become a significant source of funding, a few schools appear to have become dependent to a large degree upon the finance it brings.

Private schools and elite status

One of the consequences of the small size of Scotland in comparison to most of the other countries considered in this volume is that there are correspondingly fewer educational researchers. The Scottish educational system as a whole, and the private schools in particular, are under-researched. Delamont (1984a), for example, has made it clear that she sees a serious lack of educational research on Scottish elites. Thanks to her own ethnographic work on girls in one independent school (Delamont, 1976, 1983, 1984a-c), there is now more information on the experiences of upper middle-class girls and the cultural reproduction of female elites than there is on boys. There have been no ethnographic studies of boys in Scottish independent schools.

While such ethnographic accounts are a rich source of detailed case-study data, and can give information on the characteristics of pupils who enter particular schools, large-scale social surveys are necessary to assess the overall extent to which advantage can be gained through attendance at such schools. One of the reasons that parents wish to send their children to independent schools is that they believe that these schools, in particular through their academic emphasis, will give their children a better chance of entering university and/or well paid, prestigious, elite occupations (Fox, 1985). It is extremely difficult to test whether such parents are correct. For example, in the conclusion to his report on education and social mobility using the Scottish Mental Health Survey data, Hope (1984) states that the move towards a near fully comprehensive system in the local authority maintained sector will mean that, in the future, the higher positions in society are more likely to be filled by the products of private schools. But such a conclusion is mere speculation, for his analysis actually omits any consideration of the boys in his sample who attended private schools!

One area where Scotland has been far better served by educational research than practically any other country is at the school leaving age. For nearly two decades the Centre for Educational Sociology at the University of Edinburgh has conducted regular postal surveys of Scottish school leavers (Burnhill et al., 1987) and the very many reports of this work have led to a high degree of understanding of educational processes for this age group (see, for example, Gray et al., 1983; McPherson and Willms, 1987; Willms, 1986). Unfortunately, while response rates have generally been very high, those for the private schools have been lower and, partly in consequence, there has been practically no analysis of this rich data source which looks at the private sector. In England and Wales, Halsey et al. (1980, 1984) have provided some information for boys through their analysis of the Oxford Mobility Survey data. In Scotland, the comparable Scottish Mobility Study has, unfortunately, not been so thoroughly analysed in terms of the effects of independent education, and there is some dispute about how the results which have been published should be interpreted. Nevertheless, it is the most thoroughly analysed relevant data available.

The Scottish Mobility Survey gathered educational and occupational information from nearly 5,000 men aged between 20 and 65 who were resident in Scotland in 1975. The published work relating to education (Payne et al., 1979; Payne, 1987) deals mainly with the relation of education to mobility into and out of Social Mobility Study (SMS) Class 1, which accounts for about the top 12 per cent of the occupational structure, and which the authors usually refer to as 'upper middle class' (UMC). They show that men with UMC origins were six-and-a-half times more likely to attend private secondary education than the sample as a whole (29.7 per cent compared to 4.6 per cent). Of the 70 per cent of UMC children who went to the state system, 32 per cent were educated in fully selective state schools, for some of which fees may have been payable. Upper middle-class parents were thus well able to secure educational privilege for their sons.

It was also found that, among those men who had UMC origins and retained their class position in later life, 44 per cent had been educated privately - almost ten times the average for the sample. One particular group within the UMC, the self-employed higher professionals, showed even higher levels of use of private education. No fewer than 79 per cent of these self-recruited, self-employed professionals went to private schools (Payne, 1987: 130). Of the 30 per cent of men with UMC origins who were privately educated, about two-thirds retained their UMC position.

The story is somewhat different in terms of inflows into the UMC. The use of private education was far less prominent among those men who started life in another social group and were upwardly mobile into the UMC. Only 12 per cent of these men went to private schools, although this is still two-and-a-half times the average. More interestingly, about half of those who were upwardly mobile into the UMC had not attended any form of selective education. Payne (1987) argues that this shows that in no sense can education be seen as necessary for entry to the UMC. There was a very considerable amount of upward mobility and status maintenance without either formal qualifications or attendance at private school, particularly in the managerial and senior supervisory categories. He argues that it seems improbable that members of the UMC share an ethic which depends on privileged secondary education, and that the private schools should not be regarded as providing a necessary socializing force. He argues that the survey findings can be explained by suggesting that the most secure groups, who can hand on their position of advantage, are <u>incidentally</u> able to purchase the badge of privileged education:

As a commodity, the schools 'hidden' (or half hidden?) curriculum is geared to attract the custom of the paying parent. The outcome may be a heightening of consciousness for its pupils, and the foundation of networks which can be activated later in careers - but the education is dependent on the client (the elite?), not the other way round.

(Payne, 1987: 142)

Kendrick <u>et al</u>. (1982) have argued against an earlier version of the interpretation of these findings (Payne <u>et al</u>., 1979) on the grounds that the term 'upper middle class' is very misleading for this top group of 12 per cent. They argue that it includes occupational categories which by no stretch of the imagination can be described as 'upper middle class'. Payne (1987: 140) admits that there is some truth in this comment, but argues that the numbers involved are small. However, Kendrick <u>et al</u>. (1982) also argue that the category has been made too large by treating the top 12 per cent as a homogeneous group. As there were only about 4.5 per cent of the entire sample who attended private schooling, to take the top 12 per cent automatically means that this group must be wider than those particular strata in Scottish society for whom a fee-paying education plays a particularly central role. Kendrick <u>et al</u>. conclude that, by terming SMS Class 1 the 'upper middle class' and then identifying a considerable degree of mobility in and out of it, Payne <u>et al</u>. bias the account towards stressing the 'openness' of Scottish society.

There is some considerable merit in this criticism, for it is highly likely that a narrower definition of the UMC would have shown a tighter relationship between private education and occupational level. While such an analysis has not been conducted using the Scottish Mobility Survey data, some limited evidence for this assertion can be obtained by looking at the educational backgrounds of a defined, smaller elite group. Walford (1987b) found that 41 per cent of a sample of 'people of achievement and influence' within Scotland had a private school background. Walford's sample was drawn from a biographical dictionary of 1986. While there are considerable difficulties in using lists of this type (Bell, 1974), and a degree of scepticism is legitimate, the size of the percentage is such as to raise questions about the openness of Scottish society.

51

Conclusion

The introduction of the Assisted Places Scheme is the major concrete manifestation of the present Conservative government's support for the private sector. It has been shown that about one in eight pupils in private secondary schools now holds an Assisted Place and, as the places are unevenly distributed, this scheme has been a major factor in the survival of some schools. This direct financial support is thus of great value to some private sector schools, but APS is also important for the ideological support that it gives to the private sector as a whole (Walford, 1987a). In establishing the scheme, the government has implied that private schools are 'better' than local authority maintained schools, and that it believes that selected pupils should be enabled to attend such schools even where parents cannot afford the fees. This action not only attacks the comprehensive principles of the local authority sector, but also implies that a private school education is to be desired and aimed for in preference to one in a maintained school.

This is a strange position for a government to support, as it (through the Scottish Education Department) is ultimately responsible for the worth and appropriateness of the schooling provided in maintained schools. Yet, there may well be a degree of truth in the general position, for the government's own actions over the last decade have led to the maintained sector of schooling now sometimes failing to meet the high standards to which most parents aspire for their children. Since 1979, the local authority system has been subject to a sustained attack and to underfunding. Central government has restricted the amount of money which local authorities have been able to spend on education, at a time when new technology, rapidly rising prices in equipment and books, new curriculum demands, and a decline in the school-age population demand that more money be spent per pupil than ever before. Additionally, from 1984 to 1986 Scottish teachers were involved in the most sustained industrial action in the history of Scottish education (Ross, 1986), as a result of central government's demands to restructure the teaching profession and refusal to fund adequate salaries. The action led to teachers working to rule, extra-curricular activities being banned, and classes remaining untaught. Although the teachers generally received high levels of support, the costs to pupils and their parents were high.

It is little wonder that the private sector, where no teachers took part in industrial action and where expenditure has increased far faster than inflation, should be finding that it is able to sustain its pupil numbers at a time of a falling school-age population. The government's indirect ideological support for the sector, and the mishandling of the maintained sector, may be as important to the private sector as is the direct financial support.

There are plans for even greater government support for private schools and moves towards the privatization of the maintained sector in the future (Pring, 1987; Walford, 1988). At the time of writing, the details are still unclear, but one issue is that city technology colleges, which were announced for England and Wales in 1986, are also being considered for Scotland. This new type of school, of which the first opened in 1988 in Solihull, England, is privately owned by a trust, financially supported by industry, but basic recurrent funding is provided by a direct grant from central government. The schools will have a heavy technological emphasis, and will be situated in inner-city areas. They will not charge fees, but will be selective. More dramatic proposals, in the form of maintained schools being given the right to 'opt out' of local authority control and become directly funded grant maintained schools are in the 1988 Education Reform Act for England and Wales. These schools, too, will not charge fees but will be under the control and ownership of a board of independent governors. These proposals, too, are now being considered for Scotland.

In short, private schools and the privatization of education are about to become key issues in Scotland. The Assisted Places Scheme has led the way, but many new forms of support for private schools are likely to follow. In the next few years the emphasis will be on selection, differentiation and inequality rather than egalitarianism and equality of opportunity.

Acknowledgements

I wish to thank the Scottish Education Department, the Department of Education and Science, the Scottish Council of Independent Schools and the Independent Schools Information Service for their help in the preparation of this chapter. The Centre for Educational Sociology, University of Edinburgh provided me with a temporary and congenial home for part of 1986, during which I was introduced to the complexities of the Scottish educational system.

I am most grateful to the Journal of Education Policy and the Scottish Educational Review for allowing me to draw heavily from articles which were originally published in those journals.

References

Aitkenhead, J. (1986) 'That dreadful school: the 'free school' at Kilquhanity', Resurgence 118, 6-9.

Bain, W. (1979) 'Information Paper 4: independent and grant-aided schools in Scotland', Scottish Educational Review 11 (2) 152-4.

Bell, C. (1974) 'Some comments on the use of directories in research on elites, with particular reference to the Twentieth-Century Supplement to the Dictionary of National Biography', in I. Crew (ed.) British Political Sociology Yearbook, Volume 1, Elites in Western Democracy, Beckenham: Croom Helm.

Burnhill, P., McPherson, A., Raffe, D., and Tomes, N. (1987), 'Constructing a public account of an educational system', in G. Walford (ed.) Doing Sociology of Education, Lewes: Falmer Press.

Delamont, S. (1976) 'The girls most likely to: cultural reproduction and Scottish elites', Scottish Journal of Sociology 1 (1), 29-43. (Reprinted in R. Parsler (ed.) (1981) Capitalism, Class and Politics in Scotland, Farnborough: Gower.

—— (1983), Interaction in the Classroom, 2nd ed, London: Methuen.

—— (1984a) 'Lessons from St. Luke's: Reflections on a study of Scottish classroom life', in W.B. Dockrell (ed.) An Attitude of Mind, Twenty-Five Years of Educational Research in Scotland, Edinburgh, The Scottish Council for Research in Education.

—— (1984b) 'The old girl network: recollections on the fieldwork at St. Luke's' , in R.G. Burgess (ed.) The Research Process: Ten Case Studies, Lewes: Falmer Press.

—— (1984c) 'Debs, dollies, swots and weeds: classroom styles at St. Luke's', in G. Walford (ed.) British Public Schools: Policy and Practice, Lewes: Falmer Press.

Edwards, A., Fitz, J., and Whitty, G. (forthcoming) The

State and Private Education: An Evaluation of the Assisted Places Scheme, Lewes: Falmer Press.

Fitz, J., Edwards, A., and Whitty, G. (1986) 'Beneficiaries, benefits and costs: an investigation of the Assisted Places Scheme', Research Papers in Education 1 (3), 169-93.

Fox, I. (1985) Private Schools and Public Issues, Basingstoke: Macmillan.

Government Statistical Service (1985) Statistical Bulletin 7/C5/1985. The Assisted Places Scheme, Edinburgh: Scottish Education Department.

Gray, J., McPherson, A., and Raffe, D. (1983), Reconstructions of Secondary Education, London: Routledge & Kegan Paul.

Griggs, C. (1985) Private Education in Britain, Lewes: Falmer Press.

Halsey, A.H., Heath, A.F., and Ridge, J.M. (1980) Origins and Destinations, Oxford: The Clarendon Press.

—— (1984) 'The political arithmetic of public schools', in G. Walford (ed.) British Public Schools: Policy and Practice, Lewes: Falmer Press.

Highet, J. (1969) A School of One's Choice, Glasgow: Blackie & Son.

Hope, K. (1984) As Others See Us: Schooling and Social Mobility in Scotland and the United States, Cambridge: Cambridge University Press.

Kendrick, S., Bechhofer, F., and McCrone, D. (1982) Social Structure of Modern Scotland Project, Working Paper 3, 'Education and Social Mobility', Edinburgh: University of Edinburgh.

MacLennan, B. (1967) 'The finance of grant-aided schools in Scotland', Scottish Journal of Political Economy 14 (2), 156-74.

McPherson, A. (1983) 'An angle on the geist: persistence and change in the Scottish educational tradition', in W.M. Humes and H.M. Paterson (eds) Scottish Culture and Scottish Education, 1800-1980, Edinburgh: John Donald.

—— (1984) 'The reproduction of an ideology of egalitarianism in Scottish education since 1860', Integrating Education, 235-52.

McPherson, A. and Willms, J.D. (1987) 'Equalisation and improvement: some effects of comprehensive reorganisation in Scotland', Sociology 21 (4), 509-39.

Payne, G. (1987) Employment and Opportunity, London: Macmillan.

Payne, G., Ford, G., and Ulas, M. (1979) Education and Social Mobility: some social and theoretical developments, SIP Paper 8, Edinburgh: Organisation of Sociologists in Polytechnics and Cognate Institutions.

Pring, R. (1987) 'Privatizing education', Journal of Education Policy 2 (4), 208-99.

Public Schools Commission (1970) Second Report. Volume III: Scotland (under the chairmanship of David Donnison), London: HMSO.

Ross, D. (1986) An Unlikely Anger: Scottish Teachers in Action, Edinburgh: Mainstream Publishing.

Salter, B. and Tapper, T. (1985) Power and Policy in Education: the Case of Independent Schooling, Lewes: Falmer Press.

Scottish Education Department (1985) Assisted Places Scheme: a Brief Guide for Parents, Edinburgh: Scottish Education Department.

—— (1987) List F Independent Schools in Scotland, Edinburgh: Scottish Education Department.

Scottish Office (1987) News Release 0154/87. Assisted Places Scheme: Details for session 1986/87, Edinburgh: Scottish Office.

Walford, G. (1986) Life in Public Schools, London: Methuen.

—— (1987a) 'How dependent is the independent sector?' Oxford Review of Education 13 (3) 275-96.

—— (1987b) 'How important is the independent sector in Scotland?' Scottish Educational Review 19 (2) 108-21.

—— (1988) 'The Scottish Assisted Places Scheme: a comparative study of the origins, nature and practice of the APSs in Scotland, England and Wales', Journal of Education Policy 3 (2), 137-53.

—— (1989) Privatisation, Privilege and the 1988 Education Reform Act, London: Routledge.

Willms, J.D. (1986) 'Social class segregation and its relationship to pupils' examination results in Scotland', American Sociological Review 51, 224-41.

CHAPTER 3

UNITED STATES OF AMERICA: CONTOURS OF CONTINUITY AND CONTROVERSY IN PRIVATE SCHOOLS

Peter W. Cookson, Jr.

Introduction

Prior to the 1980s, public interest in private schools was minimal in the United States. In the minds of most policy makers, educators, parents, and scholars, the American dream of equal opportunity began at the public-school door. Schools that actually charged money for their services seemed marginal to the march of educational progress and were perhaps even socially divisive. Earlier in the century, several states had attempted to compel all children to attend common public schools, but the courts had upheld the right of individuals and religious orders to found their own schools outside the public system (Tyack, 1968; Kraushaar, 1972). The right of choice became a fixed principle within American educational philosophy and policy (Levy, 1986; Hirschoff, 1986; Erickson, 1986). The contradiction implicit in allowing certain families to opt out of the public system, while maintaining that all children should have equal educational opportunities, was muted by a perception that the public schools were as good, if not better, than most private schools and by a general feeling that the American economy was robust and dynamic enough to reward motivated individuals whatever their educational backgrounds.

By the 1970s, however, the American economy appeared to be contracting and foreign competition began to erode American control of domestic and foreign markets. At the same time, there was a growing perception that the public-school system was producing graduates who were ill-prepared for the future. Public support for public schools began to erode. The <u>Gallop Poll of the Public's Attitudes toward Public Schools</u> reflected the growing loss of faith. In

57

1973, for example, 58 per cent of the American people had a 'great deal', or 'quite a lot', of confidence in the public schools. By 1983, only 39 per cent felt the same way (Center for Education Statistics, 1987a: 82). According to Gallup's respondents, the three major problems facing the public schools were: lack of discipline, use of drugs, and poor curriculum/poor standards.

In several states, there was a taxpayers revolt; property tax rates were capped, thus limiting the expansion of public school budgets. Fundamentalist Christians began to remove their children from public schools to avoid contaminating their religious beliefs with 'secular humanism'. There were increasing reports of academic mediocrity, violence, and indifferent teaching. Americans were becoming a nation of illiterates. By the early 1980s, the public system was under siege; several national reports declared that the failing public school system was placing the 'nation at risk' (National Commission on Excellence in Education, 1983).

Within the scholarly community, the debate concerning school effects gained momentum. McDill (1978: 2), after an extensive review of the literature, concluded:

> In the past twelve years a body of empirical knowledge has accumulated, beginning with the Equality of Educational Opportunity survey (Coleman et al., 1966), and based on both cross-sectional and longitudinal studies, which unequivocally indicates that, overall, between school differences in any measurable attribute of institutions are only modestly related to a variety of outcome variables.

In other words, where an individual goes to school has little effect on his or her cognitive growth or educational mobility. This finding is counter-intuitive because our general knowledge of the social world leads us to believe that where individuals go to school will significantly influence their life chances, and with whom they will associate. It seemed only a matter of time until scholars, in their search for school effects, discovered private schools (Cookson, 1981; Coleman et al., 1982; Erickson, 1986).

Lastly, the 1980s have been a time when the political pendulum has swung quite far to the right by the standards of twentieth century American politics. For many years conservatives have argued that government at all levels was too big and too intrusive and that some public services ought to be privatized. Milton and Rose Friedman (1980) have suggested ending all public financing of primary and secondary education, except in hardship cases. William J. Bennett, who became United States Secretary of Education in 1985, has repeatedly criticized the public school system. According to the Secretary, public schools are too lax and too liberal; he advocates a back-to-basics curriculum and tighter discipline.

The disenchantment with the public school system, the search for school effects, and the rise to power of a conservative political coalition, then, created the environment within which the study of private schools has developed. With the publication of <u>High School Achievement: Public, Catholic, and Private Schools Compared</u> (Coleman <u>et al.</u>, 1982), the stage was set for a national debate concerning the role of private schools in the American system of education.

Studying private schools in their social context

In a recent book, Coleman and Hoffer (1987: 3) distinguish between two orientations to schooling; public schools represent the state's effort to integrate 'children from disparate cultural backgrounds into the mainstream of American culture', while private schools extend and transmit the values of certain families. In their words, 'the school is in loco parentis, vested with the authority of the parent to carry out the parent's will'. According to the authors, these two traditions are not in fundamental conflict.

If the world were as simple or as neatly divided as Coleman and Hoffer hypothesize, then the study of private schools would be little more than an exercise in classification. Scholars would examine private school programmes and statistically measure school outcomes within what is known in the United States as the status attainment model. Presumably they would find, as Coleman and his colleagues have, that private schooling is related to higher test scores, which are believed to measure cognitive growth and learning. Researchers would then study how private schools 'do it better'.

The fundamental problem with this approach to studying private schools is that it inevitably leaves out an essential variable - class (Cookson, 1987). The social status of attending a private school, especially an elite one, has only a little to do with cognitive growth and a great deal to do with acquiring a social credential that can be used to gain admission to other private and elite institutions (Baltzell, 1958, 1964; McLachlan, 1970: Cookson and Persell, 1985). I will argue in this chapter that private schools are embedded in the class structure and analyses of their educational and social effects cannot wholly avoid the issue of structural inequalities. This is not to say that private schools are intrinsically antithetical to democracy, it is only to say that in studying private schools, we should remain aware of the complex ways in which education affects life chances.

We begin with an overview of today's private schools and the students who attend them. Next is a brief examination of the personnel and programmes of private schools. We then turn our attention to the critical issue of whether or not private schools increase inequalities. This discussion leads to an examination of contemporary governmental policies toward private schools. We finish with some concluding remarks concerning the relationship between private schools and the public good.

An overview of private schools and private school students in the United States

The dimensions of private schooling

Discovering how many and what kinds of elementary and secondary private schools there are in the United States is in itself a major undertaking. Even defining a private school can be problematic as a good number of private schools accept public funds. Perhaps the most up-to-date and value-free definition is the one used by the United States Department of Education. According to the Department, a private school is:

> An elementary or secondary school (1) controlled by an individual or agency other than a State, a subdivision of a State, or the Federal government; (2) usually supported primarily by other than public funds; and (3) the operation of whose program rests with other than publicly elected or appointed officials.
>
> (Center for Education Statistics, 1987a: 231)

Within this general definition, there is considerable diversity. Erickson (1986: 87) notes fifteen major categories of private schools. These include: Roman Catholic,

Lutheran, Jewish, Seventh Day Adventist, Independent, Episcopal, Greek Orthodox, Quaker, Mennonite, Calvinist, Evangelical, Assembly of God, Special Education, Alternative, and Military. It should be clear from this list that most American private schools have religious origins and affiliations. In terms of their geographical distribution, private schools are mostly located on the east and west coasts. The state with the highest percentage of private school students is Connecticut (17 per cent) and the lowest is Wyoming (1.5 per cent) (Coleman et al., 1982: 18). In this chapter, I will usually discuss private schools as either Catholic, other private, or elite private. These categories mask a great deal of variation but, in terms of student numbers and organizational structure, they describe most of the private schools in the United States.

There are approximately 28,000 elementary and secondary private schools in the United States, enrolling 5.6 million students. Private schools constitute 25 per cent of all elementary and secondary schools and educate 12 per cent of the student population (Center for Education Statistics, 1987b: 8). Of all private schools, 60 per cent are elementary level, 10 per cent are secondary schools, 19 per cent combine elementary and secondary grades, and 11 per cent provide alternative or special education programmes. The mean student enrolment of private schools is 234; 16 per cent enrol fewer than 50 students, 34 per cent enrol between 50 and 149 students, 25 per cent serve between 150 and 299 students, 19 per cent enrol between 300 and 599 students, and only 7 per cent enrol 600 or more students. Most of the larger private schools have been established for more than 25 years. Compared to public schools, private schools are quite small (see Coleman and Hoffer, 1987: 37-9).

The percentage of students who attend private schools in the United States has remained remarkably stable over time. In 1970, for example, 10.9 per cent of all elementary and secondary students attended non-special-education private schools. In 1985, this percentage was exactly the same (Center for Education Statistics, 1987a: 58). During the 1970s there was a slight dip in private school enrolment, but enrolment patterns have increased in the early 1980s and have remained stable. Within the private sector, however, there have been significant shifts. From the mid-1960s to the early 1980s the big loser, in terms of students and number of schools, was the Roman Catholic church. According to Erickson (1986: 86), 'The U.S. Catholic school enrollment diminished to a little more than half its original size, dropping from 5,573,810 [5,574,354 by another estimate] to 3,106,000'. This amounts to a 46 per cent drop in students and a 29 per cent drop in schools in the period between 1965 and 1983. During the same period, virtually every other type of private school experienced great growth in terms of students and schools. For instance, the number of students enroling in Evangelical schools increased by 627 per cent, American Lutheran church schools increased their enrolment by 256 per cent, and the enrolment in conservative Jewish schools grew by 254 per cent (Erickson, 1986: 87).

The family background of private school students

Students who attend private schools are very likely to come from homes that are affluent and stable. According to Coleman and Hoffer (1987: 30), 'The median income of parents of public sector students is $18,700, that of parents of Catholic sector students is $22,700, and that of other private school parents is $24,300'. These figures, especially as they relate to non-Catholic private-school parents, should be treated with some scepticism. Baird (1977: 9), for instance, found that in 1976 the average yearly income for private-school families was $40,000. In a study of private secondary boarding schools, it was found that 46 per cent of boarding school families had incomes of over $100,000 a year (Cookson and Persell, 1985: 58). Granted that this sample contained a substantial number of students who attended the most socially elite schools, it does indicate that Coleman and Hoffer's figure is too low. Moreover, none of these studies measure family wealth, which is a better indicator of class position than income, because wealth can be passed from generation to generation.

Occupation is another key family background indicator. While data on the parental occupations of private school students is less than satisfactory, it is safe to say that in the non-Catholic sector, most parents are professionals or managers. There is little working class representation in non-Catholic private schools. Among Catholic schools, the picture is more complicated. Elite academic Catholic schools attract upper and upper-middle class professional and managerial families, while Catholic schools located in working class neighbourhoods educate the children of blue-collar workers, lower-middle class employees and entrepreneurs, and semi-professionals.

Research has shown that parental education, especially mother's education, is highly related to student aspiration. According to Coleman and Hoffer (1987: 31), Catholic mothers have attained roughly the same level of education as public school mothers; 45 per cent of public school mothers are high school graduates, 44 per cent of public school mothers are high school graduates. Other private school mothers are more highly educated, 24 per cent are college graduates and 12 per cent have earned a graduate degree. The fathers of private school students are also well educated; two-thirds of boarding school fathers have graduate degrees (Cookson and Persell, 1985: 59).

There was a time when racial and ethnic minorities did not enrol in private schools in any significant numbers. Today, 6 per cent of Catholic school students are black and 10 per cent are Hispanic. In the other private schools only 2 per cent are black and 8 per cent are Hispanic (Coleman and Hoffer, 1987: 31). Interestingly, elite secondary boarding schools enrol proportionately more black students than other non-Catholic private schools, in part because of the elite schools' service mission. (4 per cent of the students at boarding school are black). It also should be noted that Catholic and Jewish students are attending non-Catholic private schools in growing numbers (11 per cent of the students who attend boarding school are Jewish and 27 per cent are Catholic)(Cookson and Persell, 1985: 67-8).

A consistent research finding is that private-school families have, to use Coleman and Hoffer's term, 'structural integrity' (1987: 34). This means that when compared to public-school parents, there are relatively few divorced or single private-school parents. Private-school parents are quite cosmopolitan; 69 per cent have travelled outside the United States and 51 per cent have more than 500 books in their home (Cookson and Persell, 1985: 60). Given this kind of family background, it is not surprising that private-school students have high educational aspirations. While less than 60 per cent of public-school ninth-graders plan to attend college, 76 per cent of Catholic and 70 per cent of other private-school ninth-graders plan to attend college (Coleman and Hoffer, 1987: 33). Virtually all elite private-school students plan to attend college.

Private schools in ten countries

Summary

Students who attend private schools generally come from affluent, stable, and ambitious families. While not all private-school students have upper class or elite backgrounds, they tend to come from families at the upper end of the socio-economic scale. The great majority of private-school students are white, but there is considerable religious diversity.

Private schools: organizational structure, personnel, and programmes

Organizational structure

Most private schools are organized on a non-profit basis, which means they pay few, if any, taxes. It also means that they can receive financial gifts from charitable foundations and individuals without either party paying significant taxes in the transfer. Some smaller private schools are run on a profit or proprietary basis, but most of these schools have highly specialized curriculums for students with emotional problems, learning disabilities, or other special needs. Non-profit, non-Catholic private schools are invariably supervised by a board of trustees who usually are wealthy alumni or friends of the school. Trustees are financially responsible for their school and are expected to lead the fiscal way with large donations. Trustees also select the school head. Because a private-school head has nearly absolute executive power within the school, the choice the trustees make is critical. Very few non-Catholic private schools have teachers' unions and the traditions of most schools limit faculty power to decisions about the curriculum and occasionally to participating in disciplinary actions. Private-school heads tend to be males in their early forties with little or no formal background in administration. They are generally chosen for their personal or 'charismatic' qualities. In essence, the head exemplifies the 'amateur ideal', although, since the 1970s, more and more heads have become involved in raising money.

With some exceptions, Catholic schools are operated by religious orders and are ultimately responsible to the hierarchy of the Catholic church, although most religious orders guard their autonomy. Because religious orders vary

64

considerably in terms of their rituals, traditions, and emphasis on intellectual achievement, Catholic schools are not a homogeneous group, except in so far as they teach the tenets of the Roman Catholic faith. Even here, however, there is variation in style, emphasis, and intensity. A highly academic Jesuit high school, located in a large metropolitan area, is quite different than a Franciscan missionary school, located in a remote desert of the southwest. According to Erickson (1986: 86), Catholic schools have been in a period of transition, in part because the religious orders have 'withered'. The decline in the number of priests, nuns, and brothers has meant that the Catholic schools have had to hire lay teachers and, in the minds of many Catholics, the schools have lost their traditional religious atmospheres.

The relative impoverishment of Catholic schools is evident when we look at their annual per pupil expenditures compared to public schools and other private schools. In 1979-80, public schools spent $2,016 per pupil per year, other private schools $2,777, and Catholic schools $1,353. Elite private schools spent nearly $5,000 per pupil in that time period (Coleman and Hoffer, 1987: 35).

Personnel

The profile of the private-school teacher is that of the dedicated amateur, usually without much formal preparation for teaching and quite often a graduate of a private school. When asked why they entered teaching, most private-school teachers indicated that they wanted to work with children and teach their discipline (Cookson, 1980; for a discussion of public-school teachers see Lortie, 1975). Private-school teachers rate the top three attributes of a good teacher as: 'knowledge and ability', 'dedication to children', and 'kindness' (Cookson and Persell, 1985: 86). On average, private school teachers are paid less than public school teachers (Center for Education Statistics, 1987a: 67).

Private-school teachers are less likely than public-school teachers to have an advanced degree, but are more likely to have graduated from a selective college or university. Most private-school teachers are women (76 per cent) but in the elite private schools 60 per cent of the teachers are male, and 92 per cent of all private-school teachers are white (Center for Education Statistics, 1987b: 55). There is a high turnover rate among private-school staff; whereas 68 per cent of public-school teachers have been teaching for 10 years or more, only 45 per cent of private-school teachers have been teaching for the equivalent time (Center for Education Statistics, 1987a: 54). Private and public school teachers work approximately 50 hours a week, and both groups divide their time similarly in terms of classroom teaching, school-related activities, and other activities.

Programmes

One of the key differences between public and private schools is that the latter are almost exclusively academic, while the former are nearly evenly divided between academic, general, and vocational programmes. According to Coleman and Hoffer (1987: 43), 'Two-thirds of the public schools, enroling three-quarters of all public school students, are organized as comprehensive schools'. Only half of Catholic-school students, one-third of other private-school students, and no elite private-school students are enrolled in comprehensive schools; moreover, private-school students take more semester hours in mathematics, English, foreign language, history, and science than do public school students. On average, private-school students spend more time on their homework and write more than public school students. There is little grade inflation within the private sector. In a study of grading practices, it was found, for example, that 20 per cent of the seniors at one suburban public high school had A averages. Approximately 2.5 per cent of private-school students have A averages. At one private school, 46 per cent of the graduating class had a C average or below (Cookson, 1981: 117).

American schools have traditionally offered students a wide variety of extra-curricular activities as a way of socially integrating students and preparing them for life. Catholic and public-school students participate in extra-curricular activities at roughly the same rate, but other private school students tend to engage in more extra-curricular activities than their public and Catholic school peers; for example, over 57 per cent of other private-school students participate in school athletics, compared to 37 per cent of Catholic-school students and 36 per cent of public-school students. Of all elite private-school students, 70 per cent are involved in school athletics. Public-school students who work on the school year-book or newspaper comprise 18 per cent, as compared to 29 per cent of Catholic-school students and 43 per cent of other private-school students. In elite private schools, the students who work on the school year-book or newspaper comprise 55 per cent (Coleman and Hoffer, 1987: 51).

Not only are private-school students involved in their schools' activities, but so are their parents, who attend parent conferences, school meetings, and do volunteer work. Private-school parents are often involved in fund-raising and promotion and most private schools make a concerted effort to include parents and grandparents in the community life of the schools.

Private school climates

The discipline at most private schools, especially at Catholic schools, is more demanding and consistent than in most public schools (Coleman et al., 1982: 181). Moreover, private-school teachers have high academic and moral expectations for their students. In a survey of how private school teachers ranked the importance of eight educational goals for students, the following four were the most important: 'moral or religious values', 'basic literacy skills', 'personal growth and fulfilment', and 'academic excellence' (Center for Education Statistics, 1987b: 99). When boarding school students were asked whether the statement 'many classes here are boring' was true or false, nearly 70 per cent answered false. The survey also showed that 84 per cent of all boarding school students believe most students 'try hard' to get on the honour roll and that 60 per cent think that there is 'a lot of interest here in learning for its own sake' (Cookson and Persell, 1985: 94-5). When Catholic schools were compared to public schools, in terms of teachers' perceptions of school climate, it was found that 'Catholic high school teachers are considerably more likely to report a positive school climate than are public high school teachers' (Center for Education Statistics, 1987a: 74). One possible reason for the positive school climates that are found in private schools may be their relatively low pupil to teacher ratios. The mean pupil to teacher ratio in private schools is 17 pupils; this compares to more than 32 pupils per class in New York City schools.

Summary

This profile of private schools has revealed that while there is considerable heterogeneity in the organization, personnel, and programmes of private schools, they do share certain structural and atmospheric characteristics. Most private schools, for example, emphasize academics, discipline, and morality. It is an intriguing question whether the differences between private and public schools account for differences in student achievement and educational mobility. Is there a 'private-school effect'? In the next section, we examine private-school outcomes in terms of academic achievement and college destinations. There is also a discussion of the indirect and long-term effects of a private-school education.

Private schools and inequality: academic achievement, college destination, and the reproduction of privilege

Uncovering private-school effects requires some theoretical sophistication because not all effects can be detected by simply comparing the test scores of private and public school students. Schools not only impart to students skills, but they also confer social status. Status competition is an ever-present fact of social life, and the effects of having high-status educational credentials ripple through graduates' lives like waves emanating from a central source; in time, they touch every social and economic boundary. Much of what is currently being written about public and private schools shapes the issue in terms of 'choice', a value-free term that implies that private schools are educational alternatives more or less available to all families. This is not true. Private schools, especially socially elite private schools, are similar to private clubs; admission is contigent not only on the ability of the client to pay but his or her personal and social attributes. Educational choice is not a neutral, self-regulating mechanism that acts as a kind of invisible educational hand, sorting and selecting students according to their preferences. To make a meaningful choice one must have the resources to act.

A futher point of importance. The acquisition of high social and occupational status is a cumulative process, one advantage builds on the next. Private school credentials remain with people throughout their lives and can be used to open status doors that have little to do with cognitive outcomes. In fact, I will argue later that those that benefit most from a private school education are not those with the greatest academic abilities, but the least.

In this section, we examine how private secondary schools influence students' educational and status opportunities. At the core of the discussion will be the recurrent issue of whether or not private schools 'add on' substantial advantages, taking into account family background and individual attributes. If it is found that private schools do have an 'independent' effect on students' educational mobility and life chances, then we can conclude that they contribute to inequalities; if not, then we can conclude that they do not contribute to educational and social inequalities. In order to conceptualize this process more clearly, we begin by discussing an analytic model that allows us to frame the argument in a temporal and logical form.

<u>An analytic model</u>

Figure 3.1 represents the key variables under discussion. While the model is basically self-explanatory, there are two major issues that need attention:
1. Private schools vary considerably in terms of their academic standards and social statuses. Graduating from a small Evangelical day school does not carry with it the same status as graduating from an elite eastern boarding school. From a conceptual point of view, we can think of private secondary schools as having high, middle, and low status. Determining the status of a school is a complex process, but the key indicators are: student-body social status, student-body academic achievement level, school resources, and reputation.
2. School effects can be direct and indirect. Two examples of direct effects are relatively high student academic achievement scores that can be linked to private school attendance and the ability of private schools to get their students into colleges they might not be admitted to if they had not attended a private school. Indirect effects can be assessed according to how much social power private school graduates 'earn', net of their personal attributes. By producing certain types of graduates, private schools establish their reputation and institutional power. A school's institutional power has been called by Meyer (1977), its 'charter'. Accordingly, schools are chartered to produce socially identifiable graduates who are defined by essential institutional gate-keepers as possessing special attributes. In this

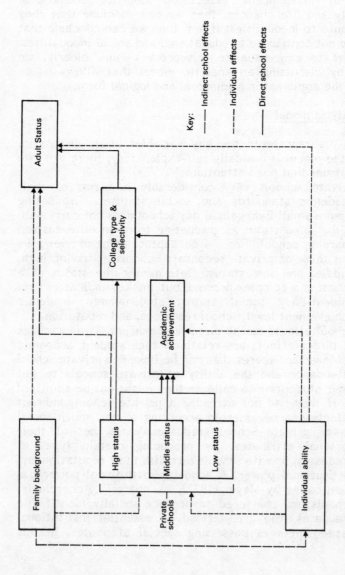

Figure 3.1 An analytic model of the relationship between individual student characteristics, private schools, academic achievement, college type and selectivity, and adult status.

Key:

········· Indirect school effects

- - - - - Individual effects

——— Direct school effects

regard, Kamens (1977: 217-8) has written, 'Schools symbolically redefine people and make them eligible for membership in societal categories to which specific sets of rights are assigned, e.g. income. The social organization of schools is a major symbolic index of the kind of socialization that has occurred and thus legitimates the conferral of specific status rights'.

Direct Effects

Academic achievement

One of the most striking findings of Coleman et al. was that when they compared the average test scores of public-school and private-school sophomores, there was not one subject in which public-school students scored higher than private-school students. In reading, vocabulary, mathematics, science, civics, and writing tests, private-school students out-performed public-school students, sometimes by a wide margin. For example, the test included 38 mathematics questions. On average, public-school students answered 18 questions correctly, Catholic and other private-school students answered on average 22 questions correctly and elite private-school students averaged 30 correct answers (Coleman et al., 1982: 124-5). The senior test scores followed the same pattern.

Having discovered that private school students have, on average, higher test scores than public-school students, the question becomes, 'Why'? Are the differences between sectors due to student selection, or are there also school effects on cognitive skills? Coleman and his colleagues created an analytic model similar to the one discussed earlier. They discovered that:

In the examination of effects on achievement, statistical controls on family background are introduced, in order to control on those background characteristics that are most related to achievement. The achievement differences between the private sectors and public sector are reduced (more for other private schools than for Catholic schools) but differences remain.

(Coleman et al., 1982: 177)

In other words, there is a private school effect on academic achievement. According to the authors, private schools produce higher achievement outcomes than public schools for two reasons: (1) 'private schools create higher rates of engagement in academic activities', and (2) 'student behavior in a school has strong and consistent effects on student achievement' (Coleman et al., 1982: 178). In short, private schools demand more from their students than do public schools. (For analyses that are highly critical of the findings of Coleman et al., see Goldberger and Cain, 1982; Alexander and Pallas, 1983. See also Haertel et al., 1987).

A key problem, however, in assessing the magnitude of school effects is that selectively bias can influence results. The problem operates on two levels: the individual and the institutional. On the individual level, it is extremely difficult to measure the kinds of motivations that impel parents and students to choose private schools. Parental and student ambitions are global characteristics of families and individuals that cannot be adequately captured by measures of parental income, education, or occupation. At the institutional level, there is strong evidence that 'the socio-economic status of fellow students plays a significant contributing role in determining students' scores.' (Murnane, 1986: 144; see also Alexander and Eckland, 1975). In a re-analysis of the data of Coleman et al., Murnane found that:

> One reason [but not the only reason] students in private schools score higher than students in public schools is that on average they come from more advantaged homes and consequently bring more skills to school with them.
> (Murnane 1986: 144)

In terms of academic achievement, then, there is a private school effect, and although the problem of selectivity bias cannot be resolved by statistical controls alone, it does appear that private schools influence achievement in three ways: through emphasis on academic achievement; tighter, more consistent discipline; and the status composition of their student bodies.

College destinations
Private-school seniors are more likely to enrol in college than are public-school seniors (Coleman and Hoffer, 1987; 154). In public schools, 28 per cent of male graduates in 1980 enrolled in four-year colleges. This compares to 51 per cent of Catholic-school male graduates and 60 per cent of other private-school male graduates who enrolled in four-year colleges. Public school female graduates who enrolled in four-year colleges amounted to 31 per cent, while those from private schools and Catholic schools amounted to 52

per cent and 51 per cent, respectively. Coleman and Hoffer observe:

There is higher college attendance among private sector students regardless of their absence levels, disciplinary behavior, or homework. At almost every level of grades and disciplinary behavior, students from either of the private sectors are more likely to enroll in college than are students from public sector schools.

(Coleman and Hoffer, 1987: 155)

Coleman and Hoffer also found that private-school students with average or below average academic records were much more likely to attend college than similar public-school students. The evidence is that about half of the differences in the percentages of public-school and private-school students who attend four-year or two-year colleges is due to individual background characteristics. The other half of the differences are accounted for by whether students graduate from a public or private school (for further discussion, see Falsey and Heyns, 1984).

In the United States, colleges and universities vary considerably in their prestige and selectivity (Hammack and Cookson, 1980). Hooper's (1971) distinction between 'educational amount' and 'educational route' is relevant here. Where one goes to college has a direct impact on one's occupational attainment and income. The most reliable indicator of a college's prestige is its academic selectivity, which is generally measured by the total average scholastic aptitude test scores of its entering class (Astin et al., 1981). In one study it was found that private-school students attend more selective colleges than did public-school students, even when the two groups of students' academic achievements and family backgrounds were similar (Cookson, 1981: 157). In another study, it was found that college advisors at elite private schools establish working and social relationships with the admissions officers at colleges, private colleges in particular. This private-school/private-college network helps students gain admission to selective colleges (Persell and Cookson, 1985).

Private schools are able to place 'floors' under their weaker students; that is, average or below-average students are protected against downward educational mobility by the mere fact of having attended a private school. Moreover, the higher the social status of the private school, the greater its effect in the secondary school to college transition (Cookson, 1981: 208). This indicates that the more

73

external institutional power a school has - its charter - the greater its effect on where students go to college.

From this discussion of academic achievement and college destinations, it should be apparent that private school attendance has a direct effect on students' educational mobility. Private schools' internal characteristics and external connections make them potent vehicles for the creation and maintenance of inequalities. Private schools also vary in their prestige and power. It is generally thought that the most socially elite private schools exercise considerable educational and social power. In the words of Baltzell (1958: 293), these schools 'serve the sociological function of differentiating the upper classes from the rest of the population'.

<u>Indirect effects</u>

Most socially elite private schools are members of the National Association of Independent Schools and are listed in such books as <u>The Handbook of Private Schools</u> (Porter-Sargent, 1987). Some of the elite schools were founded during the American Revolution, although most were founded between 1880 and 1920, during the period of the 'prep school boom'; these latter schools generally modelled themselves on the British 'public' school (Levine, 1980; for further discussion see Boyd, 1973; Wakeford, 1969; and Walford, 1983, 1986). Historically, the elite schools have educated the sons and daughters of America's upper class (Armstrong, 1979; Domhoff, 1967). Mills (1959: 64-5), has written of these schools that they are: 'the most important agency for transmitting the traditions of the upper social classes, and regulating the admission of new wealth and talent. It is the characterizing point in the upper-class experience.'

Elite boarding school students are socialized for power. The transformation of students from raw recruits into 'soldiers for their class' requires a specific rite-of-passage, the result of which is to create a sense of collective identity among elite private school students and graduates. Collective identity leads to a shared consciousness which produces class solidarity and cohesion which, in turn, reinforces the class system. Thus, private school graduates often join the same social clubs, marry other private school graduates, send their own children to private school, support important private institutions, and most importantly, support and defend the private enterprise system (Cookson and Persell, 1985).

A study by Useem (1984: 67) found that thirteen elite boarding schools educated 10 per cent of the members of the board of directors of large American business organizations. In another study, Useem and Karabel (1984) found that nearly half of the senior corporate managers in their study had elite school or social register backgrounds. A former Director of Development at the socially elite Choate School said, 'There is no door in this entire country that cannot be opened by a Choate graduate' (Prescott, 1970: 67). This network of elite private school graduates is an important element in the reproduction of privilege (for a discussion of educational and social reproduction see Bourdieu and Passeron, 1977). Inequalities based on class, which are usually highly related to inequalities based on race and gender, are in part created and justified by a private educational system that elevates its graduates into positions of influence and power.

Summary

It is clear that attending a private school has an impact on academic achievement and educational mobility. It is also evident that a diploma from an elite private school is a social credential that can be used to open, as I put it, status doors for a lifetime. The educational reproduction of privilege reinforces structured inequalities. These findings are not particularly startling, but they are unsettling if one believes in the principle of equal opportunity for all children. In the next section we examine current public policies toward private schools.

Private schools and public policy

Private schools in the United States are relatively unregulated by local, state, or federal authorities, although private schools must operate within the framework of the United States Constitution, and within certain state and local laws concerning student safety and citizenship. Private schools have not won their autonomy easily. Up to 1925, it was still a matter of legal debate as to whether private schools should be allowed to exist as alternatives to public schools. In that year, the United States Supreme Court, in

75

the case of <u>Pierce</u> v. <u>Society of Sisters</u>, upheld the right of parents to choose private schooling for their children. The court, however, did leave the door open for state regulation of private schools when they concluded, 'No question is raised concerning the power of the State reasonably to regulate all schools' (Hirschoff, 1986: 49). Since the Pierce decision, public policy towards private schools has centred on two issues: regulation and funding.

Regulation

According to Hirschoff:
> Private schools are subject to the same general laws that apply to any private business, except to the extent that their educational functions lead to the imposition of additional regulations, and their nonprofit status, if adopted, entitles them to special treatment.
> (Hirschoff, 1986: 38)

Because the American school system is decentralized, the federal government has very few regulatory powers. Most public and private school regulation is left to the states and local communities. There are four main areas of interest: control; teacher hiring and firing; student selection and discipline; and curriculum. (For further discussion, see Hirschoff, 1986: 38-40.)

Control
As long as a private school meets the technical requirements of incorporation and does not violate any federal, state, or local laws, the board of trustees may govern as they see fit. School boards are self-perpetuating and need not seek teacher, student, or parental approval for their decisions.

Teacher hiring and firing
As of 1986 only thirteen states required that private school teachers obtain a state-regulated teaching certificate. Generally, private schools can hire whoever they want, as the terms and conditions of employment are governed by a private contract.

Student selection and discipline
Private schools are free to admit whoever they wish, although they cannot discriminate on the basis of race. Major disciplinary decisions are regulated by the private

contract that parents sign when they enrol their children.

Curriculum
States vary in terms of how much they regulate private
school curriculums. Some states have no regulation, while
others require that private schools provide at least an
equivalent curriculum to that found in public schools. Some
states require private schools to teach specific courses such
as US history and civics. Occasionally, states will require
private schools to include drug and health education courses
in their curriculums and will generally require that
instruction be in English, except when teaching a foreign
language.

The rights of states to regulate private schools is a
continuing legal issue. Recent trends and court decisions
have generally upheld basic constitutional guarantees; thus,
students from Fundamentalist religious homes cannot be
forced to attend public schools, nor, as mentioned earlier,
can private schools legally discriminate against students on
the basis of race.

Public funding of private schools

Beginning with the Elementary and Secondary Education Act
of 1965, private schools have been receiving limited funds
fron the federal government. In the fiscal year 1981, schools
received $606 million from the federal government (Kutner
et al., 1986: 58). Coleman and Hoffer (1986: 40) found that,
'Substantial private school participation is limited to a few
of the Elementary and Secondary Education Act programs,
and most of this involvement is by Catholic schools'. The
last major piece of Federal legislation that affected private
schools was the Education Consolidation and Improvement
Act of 1981. While the amount of aid that goes to private
schools under federal legislation is relatively small, it does
indicate that the federal government is interested in
ensuring educational equity for disadvantaged and handicapped children, whether they are enrolled in public or
private schools. There are also several plans to help parents
defray the cost of private education.

Tuition tax credits
Essentially, a tuition tax credit allows parents, when
calculating their income tax, to deduct a certain amount of
the expenses they incur in sending their child or children to

private school. The state of Minnesota has provided tax deductions for educational expenses since 1955. Between 1967 and 1977, six tuition tax credit proposals passed the United States Senate, but never became law (Kutner et al., 1986: 65). The Reagan Administration tuition tax credit proposals have not passed either the Senate or the House of Representatives. In 1983, the Senate Finance Committee approved a phased-in plan, but it was defeated by the full Senate.

Vouchers
Under a voucher plan, parents receive a voucher worth a certain amount of money, which they then spend at a school - public or private - of their choice. Vouchers are seen by their advocates as increasing the market sensitivity of schools and, by extension, improving the quality of education. In an experiment conducted in the early 1970s, by the Office of Educational Opportunity and the National Institute of Education, it was found that 20 per cent of the parents in the voucher demonstration district chose to send their children to non-neighbourhood schools. Private schools did not participate in this study and there was little evidence that students' test scores improved as a consequence of attending a non-neighbourhood school (Kutner et al., 1986: 67).

Compensatory education grants
In order to increase the educational opportunities of disadvantaged students, some legislators have proposed a 'mini-voucher' programme where low-income families would be given vouchers to spend in either public or private schools. There are several proposals for compensatory education grants, but they have yet to become operational.

For private schools, public funding is a double-edged sword. The money that they receive allows them to admit more students and expand their programmes, but inevitably lose some of their autonomy. There is little direct evidence that tuition tax credit or voucher plans actually result in greater educational equity. As of now, it seems clear that private schools will receive limited aid from public sources but that large scale public aid, direct or indirect, is not a likely future prospect.

Summary

Private schools have attained a secure place within the American educational system. During the 1980s, they have been a topic of discussion among public policy makers and there have been some attempts to integrate them more fully within a national system of education. Most of these plans have gone for naught. Without a dramatic shift in American politics, it is quite likely that public policy towards private schools will remain the same. As long as private schools operate within the framework of the United States Constitution they will continue to function without significant governmental intervention.

Conclusion: private schools and the public good

Drawing a balanced and complete picture of American private schools within their social and educational contexts is a complex task. Linking private schools to the class system complicates the matter considerably. The goal of this chapter has been to outline the main contours of American private education and to touch on some of the more important debates concerning the effects of private schools on students and society.

Clearly, private schools play an important role in American education. They educated a relatively small proportion of students, but in real numbers, this represents a great many young people. They offer students and their families educational alternatives that are unavailable in the public system; moreover, the variation within the private school sector is tremendous. Schools differ in philosophy, practice, and personnel. Some schools are very conservative, others quite liberal. Each private school creates its own traditions and culture, yet private schools also share a common culture. I have likened attending a private school to joining a club because private schools are more than schools, they are also communities. Each one of these communities is tied into the social structure in a slightly different way. It is evident that private schools that are part of the upper-class community play a significant role in reproducing social and economic inequalities. While this may not be the intention of those who run the schools, it is the consequence.

As mentioned earlier, the 1980s have been a time when

public interest in private education has increased dramatically. This is a mixed blessing for private schools because, while they are often proud of their accomplishments, too much public exposure places them squarely at the centre of an ongoing American educational debate; how do we achieve equal opportunity for all children without sacrificing quality and the right of families to choose their own form of schooling? This issue will not be resolved quickly, nor should we expect perfect parity in a society as competitive and individualistic as the United States. By one reliable estimate, private school enrolments will increase in the future (Cooper et al., 1983). If this is true, then private schools will continue to attract the public-policy eye. Yet, unless there is a major political change in the United States, it is fair to say that public policy towards private schools is apt to remain much as it is today: curious, cautious, and cost-conscious. There is deep respect for private institutions in the United States and, with the exception of the military, a general disrespect for public institutions. Because of this, there is little chance that private schools will find themselves on the receiving end of unfavourable legislation.

Continuity is the key word in describing the private school world. As we look to the future, we can expect private schools to continue their mission of providing educational alternatives to the public system. The debate concerning their proper role in American education and society will continue as well, offering scholars, policy makers, parents, and educators recurring opportunities to debate whether or not the public good is best served by a mixed educational system.

References

Alexander, K. and Eckland, B.K. (1975) 'Contextual effects in the high school attainment process', American Sociological Review 40, 402-16.

Alexander, K. and Pallas, A.M. (1983) 'Private schools and public policy: new evidence on cognitive achievement in public and private schools', Sociology of Education 56, 170-82.

Armstrong, C.F. (1979) 'Privilege and productivity: the case of two private schools and their graduates', Ph.D. dissertation, Department of Sociology, University of Pennsylvania.

Astin, W., King, M.R., and Richardson, G.T. (1981) The American Freshman: National Norms for Fall 1981, Los Angeles, University of California: Laboratory for Research in Higher Education.

Baird, L.L. (1977) The Elite Schools, Lexington, Mass.: Lexington Books.

Baltzell, E.D. (1958) Philadelphia Gentlemen: the Making of a National Upper Class, Chicago: Quadrangle Books.

—— (1964) The Protestant Establishment, New York: Random House.

Bourdieu, P. and Passeron, J-C. (1977) Reproduction - in Education, Society, and Culture, Beverly Hills, California: Sage.

Boyd, D. (1973) Elites and their Education, Slough, England: NFER Publishing.

Center for Education Statistics (1987a) The Condition of Education - a Statistical Report, Washington, D.C.: US Department of Education.

—— (1987b) Private Schools and Private School Teachers: Final Report of the 1985-86 Private School Study, Washington, D.C.: US Department of Education.

Coleman, J.S. and Hoffer, T. (1987) Public and Private High Schools: the Impact of Communities, New York: Basic Books.

Coleman, J.S. et al. (1966) Equality of Educational Opportunity, Washington, D.C.: US Government Printing Office.

Coleman, J.S., Hoffer, T., and Kilgore, S. (1982) High School Achievement: Public, Catholic and Private Schools Compared, New York: Basic Books.

Cookson, P.W., Jr. (1980) 'The educational attitudes of private school educators', paper presented at the American Sociological Association annual meeting, New York.

—— (1981) 'Private secondary boarding school and public suburban high school graduation: an analysis of college attendance plans', Ph.D. dissertation, New York University.

—— (1987) 'More, different, or better? Strategies for the study of private education', Educational Policy 1, 289-94.

Cookson, P.W., Jr. and Persell, C.H. (1985) Preparing for Power: America's Elite Boarding Schools, New York: Basic Books.

Cooper, B.S., McLaughlin, D.H., and Manno, B.V. (1983) 'The

latest word on private school growth', Teachers College Record 85, 88-98.

Domhoff, G.W. (1967) Who Rules America?, Englewood Cliffs, New Jersey: Prentice-Hall.

Erickson, D.A. (1986) 'Choice and private schools: dynamics of supply and demand', in D.C. Levy (ed.) Private Education: Studies in Choice and Public Policy, 82-109, New York: Oxford University Press.

Falsey, B. and Heyns, B. (1984) 'The college channel: private and public schools reconsidered', Sociology of Education 57, 111-22.

Friedman, M. and Friedman, R. (1980) Free to Choose, New York: Harcourt Brace Jovanovich.

Goldberger, A.S. and Cain, G.G. (1982) 'The casual analysis of cognitive outcomes in the Coleman, Hoffer and Kilgore report', Sociology of Education 55, 103-22.

Haertel, E., James, T., and Levin, H.M. (1987) (eds), Comparing Public and Private Schools. Volume 2. School Achievement, New York: Falmer Press.

Hammack, F.M. and Cookson, P.W., Jr. (1980) 'Colleges attended by graduates of elite secondary schools', The Educational Forum 44, 483-90.

The Handbook of Private Schools (1987) Boston, Mass: Porter Sargent.

Hirschoff, M-M.U. (1986) 'Public policy toward private schools: a focus on parental choice', in D.C. Levy (ed.), Private Education: Studies in Choice and Public Policy, 33-56, New York: Oxford University Press.

Hopper, E. (1971) 'Stratification, education and mobility in industrial societies', in E. Hopper (ed.) Readings in the Theory of Educational Systems, 13-37, London: Hutchinson.

Kamens, D.H. (1977) 'Legitimating myths and educational organization: the relationship between organizational ideology and formal structure', American Sociological Review 40, 208-19.

Kraushaar, O.F. (1972) American nonpublic schools: patterns of diversity, Baltimore: Johns Hopkins University Press.

Kutner, M.A., Sherman, J.D., and Williams, M.F. (1986) 'Federal policies for private schools', in D.C. Levy (ed.), Private Education: Studies in Choice and Public Policy, 57-81, New York: Oxford University Press.

Levine, S.B. (1980) 'The rise of American boarding schools and the development of a national upper class', Social Problems 28, 63-94.

Levy, D.C. (1986) (ed.) Private Education: Studies in Choice and Public Policy, New York: Oxford University Press.

Lortie, D. (1975) School-Teacher, Chicago: University of Chicago Press.

McDill, E.L. (1978) 'An updated answer to the question, "Do schools make a difference?" ', paper presented at the National Institute of Education: International Conference on School Organization and Effect, San Diego, California.

McLachlan, J. (1970) American Boarding Schools: a Historical Study, New York: Charles Scribner.

Meyer, J. (1977) 'Education as an institution', American Journal of Sociology 83, 55-77.

Mills, C.W. (1959) The Power Elite, New York: Oxford University Press.

Murnane, R.J. (1986) 'Comparisons of private and public schools: the critical role of regulations', in D.C. Levy (ed.), Private Education: Studies in Choice and Public Policy, 138-52, New York: Oxford University Press.

National Commission on Excellence in Education (1983) A Nation at Risk: the Imperative for Educational Reform, Washington, D.C.: US Government Printing Office.

Persell, C.H. and Cookson, P.W., Jr. (1985) 'Chartering and bartering: elite education and social reproduction', Social Problems 33, 114-29.

Prescott, P.S. (1970) A World of Our Own: Notes on Life and Learning in a Boys' Preparatory School, New York: Coward-McCann.

Tyack, D.B. (1968) 'The perils of pluralism: the background of the Pierce case', American Historical Review 74, 74-98.

Useem, M. (1984) The Inner Circle: Large Corporations and the Rise of Business Political Activity in the US and UK, New York: Oxford University Press.

Useem, M. and Karabel, J. (1984) 'Educational pathways through top corporate management: patterns of stratification within companies and differences among companies', paper presented at the American Sociological Association annual meeting, San Antonio, Texas.

Wakeford, J. (1969) The Cloistered Elite: a Sociological Analysis of the English Public Boarding School, London: Macmillan.

Walford, G. (1983) 'Girls in boys' public schools: a prelude to further research', British Journal of Sociology of

Education 4, 39-54.

Walford, G. (1986) <u>Life in Public Schools</u>, London: Methuen.

CHAPTER 4

CANADA: PRIVATE SCHOOLS

John J. Bergen

General setting

Canada comprises ten provinces, each with sovereign
statutory powers, and two northern territories, the
legislatures of which have such powers as are granted by the
federal parliament. Only about 712,000 (2.8 per cent) of
Canada's population of approximately 25,310,000 belong to
the native peoples. About 15,334,000 (60.6 per cent) claim
English and 6,160,000 (24.3 per cent) claim French as their
mother tongue, and about 3,816,000 (15.1 per cent) other
mother tongues are represented by immigrants from many
countries. Only about 76,000 people reside in the northern
territories which comprise about 40 per cent of Canada's
land mass; of these, about 25,000 (33.2 per cent) belong to
the native peoples. Most of Canada's population is resident
in the southern part of the country bordering the United
States. Only about 24 per cent of Canadians are classified as
being rural residents. The provision of educational services
is largely a provincial responsibility. The federal government continues to bear the financial cost of the schooling of
natives. Private schools are found in every province;
however, the number of private school pupils in Newfoundland and each of the Yukon and Northwest territories make
up a combined total of less than 100. Of Canada's total
elementary and secondary school population of about
4,630,000, approximately 234,000 (4.8 per cent) are enrolled
in private schools.

A 'private' or 'independent' school in Canada is defined
as a school other than one under the governance of a local
public school board or of a provincial or federal government
department. Private schools may qualify for a measure of
public financial support in provinces which provide for

grants to the private education sector. Many of the private schools include instruction in religion and may be governed by their founding churches or denominations. Others may be inter-denominational or non-sectarian in nature. Still others, generally secular in nature, have been established to meet specific educational needs, such as those for physically, emotionally or intellectually handicapped children, or in order to provide instruction from the perspective of a particular educational philosophy or methodology, such as those of the Montessori and Waldorf schools. A number of elite private schools continue to serve in the interest of social selection for that sector of society which may be deemed to be relatively affluent and politically prominent. 'Separate' denominational schools, which are part of the provincially established public school systems of some of the Canadian provinces, are not 'private' schools, even though these serve a defined sector of the school population.

Early schooling

During the French regime, the first private school was founded by the Jesuits in the city of Quebec in 1635. Private schools also served the Protestant population during early British rule. The oldest continuing private school in English Canada was founded at Windsor, New Brunswick in 1788 (Wilson et al., 1970: 466). Private ventures in education during the eighteenth century were often for the education of the wealthy (Phillips, 1957: 106).

During the early part of the nineteenth century, public and private schools were not clearly distinguishable because government grants were also being provided to some of the private schools. Private schools continued to hold a dominant position until the middle of the nineteenth century. For example, in 1847 about half the pupils in Kingston were registered in private schools, and in 1867 only one-fifth of the Protestant children in Montreal attended public schools (Phillips, 1957: 296). In western Canada, schooling was first provided in 1808 by the Hudson's Bay Company for the children of its employees (Wilson et al., 1970: 244). Private initiative thus performed a public service before local education authorities were organized to serve the general population. The French in Canada had considered education 'largely as a matter of family and church responsibility' until the 1960s, following major developments in the province of Quebec, when they 'were willing to entrust more and more of educational decision-making to the state' (Wilson et al., 1970: 444).

General structure of Canadian education

Canada became a constitutional entity in 1867 following the passing of the British North America Act by the British Parliament. The place and influence of religion in Canadian education was derived from the role played by Roman Catholic and Protestant churches and officials during early developments in both private and public education. Egerton Ryerson, who laid the groundwork for free and universal education in Upper Canada, strove for equal rights for all denominations. 'Separate schools' within public school systems were established in school law for Catholic minorities in Upper Canada (Ontario) in 1853 and for Protestants in Lower Canada (Quebec) in 1841 (Wilson et al., 1970: 195-217). Section 93 of the 1867 Act gave to the provinces the exclusive right to make laws in relation to education 'in and for each province', subject to certain conditions which guaranteed Roman Catholics and Protestants the rights to denominational schools in Quebec and Ontario, and which rights were to apply to other provinces where such schools existed at the time of union or were subsequently established by law. The separate school provision was also introduced by the federal government in the northern territories in 1875, and was extended to the provinces of Alberta and Saskatchewan when these were carved out of the territories in 1905. A constitutional basis was thus laid for denominationalism in Canadian education.

Several denominational school systems comrpised the 'public schools' of Newfoundland when it joined Canada as the tenth province in 1949. Special provisions in provincial and territorial school systems can be classified as follows:
1.   Catholic and Protestant schools in Quebec;
2.   Schools for several denominations in Newfoundland;
3.   Separate Catholic schools upon request in Ontario, Saskatchewan, Alberta and in the northern territories;
4.   No provision for separate schools in the provinces of British Columbia, Manitoba, New Brunswick, Nova Scotia and Prince Edward Island.
As shown in this chapter, the foregoing arrangements have influenced private school developments across Canada.

The religious nature inherent in the Canadian school systems was not restricted to confessional and separate schools. Stamp stated that:

> Religious exercises and instruction were a central part of the school day for nearly every Canadian young person. Such an emphasis was to be expected in the openly denominational schools in Quebec and Newfoundland, and in the Roman Catholic separate schools of other regions. But is was also strong in the supposedly 'public' schools, on the basis that Canada was a Christian country, and the fundamental beliefs of Christianity could be imparted 'without insult' to mixed classes.
>
> (Stamp, in Wilson et al. 1970: 291)

No distinction is made among Protestant denominations within the terms of section 93 of the 1867 British North America Act. However, denominations may differ considerably from one another in theology and practice, and some of these may feel as keenly as do Catholics about particular theological perspectives permeating a school programme. From the very beginning, Protestants were in disagreement about what the nature of religious instruction in the 'public' schools ought to be. Nevertheless, the eventual secularization of public schools served as one of the major reasons for the establishment of new private schools, particularly during the 1970s and 1980s (Bergen, 1982). Public schools increasingly have become like the 'neutral' type of school advocated by Lupul (1969: 147) as an option -schools which would have an appeal for 'atheists, agnostics, freethinkers, rationalists, Unitarians, Quakers and liberal-minded Jews and Moslems'.

Though some moves were considered in the 1940s to give stronger emphasis to religious instruction in the public schools of Ontario (those not designated as Catholic or Protestant separate schools) these were met with opposition by Jewish leaders, the Orange Order, and some Baptists. The Committee on Religious Education acknowledged that Ontario society had changed from one predominantly Anglo-Christian to one which was pluralistic. The Committee concluded that a disregard of this fact would 'discriminate against large segments of the population', i.e. the many religious denominations and sects related to ethnic groups which had come from all parts of the world (Ontario Department of Education, 1969: 13 and 25).

In a similar vein, the Royal Commission of Inquiry on Education in the province of Quebec (Quebec Department of

Education, 1963: 63) recommended: 'establishing and operating, within the public sector and on an equal footing, both non-confessional and confessional education', which 'best correspond to ... the pluralism of the Quebec population'. Magnuson (1969: 194) pointed out that 'a spirit of confessionalism no longer permeates the cultural fabric of French Canada'. In Quebec, as in other provinces, such developments would tend to induce the continuation of private schools in which confessionalism would be promoted in contrast to the state schools which have become more 'neutral' or secular in character.

In Quebec, free public schooling was not extended to the end of the secondary school until 1943, and not until the 1960s did government initiative provide the opportunity of a secondary school education for all aspiring youth (Wilson et al., 1970: 475). Hence, a strong tradition of private schools in Quebec continued even though there was constitutional provision for Catholic schools within the provincial school system. Private Catholic schools flourished in Ontario because provisions for government support of separate schools had not been extended to include all of secondary education until 1987. Similarly, private Catholic secondary schools were established in Saskatchewan because full funding through public taxation and government grants had not been extended to include separate secondary education until 1964. Although separate schools were originally part of Manitoba's educational system, such were eliminated by provincial legislation in 1890.

No provision for separate schools was ever enacted for the province of British Columbia. A host of private Catholic and other denominational schools have been established over the years. The entrenched denominational system of Newfoundland virtually obviated the need for private schools. In New Brunswick and Prince Edward Island, Catholics reside in relatively homogeneous francophone communities, which allowed for the instruction of religion in their schools even though provincial legislation does not provide for the establishment of separate schools. In Nova Scotia, unofficial arrangements were made in some communities for the designation of certain schools as Catholic and others as Protestant. In some provinces the homogeneity of new immigrant communities allowed for religious instruction in their schools even though such were the 'public' schools of the provinces, as, for example, the schools of Mennonites in Manitoba.

Private school growth

The percentage of all elementary and secondary pupils enrolled in private schools in Canada has varied little in two decades. As is illustrated in Table 4.1, only following the last 5-year period did the proportion of all pupils in private schools exceed that of 20 years earlier in 1965-66. Private school enrolments increased from 1970 onwards, during which time public school enrolments dropped. However, had all pupils been enrolled in public schools, the total impact on their enrolments would have been less than 1 per cent.

A breakdown of enrolments by provinces is provided in Table 4.2. Private school growth in the Atlantic provinces has been negligible. Quebec and Ontario, being the most populous provinces, contribute largely to the numbers in private schools in Canada. Quebec private schools enrol 41 per cent and Ontario 33 per cent of the nation's private school pupils. British Columbia claims 14 per cent of all private school pupils and the Prairie and Atlantic provinces jointly, the remaining 12 per cent. In 1985, private schools enrolled 4.8 per cent of all pupils in Canada. The total number of secondary pupils is about twice the number of elementary pupils enrolled in private schools. However, in some provinces, about the same numbers are enrolled at both levels. Though some private schools have enrolments exceeding 1,000, the average for all schools indicates that most are much smaller. In fact, some private schools enrol fewer than ten pupils.

The affiliations for most private schools are shown in Table 4.3. As the information recorded by Statistics Canada is incomplete, a few estimates based on additional records are included in the table. Twenty-three denominational affiliations are given. There may be others for some of the schools classified as non-sectarian. No affiliation was reported for Quebec private schools, most of which are Catholic, and some of which are Protestant or Jewish. Though the table gives the enrolment in Roman Catholic private schools as approximately 40,000, probably more than half of all private school pupils were in Roman Catholic schools, and hence the actual total would be over 100,000.

The largest denominational affiliation for all private schools was Roman Catholic. The Ontario Alliance of Christian Schools and the Christian Reformed Schools, though classified separately by Statistics Canada, belong to the same general affiliation and together enrolled about

Table 4.1   Percentage changes in enrolments in five-year periods, 1965-85

Year	Percentage private of total school enrolments	Period	Percentage change during period		
			Private	Public	Total
1965/6	4.1				
1970/1	2.5	1965/6-1970/1	-22.1	13.8	12.6
1975/6	3.3	1970/1-1975/6	27.6	-5.0	-4.2
1980/1	4.1	1975/6-1980/1	15.1	-9.6	-8.8
1985/6	4.8	1980/1-1985/6	11.9	-4.3	-3.6

Source: Statistics Canada.

17,000 students. The next two largest affiliations were the Jewish and Mennonite schools, which enrolled about 9,000 and 5,600 students respectively. Seventh Day Adventists schools enrolled about 3,300 students and the Baptists schools about 2,600. The Canadian Reformed and Lutheran schools respectively enrolled about 1,700 and 1,200 students. As Table 4.3 illustrates, some affiliations are province-centred, while others are distributed more generally among the provinces. The Christian Reformed and Ontario Alliance of Christian Schools represent mainly immigrants from The Netherlands who brought with them a strong tradition of private schools.

Private schools and enrolment growth trends over a 10-year period are given in Table 4.4 The pattern for the Atlantic provinces has remained stable, with some growth indicated in Nova Scotia and New Brunswick. Even so, the proportion of all pupils in private schools has remained small. The early school developments in Newfoundland were private and denominational. However, these were institutionalized as the 'public' schools of the province. As a consequence, there has been no movement toward private schools. Though there has been some reduction in the number of private schools in Quebec, the proportion of pupils in private schools has continued to increase. Throughout Canadian history Quebec has had the highest incidence of private school education. Though there was a drop in private school attendance during the late 1960s, it has steadily increased since 1970. Government financial assistance for private schools in Quebec is superior to that found in other provinces, and may contribute to the maintenance of the private school tradition. However, the growing secularization of the provincial schools may be a stronger contributing factor.

The percentage of all pupils in private schools rose in Ontario over a 20-year period, and dropped for the first time for 1985-6. The status of secondary Catholic schools as 'separate' schools, and as a sector of the public school system for full public funding beginning in 1985, meant that Catholic students, formerly counted as private school students, became part of the public enrolment sector. As a consequence, from 1984/5 to 1985/6 the total private school enrolment for Canada dropped by about 4,000, and by 12 per cent for Ontario. Private school enrolments for all of Canada rose by 15.1 per cent from 1975 to 1980, and another 11.8 per cent from 1980 to 1985.

Table 4.2 Private schools and private school enrolment in Canada, 1985–6

	Atlantic Provinces[a]	Quebec	Ontario	Manitoba	Saskatchewan	Alberta	British Columbia	Totals
No. of schools	59	b	536	78	47	134	234	1,088[c]
Private school enrolment								
Pre-elementary	280	2,690	7,540	550	60	950	2,550	14,620
Grades 1–6	1,600	20,660	23,850	4,100	640	5,930	16,560	73,340
Grades 7–13	1,630	71,960	44,930	4,870	2,250	6,210	14,450	146,300
Totals	3,510	95,310	76,320	9,520	2,950	13,090	33,560	234,260
Approximate enrolment per school	60	470	140	120	60	100	140	215
Public school enrolment	481,270	1,041,440	1,769,450	199,010	202,560	448,020	486,780	4,628,530
Percentage private of public and private combined	0.7	8.4	4.1	4.6	1.4	2.8	6.4	4.8

a Newfoundland, Prince Edward Island, Nova Scotia and New Brunswick.
  (Private school enrolment mainly in Nova Scotia and New Brunswick.)
b Number not reported, estimated to be about 200.
c Excluding Quebec.

Source: Statistics Canada.

Table 4.3 Private school enrolments by affiliation and province for 1985-6[a]

	Atlantic Provinces	Quebec	Ontario	Manitoba	Saskatchewan	Alberta	British Columbia	Totals	Percentage of private pupils
Amish	-	-	120	-	-	-	-	120	0.05
Anglican	-	-	5,270	60	-	-	-	5,330	2.28
Baptist	650	-	1,390	130	80	300	40	2,590	1.01
Brethren in Christ	-	-	170	-	-	-	-	170	0.07
Brethren of Early									
Christianity	-	-	20	-	-	-	-	20	0.01
Calvinistic	-	-	-	-	-	270	-	(270)	0.12
Canadian Reformed	-	-	1,350	50	-	50	280	(1,730)	0.74
Christian Reformed	100	-	430	290	-	2,800	4,240	7,860	(3.4)
Church of Christ	-	-	-	-	110	-	-	110	0.05
General Church of New Jerusalem	-	-	60	-	-	-	-	60	0.03
Hutterite	-	-	-	10	-	-	-	10	0.004
Jewish	-	?	7,500	910	-	340	340	(9,090)	(3.88)
Lutheran	-	-	10	-	520	530	110	1,170	0.50
Mennonite	60	-	2,650	1,610	320	230	750	5,620	2.40
Ontario Alliance of									

Table 4.3 cont.

Pentecostal	100	–	50	10	–	–	710	870	0.37
Presbyterian	10	–	230	–	–	–	–	240	0.10
Protestant	–	?	200	–	–	–	–	(200)	(0.01)
Roman Catholic	370	?	20,470	3,370	460	100	15,120	(39,890)	(17.03)d
Seventh Day Adventist	130	–	1,150	80	150	920	840	3,270	1.40
Society of Friends	–	–	150	–	–	–	–	150	0.06
Ukrainian Catholic	–	–	230	50	–	–	–	280	0.12
United	50	–	600	–	–	–	–	650	0.28
Non-Sectarianb	1,960	?	21,400	2,650	1,280	7,550	11,130	45,970	19.6
Affiliation not reportedc	80	95,310	3,690	300	30	–	–	99,410	42.44
Totals	3,510	95,310	76,320	9,520	2,950	13,090	33,560	234,260	

a   Estimates are placed in parentheses.
b   Many of the schools reported as non-sectarian may be associated with denominations, but may regard themselves to be inter-denominational Christian.
c   Some of the schools may be non-sectarian or secular; others may belong to one of the listed affiliations.
d   The proportion of students in Catholic private schools would approach or exceed 50 percent if Quebec affiliations had been given.

Source: Compiled from Statistics Canada tables.

Table 4.4 Private schools and enrolment growth trends, 1975/6 to 1985/6*

Year	Newfoundland		Prince Edward Is.		Nova Scotia		New Brunswick		Quebec		Ontario		Total Enrolment
	N	%	N	%	N	%	N	%	N	%	N	%	
1975-6	3	0.2	1	0.2	8	0.7	4	0.1	350	6.1	310	2.6	182,000
1980-1	1	0.2	2	0.2	10	0.8	17	0.6	183	7.2	438	3.7	209,400
1985-6	2	0.2	1	0.2	28	1.1	28	0.8	(200)	8.4	536	4.1	234,200

Year	Manitoba		Saskatchewan		Alberta		British Columbia		Canada	
	N	%	N	%	N	%	N	%	N	%
1975-6	38	3.0	13	0.6	40	1.2	124	3.8	890	3.3
1980-1	53	3.8	30	1.1	42	1.4	195	4.9	971	4.1
1985-6	78	4.6	47	1.4	134	2.8	234	6.4	(1,300)	4.8

* The recorded data may be actual or reflect close approximations. Figures in parentheses indicate estimates.

N = number of private schools.

% = percentage of private enrolment is for all elementary and secondary pupils.

Source: Compiled from Statistics Canada tables.

Table 4.5 Percentage of private schools revenue from government funds and other sources, 1982-3

	Atlantic Provinces*	Quebec	Ontario	Manitoba	Saskatchewan	Alberta	British Columbia	Canada
1. Local public school boards	0	0.2	5.3	0.3	8.3	1.1	0.1	2.1
2. Government (largely provincial government)	1.2	54.9	1.7	14.8	19.5	35.3	29.3	30.9
3. Tuition fees	67.5	39.0	66.5	52.7	42.0	39.3	50.7	50.3
4. Other sources	31.2	5.9	26.5	32.3	30.3	24.3	19.9	16.8
5. Percentage provincial government private school grants is of total grants for all schools	0.1	3.5	0.1	0.9	0.6	1.0	1.2	1.6
6. Percentage total private schools revenue is of total provincial and municipal school funding	0.6	6.1	3.7	3.2	1.7	1.8	3.5	3.8
7. Percent of all pupils in private schools for 1982-3	0.6	7.9	4.4	4.7	1.2	1.9	5.3	4.6

* comprising mainly Nova Scotia and New Brunswick

Source: Compiled from Financial Statistics of Education (81-208), Statistics Canada.

Government support and control

Public financing of secondary private schooling became available in Saskatchewan in 1966. However, its impact on total private school enrolment appears to have been minimal, although the number of private schools increased from 13 to 47 from 1975 to 1985. A modest measure of funding of private schools, for all grades, was initiated in Alberta in 1967, yet substantial growth in the number of schools and in enrolment did not become evident until the 1980s. Introducting financial support for private schools in British Columbia in 1977 might have accounted for some of the growth in the 1980s. Manitoba introduced financial support for private schools in 1979. Yet many of the small private schools which were established in these provinces did not qualify nor did they expect government assistance. It is also of note that the gradual growth of private schooling in Ontario has occurred without any government financial assistance and that interest in private schooling has increased among a number of Protestant denominations.

Manitoba does not have provisions for separate schools as part of the public school sector and Catholic private schools account for more than one-third of all its private school pupils. Both Saskatchewan and Alberta have provisions for Catholic separate schools as a public school option. Hence, the Catholic enrolment in private schools is minimal in each province. Saskatchewan has some public funding for high-school private schools only, whereas in Alberta such funding is provided for elementary schools also. Private-school attendance in Saskatchewan has remained relatively stable over the years, whereas in Alberta a substantial increase has occurred since 1980.

The percentage of private schools' revenue from government and other sources for 1982-3 is given in Table 4.5. Only in Ontario and Saskatchewan was revenue from local public school boards of some note, where some public school boards purchased services from private schools. Any federal revenues related mainly to federally-financed second official language programmes. The Atlantic provinces and Ontario provided no direct funding for private schools. Financial support was most substantial in Quebec, where government grants comprised about 55 per cent of private school revenue, whereas in Manitoba such funding provided less than 15 per cent. The lower the government support, the more was derived from fees and other sources. Even for Quebec, public spending on private education accounted for only 3.5 per cent of the public cost for all provincial schools. There is a close relationship between the percentage that the total private-schools revenue is of all provincial school funding and the percentage of all pupils in private schools (see rows 6 and 7 in Table 4.5). Generally, the amount of money available per student in private schools is less than that spent per pupil in public schools. Private schools, however, generally do not include expensive vocation- or trade-related programmes which are available in many of the larger public secondary schools. Most private schools restrict their programmes to provide a basic core curriculum.

About 12,000 or 4.5 per cent of all teachers in Canada serve in private schools. For 1984-5 the pupil-teacher ratio in private schools was 19.8, and 18.4 to one in public schools. The sometimes proclaimed lower pupil-teacher ratio in private schools holds only for the relatively small proportion of elite and expensive schools.

Legislation with respect to private school attendance has been relatively liberal in all provinces. In Ontario, a private school must notify the Minister of Education annually of the intention to operate. The Minister may choose to inspect the school, and in recent years private schools have been inspected, also by their own request, by officials of the Ministry. In Alberta a private school must have the approval of the Minister to operate. In British Columbia, government involvement comes about only if the schools apply for provincial grant assistance. Manitoba and British Columbia appoint private school inspectors, whose function includes professional consultation and evaluating the adequacy of such schools. In Alberta, private schools are visited by officials located in the regional offices of the Education Department. The school legislation of all provinces allows Department officials or local school superintendents to judge whether a child is receiving satisfactory schooling 'at home or elsewhere'. Quebec is the only province which, in statute, expressed the right of parents to choose 'the institution which, according to their convictions, ensures the greatest respect for the rights of their children' (Education Department Act, 1964, preamble).

Shapiro argued against a 'legal monopoly in education', recommending public grants for private schools in Ontario (provided such schools meet certain conditions), and holding it to be discriminatory that only one denomination, the

Private schools in ten countries

Roman Catholics, should be privileged to receive full public funding as separate schools of the province's public school system (Shapiro, 1985: 40 and 48). Ghitter (1984) and Woods Gordon Management Consultants (1985) recommended the continuation of the current levels of government grant support of private schools in Alberta. As of 1987, neither the Ontario nor the Alberta governments have responded to the commissioned reports.

Choice as an issue

The tenor of debate and understanding generally is such that the option of private schooling has gained much public and also political acceptance (Bergen, 1981 and 1986a; Magsino, 1986). However, as long as the major portion of the cost of private schools is borne by the parents and associations which undergird such schools, it is unlikely that enrolments will rise much above current levels. The commitment and financial effort on the part of parents and sponsors is such that not only are new schools established, but some cannot maintain themselves for any length of time and are eventually closed. Such was also experienced by many of the 'elite' private schools of British Columbia where only eight of seventy-three such schools established from the 1880s to the 1970s survived (Barman, 1984).

From the very beginning in Canadian education, Roman Catholics have been a large enough denomination and a sufficiently unified force either to obtain separate school status and public funding at parity with other public schools, or to establish private schools and encourage their adherents to patronize them in those provinces which did not provide public funding. The general trends suggest that the major growth in private schooling in Canada is related more strongly to factors other than public financial assistance, and that parents, and also denominations, are electing to pay the costs associated with schooling under private direction.

As has been pointed out, public schools no longer could be defined as being 'Christian' and 'Protestant' in contrast to Catholic separate schools. Even as Catholics and Jews did not find the early public schools ('Protestant' in nature) acceptable, and opted for separate or private schools, even so a number of parents do not find the secular public schools of today acceptable for the education of their children, particularly so if they wish the curriculum to include a religious or a particular denominational element of instruction. The latter has been the major factor in the profusion of diverse private schools in many of the provinces, and could well contribute to the growth of private schools for religious or cultural reasons among more recent immigrant groups. On the other hand, in Newfoundland, parents desiring a secular school for their children could be inclined to opt for a private school unless the provincial school system is modified to include a non-denominational component.

Only a small number of elite private schools, about fifty across Canada and located mainly in Quebec, Ontario and British Columbia, are selective academically and affordable only to the parents of considerable means (Gossage, 1977). Most of these schools have a long history, an established clientele, and are likely to survive indefinitely. These schools have also served the social function of bringing together the children of the politically and financially prominent families. With the exception of these, most schools, including denominational schools, are open to all who wish to patronize them, and who respect their particular religious or educational perspectives. These schools are patronized by parents who believe that such schools are better for their children educationally, and who make choices divorced from any economical advantages. Some schools or their associations sponsor children of families who cannot afford to pay even modest tuition fees. It is difficult, therefore, to make any claim that most private schools in Canada result in inequalities in society.

However, public schools fear that the private schools may draw the better students, and that failing or less desirable students will be returned to them (Bezeau, 1979). Also, fears have been expressed that the more motivated and committed parents might be drawn to the private schools, and that consequently their community leadership in support of good public schools is lost. On the other hand, the competition of private schools is also seen as being good for public schools which must make a greater effort to be responsive to their communities and to retain the support of their clientele (Manley-Casimir, 1982). In a British Columbia study, good schools, either private or public, were found to have an above average degree of commitment on the part of teachers, parents and students (Erickson et al., 1979). The right of the rich to choose elitist private schools for their children has never been seriously challenged in Canada. Public school supporters have nevertheless become concerned when the average people, whose numbers have a greater impact on public schools, make such choices.

Though some fears are expressed that a proliferation of private schools may contribute to social fragmentation, there is no evidence that public schools contribute more to understanding and tolerance than do private schools. Thiessen (1983) argued that humanism and secularism do not make a public school religiously neutral, and that the pluralistic public school system could provide for religious alternatives. Wilkinson (1986) concluded that the growth of the private schools would depend on the perceived improvement in the quality of education in public schools and their perceived religious neutrality (in the sense defined by Thiessen), and on provincial financial support and the degree of government control of instructional programmes and teacher certification requirements. Also, the Canadian Charter of Rights and Freedoms included in the Constitution Act, 1982, might require 'more flexible means of accommodating those who desire different approaches' (Schmeiser, 1987: 81).

Conclusion

The complexity of the private school question in Canada is related to provincial autonomy respecting school legislation and financing, and the differences among provinces regarding defined separate and denominational schools as components of the public school systems. The right of choice among schooling alternatives has become an acceptable norm in Canadian society. Growth in private school enrolment has been regional and restricted mainly to identifiable religious and ethnic groups. Future growth might be determined mainly by the competitive ability of the public schools to provide satisfactory instructional programmes as perceived by a large majority of Canadians.

The development and growth of private schools in Canada might be summarized in the manner in which Stamp (1985) characterized the role played by private schools in Ontario during succeeding historical periods, first as the 'schools of necessity', then some serving as 'schools of privilege', the subsequent establishment of 'schools of innovation', and, in more recent times, for those who found the public schools not meeting their needs, as 'schools of protest'. Like their public school counterparts, private schools 'had become schools of Ontario' (Stamp, 1985: 205). Stamp's conclusion may be generalized to all provinces, so that it may be said that the private schools have also become the 'schools of Canada'.

References

Barman, J. (1984) Growing up British in British Columbia: Boys in Private School, Vancouver: University of British Columbia Press.

Bergen, J.J. (1981) 'Freedom of education in a religious context: the Alberta Holdeman private school case', The Mennonite Quarterly Review 60 (1), 75-85.

—— (1982) 'The private school movement in Alberta', The Alberta Journal of Educational Research 28 (2), 315-6.

——(1986a) 'Choice in schooling', Journal of Educational Administration and Foundations 1 (1), 37-48.

——(1986b) 'An examination of private school issues in Alberta', The Alberta Journal of Educational Research 32 (2), 91-108.

——(1987) 'Government sponsored private school studies in Alberta and Ontario', The Alberta Journal of Educational Research 33 (4), 292-305.

Bezeau, L. (1979) 'The public finance of private education in the province of Quebec', Canadian Journal of Education 4 (2), 23-42.

Erickson, D.A., MacDonald, L., and Manley-Casimir, M.E. (1979) Characteristics and Relationships in Public and Independent Schools, Vancouver: Educational Research Institute of British Columbia.

Ghitter, R. (1984) Committee on Tolerance and Understanding Final Report, Edmonton: Alberta Education.

Gossage, C. (1977) A Question of Privilege: Canada's Independent Schools, Toronto: Peter Martin Associates Limited.

Lupul, M.R. (1969) 'Religion and education in Canada: a call for an end to hypocrisy', The Journal of Educational Thought 3 (3), 141-50.

Magnuson, R. (1969) 'The decline of Roman Catholic education in Quebec: some interpretations and explanations', Culture 30 192-8.

Magsino, R.F. (1986) 'Human rights, fair treatment, and

funding of private schools in Canada', Canadian Journal of Education 11 (3), 245-63.

Manley-Casimir, M.E. (1982) (ed.) Family Choice in Schooling, Toronto: Lexington Books.

Ontario Department of Education (1969) Report of the Committee on Religious Education in the Public Schools of the Province of Ontario, Toronto: Ontario Department of Education.

Phillips, C.E. (1957) The Development of Education in Canada, Toronto: W.J. Gage & Co.

Quebec Department of Education (1963) Report of the Royal Commission of Inquiry on Education. Part 1, Quebec: Quebec Department of Education.

Schmeiser, D.A. (1987) 'Multiculturalism in Canadian education', in Multiculturalism and the Charter: A Legal Perspective, Toronto: The Carswell Company Limited.

Shapiro, B.J. (1985) The Report of the Commission on Private Schools in Ontario, Toronto: Ministry of Education.

Stamp, R.M. (1970) 'Education and the economic and social milieu: the English-Canadian scene from the 1870s to 1914', in Wilson et al., (1970) (eds) Canadian Education: A History, 290-313

———(1985) 'A history of private schools in Ontario', in B.J. Shapiro, The Report of the Commission on Private Schools in Ontario, 193-206.

Statistics Canada. Statistical reviews.

Statutes of the provinces and ordinances of the territories of Canada.

Thiessen, J.T. (1983) 'Is the religious alternative school useful in the public school system?' The Journal of Educational Thought 17 (3), 241-44.

Wilkinson, B.W. (1986) 'Elementary and secondary education policy in Canada: a survey', Canadian Public Policy 12 (4), 535-72.

Wilson, J.D., Stamp, R.M., and Audet, L.P. (1970) (eds) Canadian Education: A History, Scarborough: Prentice-Hall of Canada.

Woods Gordon Management Consultants (1984) A Study of Private Schools in Alberta, Edmonton: Alberta Education.

CHAPTER 5

AUSTRALIA: PRIVATE SCHOOLS AND PUBLIC POLICY

Don Smart and Janice Dudley

Introduction

Private or (non-government) schools comprise 2,500 of
Australia's 10,000 schools and they educate in excess of one-
quarter (0.775m.) of its 3 million students (see Tables 5.1
amd 5.2). Moreover, this proportion has grown impressively
over the past decade as the phenomenon of 'enrolment drift'
from government (public) schools to private schools has
gathered momentum (see Figure 5.1). (It should be noted
here that in Australia the term 'public' schools is used to
refer exclusively to government schools.) Most private
schools have a religious affiliation. The vast majority of
private students, roughly 80 per cent, attend Roman
Catholic 'systemic' (or parish) schools which form part of a
co-ordinated Catholic education system run by separate
Catholic education commissions in each state. The other 20
per cent of private students, constituting only 5 or 6 per
cent of the total Australian student population, belong, by
and large, to the so-called 'independent schools'. Most of
these latter are affiliated with the various Protestant
churches and it is this small group which is often labelled as
the 'elite' or wealthy schools. As we shall see, although they
prefer to call themselves 'independent schools', the title has
become increasingly a misnomer as they have become more
dependent on 'state aid' or direct financial grants from both
federal and state governments since 1964 (Cleverley, 1978;
Hogan, 1984; Smart, 1986).

'State aid' to private (mostly church) schools has been
one of the most acrimonious and bitter political issues to
divide Australian society over more than a century -
reflecting divisions within Australian society between the
predominantly British and Protestant middle and upper

Private schools in ten countries

Table 5.1 Schools by sector (numbers of students and percentages)

	N	%
Non-government schools		
Catholic	1,706	16.8
Anglican	104	1.4
Other	692	6.8
Total	2,502	24.7
Government schools	7,625	75.3
Total	10,127	100.0

Source: Australian Bureau of Statistics, 1986.

Table 5.2 Students by schooling sector and school type (in percentages).

	Primary students	Secondary students	Total students*
Non-government schools			
Catholic	19.3	19.0	19.1
Anglican	1.2	3.8	2.3
Other	3.2	6.0	4.4
Total	23.6	28.8	25.8
Government schools	76.4	71.2	74.2

*   total number of students = 3,006,169

Source: Australian Bureau of Statistics, 1986.

classes, and the predominantly Irish and Catholic working class (Clark, 1980). The long-standing practice of 'state aid' was abruptly curtailed during the final quarter of the nineteenth century when the various Australian colonies, influenced by notions of 'liberalism', successively legislated 'free compulsory and secular' state schools systems, thus terminating the existing state subsidies for church schools. This legislation was not achieved without acrimonious debate in the key states of New South Wales and Victoria between the political leaders and the Irish Catholic archbishops, who accused the politicians of creating 'godless state schools'.

The ultimate effect was to force the substantial Irish Catholic minority (comprising almost one-third of the population) to create and pay for its own separate schools in each state. The vast majority of Protestants embraced the new free state schools. Thus, by the time the various British colonies occupying the geographical continent of Australia became a federal nation in 1901, there were, in effect, in each state (previously colony) two major sets of schools: the state schools, run by state departments of education and open to all; and the loosely knit Roman Catholic parish schools. Only gradually and in piecemeal fashion during the latter decades of the nineteenth and the first half of the twentieth centuries did a small minority of generally more well-to-do Protestants choose to establish a variety of what were mostly Anglican, Methodist and Presbyterian single-sex schools - the so-called 'independent schools' - for their children (Austin, 1961; Cleverly and Lawry, 1972).

Education was not specifically mentioned in the new federal constitution in 1901. It was regarded as a responsibility which remained with the states, who have jealously guarded the provision of freely available public (government) education as their constitutional right. Nevertheless, in the period after the Second World War, the federal government has become increasingly involved. Through a very broad interpretation of the power of the federal purse under section 96 (the 'states grants' power) of the federal constitution, and through the 'benefits to students' power given to the Commonwealth in 1946, the federal government has, in fact, gradually come to play an increasingly influential and sometimes dominant role in both schools and tertiary education policy in Australia (Birch, 1975; Birch and Smart, 1977; Smart, 1978; Harman and Smart, 1982; Boyd and Smart, 1987).

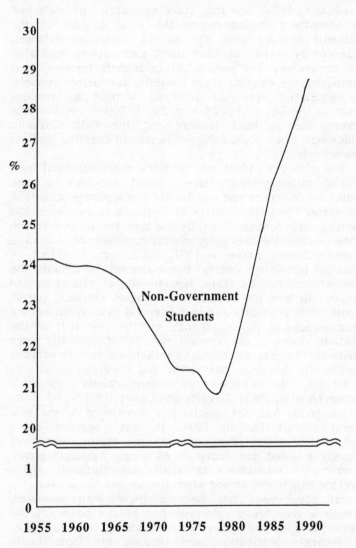

Figure 5.1 Proportion of students attending non-government schools, as a percentage of all students attending schools, 1955-1990 (actual and projected).

Sources: Schools Commission, 1981; Department of Employment Education and Training, 1987

Following the bitter 'historic settlement' of the state-aid issue in Australia in the 1870s and 1880s, the matter of state aid was effectively 'buried' for almost a century. Politicians of all persuasions studiously avoided the issue and there was bi-partisan opposition to its reintroduction. It was not until 1963 that an opportunistic Prime Minister, Robert Menzies, in a desperate quest for Catholic votes, re-established a state-aid precedent through an election promise to build science laboratories for all secondary schools - state and private. This was an awesome precedent. To the surprise of his political colleagues, Menzies incurred little criticism, won strong Catholic support, and snatched a narrow electoral victory (Smart, 1978; Bessant, 1977).

Menzies' state-aid experiment was cautiously built upon during the 1960s by politicians of all parties at both state and federal level. With some notable exceptions, there was general public tolerance of limited forms of government assistance for the private schools and, of course, enthu-siastic encouragement from those schools and their supporters (Smart, 1978). Despite some subsequent periods of heightened public disquiet over state aid (to which we will allude in the next section), the broad general pattern has been one of increasing government financial support - both state and federal - for private schools over time. In fact, it has been a 'quiet revolution'. Federal aid to private schools alone has increased from about $A2 million in 1964 to over $A0.5 billion in 1988 (it should be noted that billion here is equal to a thousand millions). If we add state government subsidies then the total financial support of Australian governments to private schools is now approx-imately $A1 billion annually. Such has been the scope of the revolution that by 1986, for every dollar the federal government spent on a state school child, it spent three dollars on a private school child. However, it needs to be understood that the federal government contributes only 10 per cent of the total funds spent on state schools, with the state government providing the other 90 per cent. Furthermore, from being totally self-funding prior to 1964, the average private school now receives more than 30 per cent of its running costs from government sources, and in the case of many poorer Catholic schools, this figure is well in excess of 50 per cent.

We will first turn to a more detailed account of the policy shifts at federal level over the past decade-and-a-half, for it is these developments which have largely shaped

- indeed transformed - the present economic and political context within which private schools exist in Australia. We will then discuss some of the immediate policy issues currently occupying Australian private schools. Next, we will address the Australian evidence on the relationship between private school attendance and social inequality and, finally, we will offer some concluding observations.

The end of the Menzies era

Robert Menzies' 1963 science-laboratories scheme was a far-reaching double-barrelled precedent. It simultaneously provided the first-ever direct federal aid for all schools and breached the wall of resistance to 'state aid' for private schools. However, it was to be the last of Menzies' personal initiatives for private schools, as he retired in 1966, having been prime minister for the previous 17 years. After Menzies' departure, a leadership vacuum enveloped his conservative Liberal-County Party coalition government, although it managed to retain office until 1972. During these latter years, a combination of buoyant economic conditions, strong private school lobbying, sympathetic support from conservative cabinet ministers (most of whom had attended or patronized private schools), and electoral pragmatism, led to further federal financial initiatives for private schools - each announced just prior to a federal election! (Smart, 1978).

In 1968 a secondary-schools libraries scheme paralleling the science-laboratories scheme was announced. Then in 1969, a massive 'breakthrough' for private schools came when Malcolm Fraser, the Minister for Education and Science, introduced a scheme of federal per capita recurrent grants for private schools only. Unlike the previous science and libraries schemes which provided finance only for capital buildings and equipment, the per capita grants were an open-ended commitment to the recurrent costs of private schools. As such, they would be almost impossible for any future federal government to terminate - it is much more likely that the size of the grants will gradually increase over time. By 1972, this private-school per capita grant had been formalized by the Liberal government at 20 per cent of the standard per-pupil costs in government schools. Amidst growing expressions of concern about federal financial favouritism towards private schools, Gough Whitlam's Australian Labour Party (ALP) federal opposition advocated the creation of an Australian Schools Commission to develop procedures for allocating and administering federal finance to all schools on a needs (as opposed to per capita) basis. Whitlam believed that the growing sparks in the renewed state aid debate could be doused by providing federal aid to government and private schools according to a needs-based formula (Smart, 1978).

The Whitlam government (1972-75) and the Schools Commission

On winning office in 1972, the Whitlam government implemented ALP policy by establishing an interim committee of the Schools Commission (Karmel committee) to propose a more equitable system of funding all schools based on the actual financial 'needs' of individual schools. After devising a complex schools recurrent resources index (SRRI) the Karmel committee classified private schools into eight categories of need (A to H, with A being the wealthiest or least 'needy') and proposed different levels of per capita funding for each category. It proposed a massive increase of almost a half billion federal dollars for government and independent schools over the two years 1974 and 1975. Sympathetic to ALP redistributionist ideology, it also proposed that federal aid to the two wealthiest categories of private school (A and B) be phased out altogether over the same two years. This latter proposal was rejected by the Whitlam cabinet in favour of immediate cessation of aid to such 'wealthy' schools (Smart, 1978; Weller, 1977).

Fear that such a 'phase-out' would gradually be extended to all private schools, led to strenuous opposition by the parents and supporters of all such schools. Surprisingly, given the virtual absence of Catholic schools in categories A and B, some of the strongest opposition came from the Catholic bishops and the Catholic education hierarchy, which argued forcefully that no student should be denied a basic per capita grant by virtue of parental wealth. Ultimately, when the legislation became bogged down over this issue in the opposition-controlled Senate, the Country Party achieved a compromise with the government, part of which conceded that all private students, regardless of wealth, were entitled to a basic per capita grant. The resultant Whitlam policy of substantial additional funds for all schools (though with a 'needs' bias) successfully 'defused' the bitter state-aid debate for almost a decade (Weller, 1977).

In retrospect, it is clear that the conflict and passion generated during 1973 by the ALP's initial attempt to enforce the principle of removing aid from the few very wealthy schools was counterproductive. The amount of money to be saved was relatively small and the bad feeling, media publicity, and conflict generated was disproportionate to the potential gains. However, apparently lacking a sense of history in relation to this issue, the Hawke ALP Government on winning office in 1983 duplicated this bitter episode with essentially the same outcome!

The Fraser government's pro-private schools policies (1975-83)

Under prime minister Malcolm Fraser's conservative Liberal government between 1975 and 1983, a less sympathetic attitude to the 'needs' approach saw a telescoping of the Schools Commission's relatively sophisticated eight categories of need into just three, a re-establishing of a generous 'nexus' (or indexing) with government school costs for even the wealthiest category of private schools, and a consequent acceleration of private school enrolments and of the total proportion of schools commission (federal) funds going to the private sector. By the end of the Fraser era, the 24 per cent of students in private schools were receiving 50 per cent of the Schools Commission's budget - a proportion which the Hawke government had been unable to reserve by 1986 (Smart et al., 1986).

The explanations for this dramatic drift of Schools Commission resources to the private sector are complex. They are in large measure attributable to: the failure of the Schools Commission to impose maintenance-of-effort conditions on recipient private schools; to more and more lenient categorization of such schools; and to the dynamic growth of new private schools and of enrolments in existing private schools as a result of sympathetic Schools Commission policies. In particular, the Catholic system, which was near collapse in 1973, underwent significant renewal and growth as a result of the massive infusion of federal and state needs-based funding which flowed from

Schools Commission policies and support (Ryan, 1984; Praetz, 1983; Marginson, 1985).

State school disenchantment with the Schools Commission (1980-3)

Initially, the creation of the needs-oriented Schools Commission in 1973 defused the state aid conflict by creating a bigger cake and by promoting a consensual settlement which effectively co-opted or disarmed supporters of government schools who were later to oppose its implications. Initially there was more money for all. However, by the early 1980s, as a result of enrolment 'drift' and associated funding policies which transferred a growing proportion of Schools Commission money to private schools, dissatisfaction among government school supporters re-emerged. This dissatisfaction was partly fuelled by Fraser's reduced emphasis on 'need' and the change of chairmanship of the Schools Commission in 1981. When the term of the original ALP-appointed chairman, Dr Ken McKinnon, expired, the Fraser government appointed Dr Peter Tannock who was closely identified with the Catholic schools sector.

In 1981, the government-school parent and teacher representatives on the Schools Commission prepared a minority report condemning what they saw as the Fraser government's interference with Schools Commission policy and the continued funding drift to the private schools. Opposition hardened, and in January 1982, the national teachers union adopted a 'no state aid' position and, as a gesture of dissatisfaction, when its member's term expired on the Schools Commission at the end of 1982, it refused to nominate a replacement.

ALP rejects 'wealthy school' aid prior to the 1983 federal election

This growing dissatisfaction amongst state-school supporters was reflected in a hardening of the federal ALP opposition's education policy prior to the March 1983 election. The revised 1982 party policy required 'that commonwealth funds be available only to those non-government schools whose total private and public resources do not exceed the resources of comparable government schools'.

According to the architects of this policy, Labour had decided that, if it won office in 1983, it would 'make a decisive move to break the log-jam' on the 'divisive state aid issue' and phase out aid to wealthy private schools. This was to be done by abandoning the 'nexus' and having the Schools Commission develop a 'community standard', 'a level of resources which the community at large will accept as necessary for children in various settings to get a high standard of schooling' (Department of Education and Youth Affairs, 1983). Once the 'community standard' was defined, wealthy private schools which spent more were to be denied aid (Dawkins and Costello, 1983).

The Hawke ALP government in power (1983-8)

The Hawke government's 'hit list' of forty-one private schools

In July 1983, just a few months after Hawke won office, Senator Susan Ryan, Minister for Education, took the first decisive (though historically and strategically naive) step towards implementing the ALP's new policy. She announced in her guidelines to the Schools Commission that the nexus was to be abandoned and the recurrent grants of the forty-one wealthiest private schools were to be reduced by 25 per cent. In a predictable response - almost a re-run of the 1973 conflict - the private sector sprang, as one, to the defence of its wealthiest members. As in 1973, the Catholic sector staunchly defended the right of wealthy non-Catholic independent schools to retain their grants at existing levels and argued for the retention of the percentage link or nexus (Hogan, 1984).

The ALP's policy proved to be a political fiasco. Ryan was obliged almost daily to address large and frequently hostile gatherings of anxious private-school parents across the country. Ultimately, prime minister Hawke himself, was obliged to intervene. He joined Ryan in the unpopular task of addressing parent meetings and lobby groups to reassure them that this decision was not the 'thin end of the wedge' and there was no intention to phase out aid to private schools (Smart et al., 1986).

Hawke becomes more conciliatory to private schools

In a further measure to calm anxiety in private schools, Ryan and her department prepared a widely distributed booklet, reassuringly titled, Commonwealth Support for Non-Government Schools (1983), providing information about the government's 'policies for non-government schools in 1984 and beyond'. It described the decision to 'break the percentage link' (nexus) and move to a 'community standard' as the only way to overcome the continuing inequalities in school resources by a more redistributive approach. However, it reassured schools that because there would be more money available overall, redistribution would harm few and 90 per cent of private schools would receive increased grants in 1984. Clearly the ALP had been rocked by the extent of the reaction to its policy and by early 1984 the signs were obvious that the cautious and pragmatic Hawke government would neither pursue its declared intention to 'phase out' aid to the wealthiest schools nor reduce or even hold constant the total funds for the private schools sector (Smart 1986).

The Schools Commission's report on funding policies (1984)

In March 1984 the Schools Commission's eagerly awaited report, Funding Policies for Australian Schools was released. This controversial document contained minority reports form two commissioners representing government school interests. The report detailed the 'community standard' and spelled out funding options for the federal government to be examined in the context of the forthcoming 1984-5 budget deliberations. Amongst its key recommendations, the report proposed a 'community standard' of $A2,195 per primary student and $A3,240 per secondary student with an additional loading for government schools because of their 'different circumstances' and obligations. The report also stressed the vital need in the school community for 'a period of stability and agreement about the future direction of commonwealth and state general resources funding'. The Hawke government was well aware of this need after the turbulent debate of the preceding 8 or 9 months! Nevertheless, it was also aware of the desperate need for federal budgetary restraint.

Urging the government to boost confidence by providing guaranteed levels of funding for the 4 years 1985-8, the commission proposed three options for the recurrent funding of government schools. Each option was premised on an annual increase in the federal contribution and the options ranged in cost over 4 years from an additional $A140m to $A240m. Option 1 would result in the Commonwealth reaching a target of contributing 10 per cent of the community standard by 1988. Option 2 would result in the Commonwealth meeting a constant 8 per cent of the community standard. Option 3 would involve an annual 10 per cent increase in Commonwealth contribution over the four years. For private schools, the commission advocated a new twelve-category system of need linked to the community standard with <u>all</u> schools entitled to a grant. This scheme would cost the federal government an additional $A106m over the 4 years.

Clearly, the Hawke government was faced with a most uncomfortable and highly public decision involving sensitive ideological and budgetary considerations. On the one hand, it wished to avoid the demonstrable fury of the private schools lobby and it had the diplomatically-couched but clear-majority advice of its increasingly pro-private-schools Schools Commission to abandon the 'phase-out' strategy and give the wealthy private schools, instead, a Category I grant. On the other hand, it had the 'minority report' from the government-school parent and teacher organization representatives on the Commission - both traditionally strong pro-ALP organizations - urging it to cease the pattern of excessive transfers of federal funds to promote private schools at the expense of the government schools. As if this were not difficult enough, in July 1984 - just a month before the government's crucial budgetary announce-ments on school funding - the ALP's supreme policy-making conference passed a motion calling upon the federal government 'to continue to phase out all funding support for the most wealthy private schools . . . and redirect these funds to government and non-government schools on the basis of need'.

An expensive 'historic settlement' of the state-aid conflict

On 14 August 1984, the government announced its new funding policy for schools. Both Hawke and Ryan took great pains to describe it as an historic settlement designed to 'take off the political agenda of the 1980s the tired old state-aid rhetoric of the 1960s' (Ryan, August 1984). On closer analysis, it is an extremely expensive funding solution, pragmatically designed to defuse the state-aid debate and ensure consensus by making more money available for virtually all schools and simultaneously giving long-term stability by promising legislation guaranteeing levels of funding for 4 years. Effectively, the government choose to find additional money rather than attempt to redistribute the existing cake away from private schools. This was described as a 'betrayal' of government schools by their parent and teacher organizations and Hawke was accused of becoming 'Fraser' (Marginson, 1984). However, the opposition was relatively short-lived.

The Schools Commission's 'twelve-category option' for private schools and the 'community standard' were both endorsed, as was the recommendation that all schools continue to receive some aid. The wealthiest private schools (categories 1 and 2) were guaranteed that their existing money grants would be maintained in real terms, although without the real increases applying to schools in all other categories. Government schools were to be given a real increase in commonwealth funds of 50 per cent over 8 years -as contrasted with a real decrease of 1.9 per cent during the 7 years of the Fraser government. This policy provided guaranteed funding from 1984-8 and resulted in 4 years of remarkable tranquility.

The decline and fall of the Schools Commission

From its inception under Whitlam in 1973, the Schools Commission's role of advising the federal government on funding and policy for all Australian schools had been a difficult and tortuous one. It continually had to negotiate a delicate policy balance which was satisfactory to the powerful lobbies of both government and private school groups. The state aid 'minefield' was constantly present. When the conservative Fraser government replaced the Whitlam ALP government in 1975, it was widely expected that Fraser would abolish the commission and transfer its functions back into the Department of Education. Instead, between 1975 and 1983 Fraser successfully eroded the commission's authority and legitimacy by frequently refusing its advice and by gradually 'stacking' it with private school representatives so that the neutrality of its membership and policies increasingly came into question.

It might have been assumed that Fraser's defeat and

117

replacement by a sympathetic Hawke ALP government in 1983 would have secured the ALP-created commission's future. Quite the reverse. A combination of widespread public disenchantment with 'government by commission' and shifting fortunes in bureaucratic power and personnel conspired to bring the Schools Commission down. Gradually, between 1983 and 1986, the initially vulnerable and uninfluential Federal Department of Education strengthened its influence with the minister. This was done through changes in its leadership and through expansion of personnel and budget at the expense of the Schools Commission. During the first half of 1985, whilst a new Schools Commission chairman was being sought, a cabinet-inspired inquiry into the commission's activities (Quality of Education Review Committee) and a Public Service Board review were instrumental in ensuring that cabinet would agree to the transferring of the Schools Commission's two key programmes - together with their billion-dollar budget - and almost half of its staff to the Department of Education. By the time the new chairman, Garth Boomer - a curriculum rather than a policy specialist - was appointed, the Schools Commission was clearly destined for a significantly downgraded role (Smart et al., 1986).

The ultimate fate of both the Schools Commission and the Tertiary Education Commission was revealed in October 1987 when their impending abolition was announced by John Dawkins, the Minister for the new 'mega-ministry' of Employment, Education and Training. Under this sweeping structural reform, designed to tighten central control of the whole portfolio, these commissions are to be replaced by a statutory national Board of Employment, Education and Training, which will have four small and very limited advisory councils - including a schools council and higher education council. How all client groups, including private schools, will fare in this dramatically new multi-sectoral structure is yet to be seen. We certainly believe it to be inherently dangerous to reduce so drastically the role of expert, statutory, publicly-reporting advisory commissions and to place so much potentially secretive power in the hands of a single ministerial department and minister.

Major policy issues confronting private schools in Australia

Unquestionably, the most central of the issues preoccupying

the private schools in 1988 have focused around anticipation of announcements on government funding levels for 1989-92 and threats to independence.

Independence

In an address to the 1986 Conference of the National Council of Independent Schools (NCIS) Smart observed:

As the 'accountability' process begins to 'bite' schools are beginning to be reminded of a lesson which many had forgotten for a time - that there is inevitably a trade-off in accepting government aid and that trade-off is reduced autonomy and vulnerability to government intrusion and direction. Schools which wish to insure against potential future intolerable intrusion must seek to diversity their funding sources to permit the future option of declining government aid entirely should they need to.

(Smart, 1986: 133)

Now, two years later, uneasiness is more widespread. The May 1988 issue of the NCIS Newsletter devoted its front page to an editorial headed 'The Fragility of Independence'. The editorial commenced:

There is growing concern among independent schools that their independence is being eroded by a succession of recent Federal Government initiatives. The areas of greatest current concern in this perceived whittling away of independence arise from: accountability requirements; new schools policy; the education resource index; the national board of employment education and training; and the policy for skills training in schools.

Accountability requirements

Federal accountability requirements have become increasingly draconian, bureaucratic and frustrating. Schools must provide a myriad of quarterly and/or annual returns including: commonwealth annual questionnaire (audited accounts required); commonwealth annual accountant's certificate; commonwealth recurrent grants accountability document; states grants questionnaire (audited accounts required); enrolments audit; and annual census data. In addition, schools are becoming increasingly disturbed by the growing range of non-financial disclosures required in areas

119

such as enrolment policy, educational objectives and system of governance. Whilst some of the federal financial and non-financial accountability requirements are legitimate, much of the accountability thrust is deliberately designed as a strategy to stem 'drift' to the private schools.

So far as financial accountability is concerned, the NCIS is arguing strenuously that schools should only have to account publicly for income from government sources and that the current requirements about disclosure of income and expenditure from private sources and ownership are unreasonable. Nor have schools been happy about government attempts to use accountability disclosure as a means of forcing 'wealthy schools' to limit their 'private effort' or risk losing their grants. Schools argue that innovation and creativity is being stifled by such federal policies which, in the name of equity, penalize schools for seeking additional outside funds and/or students.

Restrictions on federal funds for new schools and new places

Enrolment 'drift' to the private schools has been dramatic. Between 1972 and 1982, enrolments in private schools (which enrol roughly 25 per cent of the school population) increased by 100,000, or 17 per cent. During the same period, enrolments in state schools (which enrol roughly 75 per cent of the population) increased by 60,000, or 3 per cent. It is the enormity of this 'drift' to private schools and its 'cost transfer' implications for commonwealth funding - the state governments pay 90 per cent of the costs of each student in a government school - which is at the heart of emerging federal policy in this area. For example, the old 'open-ended' commonwealth policy of automatic per capita grants for all new places in new or existing private schools was estimated to cost the commonwealth an extra $A17-22m in 1985 alone! The situation had been exacerbated in the 1980s by the blossoming of a range of small relatively uneconomic 'alternative schools' and a variety of Christian fundamentalist schools. Many of these schools have been eligible for generous federal building grants ('establishment grants') as well as per capita grants. However, the commonwealth eventually moved to staunch this flow by bringing in measures to have establishment grants abolished in 1989.

This enrolment drift with its complex associated social, financial, industrial and educational implications has led to tensions, anxiety and vigorous debate about appropriate policy responses. The policies adopted by the federal government under the rationale of 'planned educational provision' have been fairly harsh and are designed to financially penalise private schools which seek to grow or expand - the aim, of course, is to minimise the drift to the private schools. For example, under the new schools policy adopted in 1986, schools which seek to re-locate all or part of their operations to a new site jeopardise their existing government funding. Similarly, a single-sex school which becomes co-educational or, vice versa, a day school which establishes boarding operations, or schools which amalgamate - all run the risk of having their existing funding penalized.

Such independence-sapping policies on financial accountability, school enrolments, and school planning are providing strong incentive for many private schools to explore ways of becoming, once again, totally independent of government finance. For the majority, of course, this is only a pipe-dream but it has provided a remarkable impetus to the trend towards the creation, since 1985, of fund-raising 'education foundations' among the private schools.

Issues of class, ethnicity, and gender

Class

Approximately 60 per cent of Australia's wealth is owned by only 10 per cent of the population (Raskall, 1987) and there is a very strong correlation between wealth, socio-economic status, and schools attended. Those of highest socio-economic status - Australia's elite - have predominantly been educated at non-Catholic private ('independent') schools and send their children to such schools (Higley et al., 1979). By contrast, those at the lower end of Australia's socio-economic spectrum go to government or Catholic schools.

Williams (1987) states that [private] 'school students do better ... in most of life's arenas' than do government school students. Thus it can be argued that Australia's private schools - and particularly independent schools - are instrumental in maintaining and reproducing class divisions within Australian society. This is effected more by the success of independent schools in providing access to high status tertiary education and the resultant wealth and privilege that this may provide than by any nepotism or 'old boy' network.

The rate of retention to the end of secondary schooling (Year 12) is highest in independent schools (greater than 80 per cent) and lowest (30 per cent) in government schools, with Catholic schools falling in between. Students from independent schools form a disproportionate number of those qualifying for higher education and are further 'concentrated' in the actual transition to higher education (Williams, 1987). Moreover, students from independent schools tend to choose universities in preference to the lower prestige colleges of advanced education and, within universities, opt for the socially prestigious professional faculties such as medicine and law (Anderson and Vervoon, 1983).

Thus, students from independent schools are not only 'over-represented' in higher education as a whole, but also 'over-represented' in the professions most likely to lead to elite status within Australian society. However, it could be argued that this is but a reflection of the higher socio-economic status of the 'population' of independent school students and would be the case whatever the school - the 'selective socio-economic recruitment argument' (Williams, 1987). Alternatively, it could be argued that independent school families are those which understand the value of education and so provide students with a home background supportive of academic achievement and hence conducive to academic achievement - the 'cultural capital' argument. Or perhaps, the school environment itself (both physical and intellectual) promotes higher academic achievement - the 'better education' argument. Or does this environment simply 'serve to make school a pleasant place to be and, by so doing, cultivate a commitment to education and its institutions' (Williams, 1987) - the 'differential resources' argument. Williams assesses these in the Australian context and concludes that despite all these factors 'between system differences in participation remain . . . and . . . [private] schools may do things differently' (Williams 1987).

It seems reasonable to conclude, therefore, that the relationship between attendance at an independent school and access to the more prestigious professions is not merely correlational but causal, and that private schooling is one strategy by which Australia's dominant class maintains its dominance.

Ethnicity

For most of the century Australia's dominant class has been essentially Anglo-Celtic. Immigration was predominantly from the United Kingdom and Ireland and the proportion of Australians of non-English-speaking background (NESB) was relatively low. However, Australia's post-war immigration programme expanded greatly and the range of countries from which immigrants were accepted was widened, firstly to nothern Europe, then to southern Europe and in the late 1960s to the Middle East and Asian countries.

There is growing evidence that a non-Anglo-Celtic ethnic background (apart from Aboriginality) is no longer a barrier to access to higher education and the social status a profession may provide. Anderson and Vervoon report a Victorian study from the early 1970s which concluded that:

> those of non-English European background were at least as likely to continue to higher education as those of English speaking background . . . whilst 'other' students (mainly Asian) achieved an even higher continuation rate.
>
> (Anderson and Vervoon 1983)

They noted that the educational and career aspirations of recent immigrants tended to be relatively low but that rates of participation tended to increase with length of time in Australia. Beswick (1987) reports that 'immigrants from non-English speaking backgrounds are now graduating at significantly higher rates than the old Anglo-Australian population'. In particular, he notes that for second-generation immigrants (those born in Australia of immigrant parents)

> Entry to the professions has clearly been identified as a means of social mobility . . . In the most recent cohorts admitted to the course in Medicine at the University of Melbourne, in one of the most competitive entry processes in Australia, less than half of the students have Australian born parents.
>
> (Beswick 1987)

Similarly at the University of New South Wales, between 1974 and 1987 the numbers of overseas-born students of migrant families increased substantially in all faculties and doubled to approximately 30 per cent overall (TERC News, June 1987).

As yet, there is no evidence directly linking this success in achieving access to higher education with attendance at private schools. Disproportionately high numbers of students of NESB are enrolled in Catholic schools (Sturman, 1985). However, whilst retention rates and tertiary participation rates are higher for Catholic schools than for government schools, it is not likely that all of the differential participation in higher education can be accounted within this slightly better performance. It is more likely that upwardly mobile immigrant families have clearly recognized the potential of private schooling (and particularly independent schooling) for realizing their aspirations. Private schooling, with its greater probability of access to tertiary education and the more prestigious professions, is perceived as an 'investment' that 'pays off'. Anecdotal evidence, such as the number of Greek students in several of Melbourne's most prestigious independent schools, would appear to support this conclusion.

One group of newly arrived immigrants has both the financial resources and a long tradition of private schooling to support its apparent preference for private (mainly independent) schooling in Australia. Australia's business immigration programme in the 1980s has attracted numbers of wealthy upper-middle class Asians - predominantly Malaysian Chinese and Hong Kong Chinese - who appear to recognize in private schooling the traditional, conservative, academic curriculum and social environment most compatible with their own culture and class. Similarly, upper-secondary students from South-East Asia, whose families wish them to enrol as full fee-paying overseas students in Australia's tertiary institutions, are also enrolling in increasing numbers as both boarders and day pupils, in Catholic and independent schools.

Indigenous Australians - Aborigines and Torres Strait Islanders - have the lowest participation rates in all forms of mainstream education (Anderson and Vervoon, 1983), and are conspicuous by their absence from independent schools. Most Aboriginal and Torres Strait Island children who do continue with their mainstream education, attend government or Catholic schools. This is not the result of a policy of active exclusion or discrimination (illegal under Australia's equal opportunity legislation), but of the poor socio-economic conditions of most Aborigines and Torres Strait Islanders. However, the growing development of black consciousness and the parallel growing preference among many Aboriginal communities for an education that is more supportive of their culture and aspirations than the mainstream traditional white education, cannot be discounted. Indeed, it is this desire that is fundamental to the growing numbers of Aboriginal community schools which are springing up to provide an alternative form of education for Aboriginal children - an education that attempts to bridge the gulf between the academic white curriculum and the spiritual basis of traditional culture (Wikaru, 1987).

Gender

In Australia, the vast majority of schools are co-educational. This generalization is true of both the government and Catholic systems. However, there is still a sizeable minority of the independent schools which remain single-sex. Whilst most of the newer ones are co-educational, many of the older and more prestigious ones - such as the old established 'ladies colleges' and 'grammar schools' - resisted the swing in the 1970s which saw many private single-sex schools become co-educational either by merger or by varying enrolment policy.

Superficially, females would appear to be achieving equally with males in Australian education. Year 12 retention rates for all students show that more girls than boys are now completing secondary education whilst, in higher education, females and males each constitute approximately half of the student population (Williams, 1987). However, in higher education, women are over-represented in fields such as teaching, the humanities, music and the social and behavioural sciences, whilst men are over-represented in such fields as engineering, technology, and natural sciences and architecture (Anderson and Vervoon, 1983). Moreover, women are under-represented in those undertaking higher degrees and amongst academics - the more senior the position, the less the proportion of women (Anderson and Vervoon, 1983).

So far as educational participation is concerned - whether measured as high-school graduation or tertiary enrolment - girls from independent schools participate at a higher rate than girls from Catholic schools, who in turn participate at higher rates than girls from government schools. Thus private schools would appear to be actively promoting the position of women in Australian society. The predominance among graduates and successful career women of women from private schools is often cited as 'proof' of the valuable role these schools play in advancing the status of women. This success is often attributed, at least in part, to the number of single-sex schools in the private sector. Such arguments tend to be based on evidence which indicates that girls may be disadvantaged relative to boys in co-educational settings (see Morgan (1986) for a review of this evidence). However, as most of these private single-sex schools are selective in terms of both class and initial achievement, it can be argued that it is more who the girls are than the gender of their classmates that is determining their achievement and hence life chances (in other words, that their achievement is commensurate with their class).

Much of the argument that single-sex schools are against the interests of girls and society is based on the character, style and values of such schools. As Keeves (Schools Commission, 1975) notes, implicit in the provision of single-sex schooling is the community perception of different roles for males and females in adult life and hence the need for different preparation for these roles. Kenway and Willis (1986) maintain that the role of girls' single-sex schools is to prepare and groom the 'consorts' of the privileged and powerful in Australia - that the ideology of the hierarchical social status quo is inculcated in the girls (and boys) who attend single-sex schools, whilst the traditional role of women and the ideology of motherhood and nurturance tend to remain unquestioned:

... the majority of [independent school mothers] express considerable suspicion about the feminist movement...a few are apologetically 'mildly feminist'...the majority hold quite conservative views of women's place in society, and some are quite vehemently hostile.

(Kenway and Willis 1986: 126)

Morgan (1986) reports that single sex-schools for girls in Australia tend to lack facilities for non-traditional subjects such as industrial arts, are less likely to promote non-traditional careers for girls and are less likely to provide broad-ranging careers advice to girls than are co-educational schools. Thus, according to these writers, private schools - both co-educational and single-sex - with their traditional curricula and conservative social environments are unlikely 'sites' for any 'feminist reconstruction of reality'.

It would appear then, that many private schools may serve an important role in reproducing the class-ordered structures of Australian society - instrumentally through their greater success in providing access to higher education and ideologically through their inculcation of the cultural and social values of the hierarchical status quo. However, their role in maintaining ethnic and gender disadvantage is less clear. Through their growing enrolments of the children of upwardly mobile immigrant families, Australia's private schools may be playing a significant role in diluting the traditionally British background of Australia's elites. Private schools also appear to be enabling girls of higher socio-economic background to achieve equally with boys of similar socio-economic background. However, they do not appear to be contributing to the life chances of Australians of lower socio-economic status to the same extent - by they Australian born or of immigrant background, be they female or male. As Jakubowicz (1984) argues, the primary allegiance of Australia's ruling class is to class and ideology rather than ethnic background. Moreover, it could be argued that as private schools do not support any radical re-appraisal of women's roles in society, they contribute to the maintenance of the second class status of women.

Concluding observations

Enrolling more than one-quarter of Australia's students, private schools are inevitably major players in the national education system. This is reflected in their disproportionate political 'clout' and capacity to attract generous support from governments. The generosity of government support has been a major factor fuelling the drift to private schools as they are now, in general, more affordable than at any time since the early 1960s (Williams, 1984). However, there are a host of other complex factors not discussed in this paper which have contributed to the drift from government schools - in particular, parental concerns about: youth unemployment, academic standards, moral and religious values, discipline, pastoral care, and so on (Ashenden, 1987). Part of the disproportionate 'political clout' of the private schools stems, of course, from their well organized political lobbies via such organizations as the NCIS and the National and State Catholic Education Commissions. However, it also stems from the elite status and associated power which inheres to the relatively small group of wealthy (largely non-Catholic) 'independent' schools.

These schools draw a relatively exclusive clientele

127

which, predictably, is strikingly over-represented in terms of upper school retention rates, tertiary admissions, university graduation and subsequent professional and business careers - in fact, on all the traditional predictors of life-chance enhancement. Many observers believe that these exclusive independent schools - both single-sex and co-educational - serve the explicit function, through their values and practices, of the social reproduction of an Australian 'ruling class' (Kenway and Willis, 1986; Connell et al., 1982).

There is no doubt that public and media perceptions of the 'exclusiveness' of the independent schools and the 'separateness' of the Catholic system create a sense of social division in Australia. It is this perpetuated, though now muted, sense of divisiveness - partly borne of the acrimonious anti-Catholic state-aid debates of the distant past - which stil produce a sense of 'temporary political settlement' and uneasy calm so far as government funding policy towards private schools is concerned. In such a context, it is hardly surprising that private schools live in a continual state of suspended anxiety about their independence and financial security. In May 1988, as this chapter went to press, the federal government allayed some of these immediate fears by announcing guaranteed real increases in funding levels for virtually all schools for the years 1989-92. In effect, no school will receive less than before and most will receive modest annual increases (see Table 5.3).

Prior to the 1970s, the dire financial circumstances of many schools meant there was a very real question mark hanging over the future of private schools, especially the Catholic sector. However, the increasing role of the commonwealth government in the 1970s and 1980s, as a policy-shaper and funder, has both guaranteed and legitimized the permanence of private schools in Australian education.

References

Anderson, Don S. and Vervoon, A.E. (1983) Access to Privilege: Patterns of Participation in Australian Post-Secondary Education, Canberra: A.N.U. Press.
Ashenden, Dean (1987) Private or State? Time Magazine (Australia), May 4.

Table 5.3 Federal needs-based per-student grants for private schools 1988-92

Category	1988	1989	1990	1991	1992
Primary	$	$	$	$	$
1	314	314	314	314	314
2	419	419	419	419	419
3	468	488	509	516	520
4	633	633	633	633	633
5	683	701	715	724	729
6	715	748	784	797	806
7	754	801	851	874	884
8	919	938	954	960	963
9	945	973	997	1,008	1,015
10	971	1,010	1,041	1,059	1,067
11	998	1,046	1,087	1,110	1,119
12	1,026	1,082	1,131	1,160	1,171
Secondary					
1	498	498	498	498	498
2	664	664	664	664	664
3	715	735	755	764	768
4	1,007	1,007	1,007	1,007	1,007
5	1,040	1,053	1,065	1,072	1,075
6	1,097	1,133	1,169	1,184	1,190
7	1,156	1,212	1,269	1,295	1,307
8	1,398	1,407	1,414	1,419	1,422
9	1,441	1,465	1,486	1,494	1,499
10	1,484	1,524	1,554	1,569	1,575
11	1,522	1,577	1,618	1,642	1,652
12	1,561	1,627	1,679	1,714	1,729

Source: Minister for Employment, Education and Training media release 87/88, 25th May 1988.

Austin, A.G. (1961) Australian Education 1788-1900: Church, State and Public Education in Colonial Australia, Melbourne: Pitman.

Australian Bureau of Statistics (1986) National Schools Statistics Collector (Catalogue No. 4220.0), April.

Bessant, Bob (1977) 'Robert Gordon Menzies and education in Australia', in Stephen Murray-Smith (ed.) Melbourne Studies in Education.

Beswick, David G. (1987) Prospects for the 1990s: a New Phase of Development in Australian Higher Education, Centre for the Study of Higher Education, University of Melbourne, Research Working Paper No 87.17.

Birch, Ian K.F. (1975) Constitutional Responsibility for Education in Australia, Canberra: Australian National University Press.

Birch, Ian K.F. and Smart, Don (1977) The Commonwealth Government and Education, Melbourne: Drummond Press.

Boyd, William Lowe and Smart, Don (1987) Educational Policy in Australia and America: Comparative Perspectives, London: Falmer Press.

Clark, Manning (1980) A Short History of Australia, Sydney: Collins.

Cleverly, John (1978) Half a Million Children: Studies of Non-Government Education in Australia. Melbourne: Longman Cheshire.

Cleverly, John and Lawry, John (1972) Australian Education in the Twentieth Century: Studies in the Development of State Education, Melbourne: Longman.

Commonwealth Schools Commission (1984) Funding Policies for Australian Schools, Canberra: Commonwealth Schools Commission.

Connell, R.W., Ashenden, Dean, Kessler, Sandra, and Dowsett, Gary (1982) Making the Difference, Sydney: Geo. Allen & Unwin.

Dawkins, J. and Costello, R. (1983) 'Education: progress and equality', in J. Reeves and K. Thompson (eds) Labor Essays 1983: Policies and Programs for the Labor Government, Melbourne: Drummond Press, 73-9.

Department of Education and Youth Affairs (1983) Commonwealth Support for Non-Government Schools.

Department of Employment, Education and Training (1987) Schooling in Australia: Statistical Profile No. 1, Canberra: Australian Government Printing Service.

Harman, Grant S. and Smart, Don (1982) Federal Intervention in Australian Education, Melbourne: Georgian House.

Higley, John, Deacon, Desley, and Smart, Don (1979) Elites in Australia, London: Routledge and Kegan Paul.

Hogan, Michael (1984) Public Versus Private Schools - Funding and Directions in Australia, Victoria: Penguin Books.

Jakubowicz, Andrew (1984) 'Ethnicity, multi-culturalism and neo-conservatism', in Gillain Bottomley and Marie de Lepervanche (eds) Ethnicity, Class and Gender in Australia, Sydney: Geo. Allen & Unwin.

Kenway, Jane and Willis, Sue (1986) 'Countering sexism the single-sex way: a flawed proposition', in Paige Porter (ed.), Gender and Education, 116-238, Victoria: Deakin University Press.

Marginson, Simon (1984) 'The schools guidelines: Hawke in Fraser's clothing', A.T.F. Research Notes No. 2, September.

—— (1985) 'The collapse of the Karmel consensus, A.T.F. Research Papers No. 9.

—— (1987) 'Trends in commonwealth spending on Australian schools: 1975-1976 to 1985-1986', A.T.F. Research Notes No. 21, June.

Morgan, Dorothy (1986) Girls, Education and Career Choice: What the Research Says, (N.S.W. Joint Non-Government Schools P.E.P. Committee), Commonwealth Schools Commission.

N.C.I.S. Newsletter (1988), The Fragility of Independence, May.

Praetz, Helen (1983) 'The non-government schools', in R.K. Brown and L.E. Foster (eds), Sociology of Education, Melbourne Drummond.

Raskall, Phil (1987) 'Wealth: Who's got it? Who needs it?', Australian Society 6, (5), May.

Ryan, Susan (1984) Address to the National Press Club, 15 August.

Schools Commission (1975) Girls School and Society, Canberra: Schools Commission.

—— (1981) Report for the Triennium 1982-84, Canberra: Schools Commission.

Smart, Don (1978) Federal Aid to Australian Schools 1901-1975, St. Lucia: Queensland University Press.

—— (1986) 'The shifting sands of commonwealth policy towards independent schools: Where have we been? Where are we headed?' in Proceedings of the Sixth

National Conference of the National Council of Independent Schools, 132-62, Perth.

——— (1987) 'The Hawke Labor Government and public-private school funding policies in Australia, 1983-1986', in William Lowe Boyd and Don Smart (eds), Education Policy in Australia and America: Comparative Perspectives, 141-62, London: Falmer Press.

Smart, Don, Scott, Roger, Murphy, Katrina, and Dudley, Janice (1986) 'The Hawke government and education 1983-1985', Politics 21, (1), 63-81.

Sturman, Andrew (1985) 'Immigrant Australians and education', Australian Education Review, no. 22, Victoria: Australian Council for Educational Research.

University of New South Wales (1987) TERC News, University of New South Wales Tertiary Education Research Centre, no. 54, June.

Weller, Patrick (1977) 'The establishment of the Schools Commission: a case-study in the politics of education', in Ian K.F. Birch and Don Smart (eds) The Commonwealth Government and Education 1964-1976, Melbourne: Drummond Press.

Wikaru, Journal of the Institute of Applied Aboriginal Studies (1987) Western Australian College of Advanced Education, no. 14, June.

Williams, Ross A. (1984) The Economic Determinants of Private Schooling in Australia, A.N.U. Centre for Economic Policy Research, Discussion Paper no. 94.

Williams, Trevor (1987) Participation in Education, A.C.E.R. Research Monograph no. 30, Australian Council for Educational Research: Victoria.

CHAPTER 6

FRANCE: CATHOLIC SCHOOLS, CLASS SECURITY, AND THE PUBLIC SECTOR

Richard Teese

On Sunday 24 June 1984 more than one million people converged on Paris in protest against a law to integrate private schools within the public education system. This 'mega-demonstration' was the culmination of 3 years of opposition to the Socialist Party's plans to bring to an end the dual system of public and publicly-subsidized schools which had operated in France since the Debré law of 1959. Held a week after elections for the European Parliament, at which the ruling parties of the Left had suffered a major defeat, the méga-manif fuelled a political crisis whose origins were broader than the school question itself. The defence of the école libre served to organize conservative opposition to a government whose record on unemployment, fiscal policy, and industry adjustment had eroded its popular support. That the school issue could play such a role and produce such casualties - the Minister for National Education, M. Savary, the Prime Minister, M. Mauroy, as well as the Savary bill itself - shows that it was not simply a pretext for the warring factions of the Right to war against the Mitterrand government. On the contrary, private schooling lent itself well to this political conflict because it is a major source of class security.

Official statistics tend to mask the full importance of non-public schools in France. Neither sector size, nor enrolment trends, nor examination success rates would suggest that public institutions, like the state lycées, should fear 'competition' from this quarter. It is true that in a few regions the private sector is large (e.g. in Brittany, where it gathers as many as 44 per cent of all high-school students (MEN, 1987: 115). Nationally, however, only 14 per cent of children in primary and pre-school education and only one in five students at secondary level attend non-government schools. Moreover, this represents a decline over the position 25 years ago when the state began financing recurrent costs in the sector (ECD 1984: 951). Public lycées, as a group, have better exam results than private establishments. This applies across the general baccalaureat, except for the small science and technology E-series, where private schools do marginally better (but present only 7 per cent of candidates). Examination statistics also show that students in state lycées have a better chance of entering the most prestigious baccalaureat series – the mathematics and physics C-section – as well as passing in greater numbers (MEN, 1987: 6.2, 3). Private schools thus do not have the influence in France that they enjoy in other countries, such as Australia, where their sector size is greater (and growing), their success-rates higher, and their share of university places disproportionately large (Teese, 1986b). On the contrary, the class security supplied by the non-public sector in France is based on the ancillary roles it plays within the school system, not structural dominance over it.

The main suppliers of private education in France are Catholic schools. Only in the academic region of Paris does non-Catholic, non-public schooling attract significant numbers – every fifth lycéen (ECD, 1984: 932). Belonging to the Catholic system is, as we shall see, a real and important attribute. Of even greater significance is the extent of diversity within this system, for it is the functional differentiation of Catholic schools around the public sector and the differential social appeal of these establishments that makes them a source of class security. To appreciate the ways in which a once-confessional sector of schooling has adapted to particular 'markets' of secular education, it is important to see how consumer demand is shaped by the operations of the much larger public system, and how in particular that system generates insecurity.

The origins of academic insecurity in France

In theory, French education up to the end of junior high school is non-selective. That is, pupils follow a common programme and are not streamed by results into different courses. But this is not true in practice. In the first place, over 12 per cent of all pupils reach the end of primary school 2 or 3 years behind (Paty, 1980: 25). Pupils have already begun to move out of the mainstream programme into pre-vocational or pre-apprenticeship classes. Moreover, at least 4 per cent of children leave school altogether (MEN, 1987). Transfer to pre-vocational classes - a phenomenon known as 'relegation'-increases at the end of the first year of junior high school. Tracking into short vocational courses also begins at this time, though the numbers are very small. Within a year, however, a major exodus takes place, with 16 per cent of students entering pre-vocational or vocational classes, and a further 2 per cent dropping out. At the end of junior high school, an even larger exodus occurs, this time with a quarter of students giving up academic work.

Non-promotion within the common course has also risen by this time. At the end of the sixième (first year of high school) 11 per cent of students are kept back; at the end of the next year, 14 per cent. Grade-repeating falls after classes have been 'relieved' of less-able or less-motivated pupils transferring to vocational courses, but rises at critical transfer points (e.g. the last year of junior high school or the first year of senior high school - when key decisions on baccalaureat streams have to be made). By the last year of academic schooling in France, when relegation and attrition have already taken half the class, as many as one in five students are repeating the year (MEN, 1985: 43).

If vocational schooling acts as a kind of safety-net for failure in the mainstream programme, it offers a very uncertain future for those caught in it. Many young people fail to complete vocational courses, and many of those that do will find themselves unemployed 9 months after finishing school (Coëffic, 1987: 14). Insecurity arises not only because of high rates of vocational relegation and of early leaving without qualifications. While rates of school completion have risen in France, the 'democratization' of senior high school has come about through the technical rather than the general baccalaureat (Prost, 1983: 19). More recently, vocational baccalaureats have been added. Technical sections, however, give limited access to higher education, and even the 'short technical courses' that once were accessible are now being 'crowded out' by students from more prestigious sections who are anxious to find work. Streaming in senior high school - both across the general, technical, and vocational baccalaureats as well as within the general series - is thus a further source of insecurity. So, too, is failure. Just over two-thirds of students were successful at the baccalaureat exams in 1986 (MEN, 1987:

221), but over 120,000 failed.

Parents have little real control over the selection processes in public high school. The promotions committee, or _conseil de classe_, has both parent and student representatives, but in practice their influence is very limited. Problems of making time available, the question of status, and uncertainty over roles all tend to exclude parents and to make decisions about individual pupils the prerogative of the _conseil des professeurs_ (LME, 1984: No.110). Although grade-repeating must be requested by parents, they are dependent on school reports. Non-promotion may be seen as a 'second chance', but it also operates as a mechanism of elimination, in part because of the psychological effects on the child, especially one who is already over-age for his or her class. When children reach the end of a particular phase or cycle of schooling (e.g. junior high school), orientation decisions are made by the _conseil de classe_. Though there are appeal procedures, parents cannot veto decisions made at these critical turning-points.

This overview of the origins of academic insecurity has focused on the high rates of selection in French schools, on the practices of selection, and on the generally limited power of parents to countermand verdicts. With this background, we are more able to understand how a sector which is _less academically efficient_ can still be a major source of class security.

Types of private schooling

Demand for private schooling arises from failure or anxiety in the public sector. For some parents, the private school is a last refuge against relegation or against zoning to a school with a poor reputation. For others, it is meant to ensure against failure, for example, because of the reputed qualities of the teaching staff, the more disciplined tone, or the moral or even religious orientation (Coutty, 1982: 14). The search for security through private schooling involves a range of benefits which vary across social groups, depending on their degree of dependence on school, the 'stakes' of success and failure, and the quality of their relationship with the public sector.

Research by Ballion (1982) shows how much diversity exists in the Catholic sector, particularly in Paris where it is most diverse. We also gain an idea of the overall balance of activity within the sector according to roles and clientele. According to Ballion, there are five main types of establishment. Schools of academic excellence are the older, highly reputed institutions, mainly for boys. Like the lycées of old, they offer both primary and secondary education. They provide traditional instruction in Catholic doctrine and they are frequented by upper- and upper-middle-class children. These schools represent 24 per cent of all the pupils in Ballion's sample (though a much smaller proportion of schools). Schools for upper-class education are less academically selective and are mainly for girls. The visual and performing arts receive special attention along with Catholic doctrine and the notion of social service. This group represents 23 per cent of pupils. Innovation schools are not numerically significant. Mainly primary, they see themselves as offering alternative 'whole-child' approaches to learning and appeal to the younger modern-minded families of the middle and upper classes. Proportionately the most important group is what Ballion calls 'substitution' schools. These represent over a third of all pupils. They are viewed as replacing a public system marked by politicization, strikes, teacher absenteeism, drugs, sexual deviance, delinquency, and lack of pupil supervision. Substitution schools are much less selective in academic terms and achieve lower standards than public schools - the reverse is true of 'academic excellence' establishments. Pupils are drawn from all social ranks, but are predominantly middle and upper middle class. Finally, refuge schools (15 per cent of all pupils) serve working class areas and offer short vocational courses.

This analysis suggests that there are four key services performed by Catholic schools - academic security, social training, moral security and social distance. Academic security is the likelihood of reaching a certain level of schooling or obtaining a qualification, the loss of which would result in social demotion. It is a benefit whose content varies according to the chances of success that are typical for the group. For example, the children of farm workers have less than 5 chances in 100 of entering university, but the children of doctors, lawyers and other professionals have nearly 1 chance in 3 (MEN, 1987: 193). Moral security is the likelihood of achieving a certain quality of interaction between persons by prescribing their roles and attributes (e.g. sex, race, speech, scholastic aptitude). This interaction is again linked to status conservation - the protection or enhancement of life-style - and may consist in academic productivity itself or in the inculcation of suitable ethical or aesthetic values.

By looking at each category of school in turn, we can see that, within the division of labour which exists across the sector, schools at the top end of the market accumulate roles (i.e. combine and integrate functions), whereas schools on the downside specialize (i.e. provide a specific and limited service - e.g. personal supervision). The schools of academic excellence, just because they select on academic lines, provide a socially-filtered environment and training in cultural values, manners, and outlook (although this may not be as formally organized as in the académies for young ladies). The mixed 'primary-secondary' nature of these institutions emphasizes their globally formative role.

Substitution schools, by contrast, cannot offer academic security in the sense of superior exam results or a high probability of access to the most profitable baccalaureat series. They can, however, provide security in the form of close pupil management, with the potential to restore lost chances through intensive supervision. Parents who choose private over public schools more often stress method and application. Their focus is on what Bonvin (1980: 77-8) calls the 'moral conditions of success'. They expect an inculcation of serious work attitudes and habits, and they are rewarded by practices such as being required to sign homework, receiving frequent school reports (e.g. weekly), or having their children spend longer hours at school, including in special remedial classes (LME, 1987: No.139).

By using a substitution school, parents are not only seeking to prevent or compensate for failure. They feel - whether rightly or wrongly - that their capacity to intervene in the educational process is greater than in public schools. They report a sense of power over teachers, exercised vicariously through the hire and fire rights of the school head. We might see in this a sense of retribution against the class of professionals responsible for the verdict of 'failure', or more simply a sense of restored rights in the process of educational selection and guidance from which, in the public system, they felt excluded. Substitution schools may be more or less successful in reversing a verdict of relegation, under which pupils are tracked into vocational streams, or in postponing it or assuring against it. However, they can compensate for failure through a range of moral and symbolic benefits. These include not only a sense of power over teachers, but the distance the school achieves from 'undesirable' children.

Private schools are socially selective. There are important regional variations which reflect the relative degrees of implantation of the two sectors. For example, where the use of private schools is weak, upper-class recruitment is very much more marked than in regions of traditional high use. In the latter, especially in rural areas, liberal professions and senior management are more highly represented in public schools (Oeuvrard, 1984: 35). In an early study of intake patterns, Tanguy (1972: 360-1) found that, within more socially-favoured urban zones, private schools drew predominantly from upper-class backgrounds (manufacturers, liberal professions, executives), while public schools took in the 'middle classes' (technicians, office workers, self-employed tradesmen, and shopkeepers). In working class areas, the social cleavage across the sectors was accentuated.

Recent research has found that, at primary-school level, private schools contain proportionately twice as many children from the upper classes of French society as are found in public (i.e. state) schools. As we should expect, this pattern is weaker at the level of French schooling which is the most socially selective, that is, the 'long cycle' of senior high school leading to higher education. There the owners of large businesses, members of the liberal professions, and senior management represent 31 per cent of private school intake as against 20 per cent in public lycées (Oeuvrard, 1984: 32). Ethnic segregation - above all, social distance from Arab children - is more difficult to document. But it is recognized as one of the motives favouring migration from public to private sectors (Coutty, 1982: 14; LME, 1984: 9).

If Catholic schools display a diversity of roles in France, this is because their social users stand in a variety of different relationships towards the public system. The severity of scholastic selection which takes place in public high schools, where over half the intake population is eliminated before final year, imposes on those individuals for whom this risk is unacceptable the need for counter-measures and resources. Within public schools, these strategies include early entry to primary school, tactical grade-repeating, choice of living or ancient language, and exploitation of the school map (Oeuvrard, 1979).

But the risk of selection in the public sector also

creates roles for private schools. Thus the schools of 'academic excellence' can offer their clients success rates of over 80 per cent (Ballion, 1982: 274). The users of these schools are able to bypass the hazards of selection in a system which, thanks to the nature of the curriculum, pupil selectivity in 'good' neighbourhoods, parental know-how and teacher expectations, is already biased in their favour. Children of executives, for example, have twice the chance of entering a lycée as the children of shop workers, and nearly four times the chance of the children of farm workers (MEN, 1987: 131). Academic excellence schools serve to reduce the marginal probability of failure which remains after advantages of structure and strategy in the public sector have been exhausted.

However, not even the schools of excellence are foolproof against failure. Their high rates of academic success depend on selection, including the 'culling out' of weaker pupils. These may be forced to resort to expensive, unsubsidized private schools specializing in remedial work and coaching. Chartreux, a Catholic school in Lyon, prides itself on academic results. It provides the full range of education, from primary school to preparatory classes for the grandes écoles. It refuses every third application, admits into secondary school only those pupils who are 'on time' (i.e. have not repeated a grade), and at the end of junior high school prunes out a third of all survivors, including some with good results (LME, 1987, 139: 37).

Descending the social scale, the relationship of individuals to the education system becomes weaker. Private schools can compensate for the increased risks of scholastic selection which children owe to their social origins by substituting surer, but less prestigious, academic goals or by renouncing academic in favour of vocational training. Thus, while private schools have lower pass rates on the general baccalaureat, this trend is reversed in the most popular of the technical baccalaureats, notably applied science and technology, and business studies. Within vocational high school, we also find higher pass rates in the examinations leading to the Certificate of Vocational Proficiency (CAP) and the Certificate of Vocational Studies (BEP)(MEN, 1986: 6.1, 4).

As a comparison with Chartreux, the college of Notre-Dame de Mont-Roland shows how schools in the Catholic sector have evolved to meet the problems of failure - problems which are linked through the action of the school system as a whole to the success produced by schools like Chartreux. Run by the Jesuits for four centuries, the college of Mont-Roland was relinquished to the diocesan clergy in 1961 and came under lay direction in 1979. This college specializes in the 'personalization' of the teaching process. It displays two important characteristics of Catholic education - streaming of pupils (the 'academic' pupils are taught in a separate part of the school) and close personal supervision. For the teachers, the school's major success has been its ability to re-integrate into the mainstream programme young people who had been relegated to pre-vocational classes in public school midway through junior high school and would have left school as failures (Vandermeersch, 1982: 75-81). These children represent a quarter of the school's intake at this level.

Class security takes on different meanings and has a different content depending on relative, not absolute, risks. Children of business owners, teachers, doctors, and other professionals have, as a group, excellent chances of reaching the baccalaureat exams. But selection to the most profitable series within the baccalaureat programme - and therefore to the preparatory classes for the <u>grandes écoles</u> -gives some of these groups advantages over others and thus establishes another social hierarchy. To the sons and daughters of office workers and factory hands this hierarchy is remote. To them, failure means exclusion from the 'long cycle' as such. The technical series within the baccalaureat, through which 'democratization' over the last two decades has mainly occurred, offer them a form of security which is of little value to their upper-class cousins. Private schools, both Catholic and non-Catholic, are a refuge against the unthinkable - failure amongst the most privileged sections of society (Ballion, 1977) - but also against the predictable failure to leap the scholastic boundaries surrounding the resources and expectations of less advantaged groups.

Private schools and the public sector

The multiple points at which the private sector offers security against the action of the public system represent a major benefit to the individuals who can access them but tend to increase selectivity and to reinforce the processes of rejection which create the need for refuges in the first place (Bonvin, 1980: 103). This is because private schools permit successively higher levels of educational selection in the public sector to be 'cleared' of pupils who have fallen behind or cannot cope. Thus private schools offer security not only to individuals, but to the institution of public schooling itself (Dreyfus, 1981: 93-94), that is, by tending to ensure the efficiency of its action as the selector of elites. We ought to say, not only 'efficiency' (the continuing ability of schools to make distinctions between pupils) but 'legitimacy' as well. For without the avenues of scholastic, or at least moral, indemnity which private schools represent, the instruments of selection in the public sector (the conseil de classe, the school map, grade-repeating, streaming) would be confronted with resistance from a range of influential social groups.

The legitimacy of the school system as a neutral arbitrator of ability differences becomes a more crucial political consideration in proportion as more and more social groups are drawn completely into its net and cannot protect themselves from its classifications by wealth or economic location (Bourdieu 1978). The post-war period in France has seen the role of formal education in the transmission of status become decisive. Groups whose historical reliance on credentials has been weak, such as small farmers, independent artisans, and shop-owners, represent a declining proportion of the workforce. The transmission of these economic roles, along with the property on which they are based, has become increasingly problematic. Business ownership has declined as a strategy for accumulating and communicating wealth across generations. The growth of big corporations has meant that, with concentration of ownership, alternative forms of property have been utilized as ways of securing or advancing family position. Educational capital - credentials - is a road, if not to outright ownership, then to management and control. The increasing demand for credentials has come both from families seeking to 'convert' economic into educational capital and from those who rely on schools to produce qualifications for them, without the advantages of social position. The variety of these social users as well as the absolute increase in numbers seeking to occupy the most valuable locations in the school system has resulted in an inflationary spiral and a constant search for the higher ground effective against competition.

If the long-term changes in the strategies of family reproduction have created a framework of global dependence on formal education, the exploitation of this structure has intensified in the wake of economic downturn since 1974. Rising unemployment, the erosion of the value of the baccalaureat, labour market changes, and new or revalued programmes in higher education have made success and failure less predictable. The monitoring of the productivity of different routes through education in terms of employment status, occupation, or higher education access is now institutionalized through official and popular research literature. A range of indicators points to increasing competition among users and institutions, and to increasing severity of selection. Grade-repeating has risen in high school, the socially weakest students now spend more time in school through non-promotion, and even the least valuable courses are recording higher rates of completion.

In this context, defence against scholastic failure, or the redemption of failure once it has occurred, draw into the private sector at one strategic moment or another a very much larger proportion of the school population than static measures of sector share suggest. It has been estimated from the school careers of the 'class of '73' that as many as every third pupil has been at one time or other enrolled in a private school (Langouet and Léger, 1987: 50). The same research shows which social groups benefit from the pattern of transfers across the sectors. The children of business executives, for example, tend more often than other groups to remain in private schools, and are also more likely to abandon the public sector. By contrast, the children of factory workers, who are poorly represented in the private sector, are the least likely to transfer out of government schools. In general, as was observed by Tanguy in her pioneering study of the social origins of private school users, middle- and upper-middle-class groups are much more likely to exploit private schools, either through continuous use as 'loyal clients' or through use as 'passengers' (Langouet and Léger, 1987: 50-1; Tanguy, 1972: 360-3).

Functional relations between public and private sectors (e.g. the absorpition of students in difficulty by private establishments) depend on a key condition - the exchange of populations. If Catholic education had retained its traditional confessional character, it would have been confined to distinct segments of the school population (e.g. the children of farmers or of the most conservative factions of the upper class). It would not have been able to underwrite the process of academic selection in public

143

schools because of the narrowness of its appeal. The exchange of populations between sectors is in fact limited, as is shown by the social composition of Catholic schools (particularly in major urban centres). But it is just because of the socially selective nature of transferring students that the system of public-private exchange is politically effective. If markets for academic security support the operation of formal scholastic selection practices in the public high schools, it is because the social traffic across the sectors consists of those groups with the most to lose from academic failure, either by status-demotion or the dashing of hopes. Conversely, the skew in the traffic away from the lower sections of French society ensures that the full range of scholastic ability is represented in the sector where formal openness and neutrality of selection must be confirmed. Consequently, it is the selective nature of population exchange between public and non-public sectors that is crucial to their functional inter-dependence.

Interactions between Catholic and public schools have become possible because Catholic education has undergone a process of de-confessionalization, making it open to multiple points of exchange with the state system. The 'crisis in vocations' has removed most religious staff from the classrooms to be withdrawn into positions of administrative control (Bonvin, 1980: 24-29). Catholic schools offer the same curriculum as public schools. Differences in teaching resources and class-sizes have dwindled, though not disappeared. While diverse in themselves, the two sectors are far from identical in pupil management, social intake, and pupil selectivity. However, in terms of staff qualifications and programme content, there is now such overall similarity between the sectors that cries of alarm have been raised over the identity of Catholic education as a separate moral force (e.g. Vallet, 1980).

Many of the most important changes in Catholic education have come about as a result of its relationship with the state. After 1959, public authorities began to assume most of the recurrent costs of Catholic schools, but on condition that these supplied 'public education'. The curriculum had to conform or at least to 'make reference to' the programme in public schools: pupils were not to be charged tuition fees and the conduct of classes had to be secular (non-discriminatory). The Debré law enabled schools to maintain their specific character through additional activities and through effective control over their staff.

Moreover, ministerial intervention prevented the public administration from incorporating 'classes under contract' within their development plans. The budgets of the public sector and the 'contractual sector' were separate and operated on different lines, favouring independent action on the part of private school administrators. Since 1959, successive amendments to the law have increased financial benefits, enforced participatory obligations on local authorities, and freed the contract regime of residual legal powers vested in the academic rectors (Teese, 1986a). These changes, along with the laicization of teaching staff, have transformed Catholic education. Its progressive secularization in practice is reflected in the predominantly secular motives reported by parents and in the ideology of the Catholic education leadership which stresses the 'liberal', not the confessional, nature of Catholic schools.

If the functional alignment of Catholic education on academic selection in public schools results from a multiplicity of market adjustments at the local level, these exchanges themselves depend upon the juridical and administrative framework linking the suppliers of private education to the state. This raises doubts about how meaningful it is to speak of the 'non-state' sector in France. For the extent of legislation maintaining the contractual sector - primary and pre-school education, secondary education, teacher training, management training, some capital costs, loan guarantees, etc. - the provisions assuring autonomy, and the implementation of the law through a large private education authority interacting with government make it difficult to see the state merely as the 'guarantor' of private schooling, and not as a supplier. Non-public schooling is not a sector of autonomous units. Although there is a small group of independent establishments, denominational and non-denominational, most private schooling is organized by Catholic education authorities. Through its diocesan and national structures, the Church operates as a de facto intermediary between various levels of government and the individual schools contracting to the state. These administrative structures limit the real autonomy of the schools in favour of a tutelary role for the Church. But they tend, on the other hand, to protect key aspects of the 'liberal' regime which private schooling represents.

Insecurity of teaching staff, the containment of teacher unionism, and diocesan control over employment and training are examples of how the agencies through which the Church asserts its authority over Catholic schools work at the same time to clear the sector of influences inimical to the images of discipline and staff supervision. At the national level, the powerful Secrétariat-général de l'enseignement catholique (SGEC) and its specialized committees operate through legal and political action to assure the flow of funds into the contractual sector. SGEC, too, is responsible for the symbolic brokerage which provides Catholic schools and teachers with the images and slogans that differentiate their product from the 'troubled' public sector. The authority which the Catholic education bureaucracy exercises through internal statues governing relations between the various parties (teacher unions, management boards, diocesan directors, religious orders), and the power that it has accumulated through legal, technical and political expertise, have developed this apparatus into that 'vast intermediary corps' which the founder of state-aid legislation argued would be intolerable to the operation of the public school system (Goureaux and Ricot, 1975).

Yet, thanks to the roles performed by this bureaucracy (acting, as it were, on relay to the state), the liberal regime of private schools actually serves the public system. It assures the efficiency (in social as well as scholastic terms) of selection practices, cushions their effects, and protects their legitimacy. Slogans such as 'Put the state back in its place!' or 'Education à la carte!' - derived from titles of books published by conservative politicians (Saunier-Seïté, 1984; Madelin, 1984) - conceal the managed nature of the relationship between public and private schooling. The image of the école libre breaking through the prison bars erected around school by the state - a poster chosen for a major demonstration in Versailles in 1984 - could not be more profoundly misleading. The liberated consumer who declares, 'I am free, I choose my school!', correctly views freedom as the ability to manipulate the total wealth of resources represented by the dual system of schools put at his disposal by the state.

Conclusion

In our discussion of Catholic schools in France, we have focused on four main questions: the academic and social benefits produced by private schools; the origins of the demand for these benefits in the operation of public education; the consumers of private schooling; and the effects of the consumption of private education on the public sector. We have stressed that private schools in France are an administered system, not a free market sector. At the centre of our attention has been the selective and allocative role of public schooling, the dangers which its formally neutral practices pose even for its socially most advantaged clients, and the problems of its legitimacy.

Private schools help assure social selection in public establishments by making scholastic selection more efficient. They do so by relieving the classrooms of weaker pupils and thus enhancing pupil homogeneity. This improves the learning environment for children whose cultural resources have enabled them to survive selection, with the result that the academic claim on which they base their quest for social promotion is strengthened. At the same time, the outflow of 'failures' into the private sector weakens the situation for children without social advantages because it frees the curriculum of the challenge to change, which greater diversity of pupil backgrounds would impose. Because scholastic selection is reinforced, the neutrality of school as the arbitrator of fates is upheld. This partial solution to the problem of failure is politically effective, partly because it restores chances to the most influential users and partly because it compensates a wider range of clients with moral indemnities.

However, it is only a partial solution. Not only can it not be generalized, but the consumption of public resources required to sustain it - even on its present scale - limits the potential for reform within the state system. A key aim of the Savary proposals was to link public and publicly-subsidized schools operating at the same level within the same geographical area so that there could be a global improvement of parental choice across an integrated school map (Teese, in press). But this would have exposed the contractual sector to the very diversity of demand which its present freedoms of selection, pupil grouping, and specialization are proof against. Consequently, this part of the Savary plan was dropped.

If the use of private schools tends to impede educational reform, this is not only because the funds used to finance private choices are no longer available for reforms generalizable to the school community as a whole

147

(e.g. smaller classes, specialist teachers, pre-school provision). More importantly, perhaps, it is because a particular mode of access to schooling becomes established as a model solution and is substituted for policies directed at the production of scholastic failure itself. Liberating the consumer by financing more private sector places or by 'deregulating' (de-zoning) the public sector, as piloted under the Chirac government, is simply to make more visible and to intensify the transactions which public policy and school administrations have institutionalized over the last quarter of a century to protect rather than reduce scholastic selection.

Today, private sector choice in France operates to preserve or to restore relative social user advantage. While some 'refuge' schools cater for very disadvantaged groups, the origins of scholastic failure cannot be tackled simply by making private establishments available to the poor. These will continue to work within the sphere of a curriculum which is culturally selective. The relative inefficiency of the teaching process for the social groups weakest in 'cultural capital' - language mastery, educational background, and know-how (Bourdieu and Passeron, 1977) - translates the selectiveness of its content into something foreign and arbitrary to many of its would-be 'consumers'. Through space (the differential effects of pupil-mix by urban geography, the distribution of resources, the differential implantation of types of schools, teachers and programmes) and time (the institutionalization of curriculum content and selection practices), the school system undergoes a pattern of social occupation. This pre-exists and relativizes the categories of public and private by accumulating private resources within the education system and by translating these historical resources into public institutions, above all in curriculum selection. The use of private resources, and the resources of the state supplied through the private education authority represented by Catholic education in France, supports a multiplicity of individual adjustments and evasions around this pattern. At the local level, the threat to 'social logic' posed by 'school logic' can be averted (Bonvin, 1980: 103). However, this only serves to enrich the 'social logic' at work within the school system overall, for it gives additional instruments for its contemporary manipulation to those social users whose historical presence in the system is already fullest.

Acknowledgements

The author gratefully acknowledges the kind assistance of Pierre Bourdieu, Monique de Saint Martin, and François Bonvin of the Centre de Sociologie Européenne.

References

Ballion, R. (1977) L'argent et l'école, Paris: Pernoud/Stock.
—— (1982) Les consommateurs d'école, Paris: Stock/Pernoud.
Bonvin, F. (1980) Systèmes d'encadrement et demandes de familles dans l'enseignement privé. Deux collèges secondaires dans leur marché. Université Paris V, unpublished doctoral thesis.
Bourdieu, P. (1978) 'Classement, déclassement, reclassement', Actes de la Recherche en Sciences Sociales 24, 2-22.
Bourdieu, P. and Passeron, J-P. (1977) Reproduction in Education, Society and Culture, London and Beverly Hills: Sage.
Coëffic, Nicole (1987) 'Les jeunes à la sortie de l'école: poids du chomage et risque de déclassement', Formation-Emploi, 18, 13-23.
Coutty, M. (1982) '"Ils" ont choisi le privé', Autrement 42, 12-23.
Dreyfus, Evelyne (1981) Libres écoles? Enquête sur l'enseignement privé, Paris: Le Centurion.
ECD (1984) Comité national de l'enseignement catholique, Enseignement Catholique Documents (various numbers).
Goureaux, G. and Ricot, J. (1975) Autopsie de l'école catholique, Paris: CERF.
LME (1984-1987) Le Monde de l'Education (various numbers).
Langouet, G. and Léger, A. (1987) 'Parcours scolaires et transferts public-privé', Société Française 22, 42-50.
Madelin, A. (1984) Pour libérer l'école. L'enseignement à la carte, Paris: Robert Laffont.
MEN (1985) Ministère de l'education nationale, Statistiques des enseignements, 1983-84, SPRESE: Vanves.
—— (1986) Ministère de l'education nationale, Statistiques des enseignements, 1984-85, SPRESE: Vanves.
—— (1987) Ministère de l'education nationale, Repères et références statistiques sur les enseignements et la formation, édn 1987, SPRESE: Vanves.

Oeuvrard, Françoise (1979) 'Démocratisation ou élimination différée? Note sur l'évolution du recrutement sociale de l'enseignement secondaire en France entre 1958 et 1976', Actes de la Recherche en Sciences Sociales 30, 87-97.

—— (1984) 'Note sur la clientèle des établissements privés: l'origine sociale des élèves', Education et Formations 6, 32-8.

Paty, Dominique (1980) 12 Collèges en France. Enquête sur le fonctionnement des colleges public aujourd'hui, Paris: La Documentation française.

Prost, A. (1983) Les lycées et leurs études au seuil du XXI siècle, Paris: Ministère de l'education nationale, Service d'information.

Saunier-Seïté, Alice (1984) Remettre l'Etat à sa Place, Paris: Plon.

Tanguy, Lucie (1972) 'L'etat et l'école. L'école privée en France', Revue française de sociologie 13, 325-375.

Teese, R. (1986a) 'Private schools in France: evolution of a system', Comparative Education Review 30, 247-59.

—— (1986b) 'The traditional structure of the university market in Australia', The Australian Universities' Review 29 (1), 17-21.

—— (in press), 'Catholic school integration in France and the fall of the Mauroy government', History of Education Review (Spring 1989).

Vallet, O. (1980) 'L'école catholique dans la société politique française', Etudes 479-91.

Vandermeersch, E. (1982) 'A Mont-Roland, le collège de la dernière chance', Autrement 42, 75-81.

CHAPTER 7

FEDERAL REPUBLIC OF GERMANY: THE SITUATION AND DEVELOPMENT OF THE PRIVATE SCHOOL SYSTEM

Manfred Weiss and Cornelia Mattern

The general significance and function of the private school system

In the Federal Republic of Germany (FRG), private educational institutions are engaged in providing a wide range of educational services, from kindergartens to schools (with universities also included recently) to further education. The following chapter focuses upon the private school system. The execution of educational tasks in this sector by private bodies has received prominent sanction by its official regulation in Article 7 of the Federal Constitution (for further details, see pp. 168-172). This article guarantees the statutory right to establish and run private schools parallel and with equal rights to state schools, and thus represents a clear rejection on the part of the legislators of a state monopoly on schools, with the aim of creating the basis for the diversity and freedom of choice in the educational system appropriate to a liberal democracy and a pluralist society. The private schools are expected, as the private school legislature of some <u>Länder</u> (states) specifically stipulates, to enrich the state school system by providing special forms of instruction and education or to complement it by supplying forms and categories of school which are not part of the standard state repertoire (Vogel, 1984: 6).

These general functions which the legislators have allotted to private schools are supplemented by specific functions, which have actually led to private bodies taking over educational tasks. Here we would first mention the <u>compensatory</u> function of private schools. 'Private schools have always emerged in those areas where a societal need was not being satisfied by the state schools.' (Working Group

151

of Free Schools, 1984: 33). This suggests that the founding of schools based on private initiatives always signals gaps and inadequacies in the education provided by the state. It should be noted here that state education in the FRG is characterized by its tripartite structure, i.e. the co-existence of three - hierarchically ranked - types of secondary school: the Hauptschule (secondary modern school), Realschule (intermediate school), and the Gymnasien (grammar school). In some states (Länder), comprehensive schools have been established as standard institutions alongside the traditional types of secondary school. In 1986, 36 per cent of 13-year-olds attended Hauptschulen (70 per cent in 1960), 26 per cent attended Realschulen (11.3 per cent in 1960), and 28 per cent attended Gymnasien (15 per cent in 1960). Nationwide, 5 per cent were enrolled at comprehensive schools (for details, see Weiss, 1987).

In the past there was frequently an inadequate supply of public (state) secondary schools (i.e. intermediate/Realschule and grammar schools/Gymnasium), especially in rural areas, which was compensated for primarily by schools run by religious providing bodies. However, in the course of the expansion of the state school system which started in the middle of the 1960s, this function became increasingly less relevant. A further reason for the founding of private schools was inadequate state provision of girls' and, to an extent, vocational education. At the beginning of this century, a girl who aspired to a higher school education was, in effect, restricted in her choice to private educational institutions and, as late as 1921, almost half of the higher girls' schools were still in private hands (Roeder, 1979: 15). In the meantime, however, the state sector is no longer deficient in fulfilling its tasks in this area, as is strikingly shown by comparing enrolment quotas according to sex at grammar schools, which are now attended by more girls than boys.

This does not mean that the compensatory function of private schools has become obsolete; it has merely undergone a change. If in the past more emphasis was placed on making up for deficits in the supply of state education, today more stress is placed on compensating the alleged deficiencies of the 'process and output quality' of the state schools, which are often associated with anonymity, lack of stable social relationships, neglect of the broader pedagogical tasks, egalitarian mass education, erosion of academic achievement, bureaucratization, and resistance to reform.

The uniformity of the state school system is regarded as a serious defect. Private schools are therefore expected, as mentioned above, to guarantee the necessary diversity in education. This is a function which has gained in importance and will continue to do so even more in the future, when one considers that the increasing pluralism of values and diversity of lifestyles will be accompanied by a differentiation of educational demands. However, this function, which is also stressed by the legislators, has so far only been inadequately fulfilled by the private schools in the FRG. Pluralism and 'alternativity' can scarcely be called characteristic of the German private school system. For traditional reasons (as in the majority of other Western industrial nations), the church schools, which in form, structure, curriculum, and pedagogical conception largely resemble state schools, dominate, being attended by more than 80 per cent of private pupils. A fundamental reason for the lack of pluralism in the private school system in the FRG lies (as will be shown in more detail) in the procedures for authorization and the restrictive regulations for state financing.

Supporters of the private system often refer to the innovatory function of the private schools in order to justify their existence. They argue that the private school is the natural terrain for pedagogical experimentation (Heckel and Seipp, 1969: 161) and thus sets the pace for pedagogical progress, from which the state school system also benefits. This statement has a certain relevance for the independent schools founded in the wake of reformist pedagogics at the beginning of this century, and also for some newly established schools based on alternative pedagogical concepts, but for the majority of existing private schools it hardly applies (Holtappels and Rösner, 1986: 213). Richter probably gives an accurate assessment of the innovatory function of private schools when he writes:

> Even if it cannot be denied that reformist initiatives were instigated by private boarding schools, Waldorf schools, Montessori schools and, in a few cases, by private church schools, which have also enriched and improved the state school system, these are on the whole rather marginal phenomena, isolated initiatives which deserved support but hardly lent themselves to wide-scale general application.

(Richter 1984: 538)

Concepts which can be mentioned in this context are, for example, the 'epoch instruction' of the Waldorf schools, the mixed-age, self-determined learning groups of some Free Schools or the stronger emphasis in the general school system on practical learning, which derives from the tradition of the private boarding schools.

The decisive point here is the reference to the limited possibility of generalizing these initiatives. Transfer to the state-school system of pedagogical concepts which have been successful in private schools is often hampered or prevented by the absence of the necessary preconditions, e.g. a body of parents and teachers with common values and above average motivation and commitment, which is a constituent element, for example, of the pedagogical concept practised at the Waldorf schools. Some private schools with a special pedagogical character, such as the 'Free Schools', which have recently been enjoying growing popularity in the FRG (see Preuss-Lausitz and Zimmermann, 1984) justify their very raison d'être with the impracticability in the existing state-school system of the pedagogical principle applied in their schools. This means that these schools cannot legitimize their existence by claiming reformist intentions aimed at the state school system. Such intentions have always played and continue to play at best a minor role for the establishment of private schools. In view of this fact and the environmental differences between public and private schools, reforming the state-school system should not be upgraded to an existential criterion for the private school system per se.

The compensatory and innovatory functions on which we have concentrated here certainly do not do justice to the de facto pluralism of functions in the private school system in the FRG. Moreover, they only take into account the manifest functions, which are quoted in order to legitimize private schools: these need to be supplemented by their other, latent functions. In this context, critics of private schools think primarily of their relevance for the creation of an elite, for social reproduction, and the acquisition or preservation of 'social capital' (Bourdieu). However, owing to inadequate empirical evidence, it is only possible to speculate about this. All that can be said with any certainty is that, with very few exceptions, private (grammar) schools in the FRG are not the elite establishments of the English type: 'On the elitist scale they rank pari passu with the better state schools and resemble them more than they differ from them' (Mason, 1986: 7). The creation of an elite and social reproduction were tasks fulfilled in the past by the state grammar schools: since they were only open to a small circle, there was scarcely any need for private schools to take over this function. It is surprising, then, that grammar schools nevertheless still represent the quantitatively most significant type of school in private hands (see Table 7.1). One reason for this may be that, in the general educational school system, the education provided by private bodies is generally aimed at a clientele with high educational aspirations. A further explanation may also be the fact that private grammar schools have also fulfilled a major substitute function, and to an extent continue to do so, in preserving the social status of those pupils who have failed in the state system. Owing to current developments in the educational and the employment system, this substitutional function has gained even more importance. As a consequence of the interaction of a demographically determined 'explosion' in pupil numbers, with a simultaneous increase in educational aspirations, a relative devaluation of educational credentials has taken place, i.e. the conversion of 'human capital' into status and income has become considerably more difficult. The entitlements gained by successful completion of grammar school (such as eligibility for university entrance) no longer automatically guarantee preservation of status or social improvement. With the gradual shift of the selection function from the educational system to the labour market, 'social capital' (i.e. the social connections of an individual or his family) has become more important for the acquisition of attractive (status-preserving) occupational positions. There can be no doubt that the private educational system (one only needs to think of the role of the 'alumni', for example) has always had a crucial function in terms of the acquisition of social capital. Owing to the tougher competition for attractive occupational positions this function has acquired greater importance in recent years.

The private school system as reflected in the statistics

In the FRG, the non-state-school system traditionally plays a less significant role than in many other Western countries. In 1986, 5.8 per cent of pupils at general schools and 6.7 per

Private education in ten countries

Table 7.1   Pupils at private general schools according to types of school (1960-86)

Year	Total	Percentage of private school pupils in:					
		Primary schools and Hauptschulen	Special schools	Intermediate schools (Realschulen)	Grammar schools (Gymnasien)	Comprehensive schools/ Waldorf schools	Evening schools and Kollegs
1960	200,079	12.6	6.8	17.6	57.2	5.8	
1965	229,706	11.5	6.6	19.9	55.2	5.3	1.6
1970	289,782	11.9	8.5	19.0	53.0	5.1	2.6
1975	352,211	12.9	9.7	17.8	50.6	6.3	2.8
1980	417,776	12.0	10.0	19.9	48.4	7.7	1.9
1981	422,293	11.9	9.9	19.9	48.2	8.1	2.0
1982	421,504	11.7	9.8	19.7	48.1	8.7	1.9
1983	418,808	11.8	9.8	19.6	47.9	9.1	1.8
1984	412,233	11.8	9.8	19.3	47.6	9.7	1.8
1985	405,556	11.8	10.0	18.9	47.3	10.3	1.7
1986	400,703	11.7	10.1	18.6	46.5	11.3	1.8

Source: Der Bundesminster für Bildung und Wissenschaft (BMBW), 'Grund- und Strukturdaten' 1986/87, 1987/88; Statistisches Bundesamt, 'Bildung im Zahlenspiegel' 1987; own calculations.

Table 7.1 continued

Private school pupils as a percentage of total pupils in:					
Primary schools and Haupt-schulen	Special schools	Intermediate schools (Realschulen)	Grammar schools (Gymna-sien)	Compre-hensive schools/ Waldorf schools	Evening schools and Kollegs
0.5	9.5	8.2	13.4		
0.5	7.9	8.0	13.2		23.0
0.5	7.6	6.4	11.1		28.2
0.7	8.7	5.5	9.6	13.3	26.1
1.0	11.8	6.1	9.5	14.6	20.4
1.1	12.4	6.3	9.7	15.2	19.7
1.1	13.0	6.5	9.9	16.3	18.7
1.2	13.7	6.8	10.2	17.0	17.7
1.2	14.3	7.0	10.6	18.2	17.3
1.2	15.0	7.3	10.9	19.3	16.9
1.3	15.4	7.5	11.1	19.0	17.5

Table 7.2 Pupils at private vocational schools according to types of school (1960-86)

Year	Total	Percentage of private school pupils in:				
		Part-time vocational schools	Institutions for supplementary vocational training	Full-time vocational schools	Senior technical schools	Specialized technical colleges
1960	88,282	14.9		46.5		38.7
1965	101,629	15.7	3.7	41.2		39.5
1970	121,636	18.9	3.1	35.2	1.6	41.3
1975	186,471	14.3	1.4	33.1	2.4	48.8
1980	171,422	22.5	1.3	27.7	2.0	46.5
1981	181,999	22.4	1.1	26.6	1.9	47.9
1982	185,594	22.2	0.8	27.3	1.8	47.8
1983	185,446	23.4	0.7	27.1	1.7	47.1
1984	186,622	23.9	0.6	26.6	1.7	47.3
1985	188,525	23.9	0.4	25.8	1.7	48.2
1986	180,516	24.7	0.3	25.0	1.9	48.5

Source: Der Bundesminster für Bildung und Wissenschaft (BMBW), 'Grund- und Strukturdaten' 1986/87, 1987/88; Statistisches Bundesamt, 'Bildung im Zahlenspiegel' 1987; own calculations.

Table 7.2 continued

Vocational schools in total	Part-time vocational schools	Institutions for supplementary vocational training	Full-time vocational schools	Senior technical schools	Specialized technical colleges
		Private school pupils as a percentage of total pupils in:			
4.5	0.8		29.5		24.1
4.7	0.9	7.2	25.0		27.5
5.9	1.4	9.3	20.9	3.2	30.0
8.1	1.6	9.4	20.9	3.7	43.1
6.4	2.0	10.0	13.5	2.5	41.6
6.8	2.1	9.1	13.1	2.2	42.8
6.9	2.2	7.5	12.8	2.1	42.7
6.8	1.6	7.9	12.4	2.1	42.5
6.8	2.4	9.0	12.4	2.2	42.5
6.8	2.4	8.4	12.4	2.3	42.5
6.7	2.3	6.7	11.9	2.5	39.8

cent of pupils at vocational schools attended private educational institutions (see Tables 7.1 and 7.2). Almost half (46.5 per cent) of the pupils at private general schools were enrolled at grammar schools, which corresponds to a proportion of about 11 per cent of the total number of pupils educated at this type of school. The largest proportion (48.5 per cent) of pupils at vocational private schools are to be found at technical schools (Fachschulen), which at almost 40 per cent also represents a considerable proportion of the total number of pupils at this type of school. The proportion of pupils at private general schools according to Länder (states) ranged in 1986 from 3.2 per cent (Schleswig-Holstein) to 7.4 per cent (Bavaria), the proportion of pupils at private vocational schools from 2.8 per cent (Schleswig-Holstein) to 13.4 per cent (Saarland).

When compared according to providing body (see Table 7.3), the largest group of private schools turns out to be the church schools, which were attended in 1983 by more than 80 per cent of the pupils at private general schools (62.8 per cent Roman Catholic, 18.6 per cent Lutheran Protestant schools); about 10 per cent attended schools which belong to the Association of Freely Supported Schools (Verband Schulen in freier Traegershaft e.V.), 7.5 per cent were enrolled in Waldorf schools and about 1 per cent in private boarding schools (Landerziehungsheime).

As to the development of enrolments in the private sector, the statistics show an increase in the total student population attending private schools over the past two and a half decades from 2.8 per cent (1960) to 5.8 per cent (1986).

A closer look at the development of enrolments reveals some interesting insights, if we compare the state and private educational sectors since the mid-1970s - when the decline in enrolments caused by demographic factors set in (see Table 7.4). The total number of pupils sank from 12.5m in 1975 to 9.6m in 1987: this corresponds to a decrease in pupils of more than 20 per cent. The demographic reduction is even clearer when we consider the development of pupil numbers at the primary schools. Between 1972 and 1984 the number of pupils decreased by 45 per cent, dropping from 4.2m to 2.3m as a result of the drastic decline in births which started in the mid-1960s.

As regards the general educational sector, the figures show a trend in favour of the private schools (with one exception - evening schools/Kollegs), which are less affected by the demographic decline than the state schools,

Table 7.3 Private schools and pupils according to associations (1983)

Association	Institutions		Pupils	
	Abs.	%	Abs.	%
Arbeitskreis kath. freier Schulen* (Working Group of Free Catholic Schools)	1,148	59.9	310,000	62.8
Arbeitsgemeinschaft evang. Schulbuende (Working Group of Evang. School Alliance)	376	19.6	92,000	18.6
Schools in accordance with the pedagogics of R. Steiner				
Waldorfschulen	80	4.2	ca.37,000	7.5
special schools (incl. residential schools)	46	2.4	3,000	0.6
Landerziehungsheime (Country Boarding schools)	17	0.9	4,000	0.8
Verband Schulen in freier Traegerschaft e.V. (Association of Freely Supported Schools)	250	13.0	48,000	9.7
	1917	100	494,000	100

* Indications for school year 1980/1.

Source: Arbeitsgemeinschaft Freier Schulen (Ed.) (1984): Handbuch Freie Schulen. Reinbek Hamburg: Rowohlt.

where pupil numbers dropped earlier and more significantly. The 'anti-cyclical' development of enrolments at the private comprehensive schools is especially striking: this is due to the major expansion of the Waldorf schools, where enrolments have doubled since 1975.

Private education in ten countries

Table 7.4 Pupils at state and private general and vocational schools according to types of school, in indices (1975 = 100)

a)

Year	Total		Primary schools and Hauptschulen		Special schools	
	Private	State	Private	State	Private	State
1975	100	100	100	100	100	100
1980	119	90	111	78	123	87
1981	120	86	111	74	123	82
1982	120	82	109	70	121	77
1983	119	78	109	66	121	72
1984	117	73	107	62	119	68
1985	117	70	105	59	119	64
1986	114	67	103	58	119	62

b)

Year	Total		Part-time vocational schools		Institutions for supplementary vocational training	
	Private	State	Private	State	Private	State
1975	100	100	100	100	100	100
1980	92	121	144	120	84	78
1981	98	121	153	118	79	82
1982	100	121	155	116	61	77
1983	100	122	163	117	47	57
1984	100	124	167	121	42	44
1985	101	125	169	122	32	36
1986	101	124	167	120	23	34

Source: Der Bundesminster für Bildung und Wissenschaft (BMBW), 'Grund- und Strukturdaten' 1986/87, 1987/88; Statistisches Bundesamt, 'Bildung im Zahlenspiegel' 1987; own calculations.

Table 7.4 continued

Intermediate schools (Realschulen)		Grammar schools (Gymnasien)		Comprehensive schools and Waldorf schools		Evening schools and Kollegs	
Private	State	Private	State	Private	State	Private	State
100	100	100	100	100	100	100	100
133	113	114	114	146	131	81	112
134	111	114	114	156	133	84	121
133	107	114	110	167	132	80	123
131	101	113	104	173	136	74	122
127	94	110	98	182	126	73	122
122	87	108	92	190	122	71	124
119	81	105	88	206	135	72	119

Full-time vocational schools		Senior technical schools		Specialized technical schools	
Private	State	Private	State	Private	State
100	100	100	100	100	100
77	147	157	112	88	93
79	155	155	126	96	97
82	167	153	134	97	99
81	170	144	126	96	98
80	168	143	118	97	99
79	165	146	114	100	102
73	160	153	115	95	109

A global comparison of the development in pupil numbers in the vocational school system gives a picture which diverges from that of the general school system. Here the strong expansion of the state school system (partly as a reaction to the shortcomings of the 'Dual System', especially the inadequate provision of apprenticeships and training places) has led to some reductions in the private sector, especially in the vocational extension schools (Berufsaufbau-schulen). While enrolments in the public sector increased by 23 per cent between 1975 and 1985, in private schools they remained at almost the 1975 level.

What are the possible causes of the disparate developments between state and private sector in the general school system with which we will be concerned in the following section? Are they manifestations of long-term and stable changes in educational preferences or factors with only short-term effects? Representatives of the private schools tend to favour the second interpretation; for example, maintaining that demographic changes first affect the waiting lists for private schools, so that effects on pupil numbers can only be expected after a certain time-lag. At the end of the 1970s, the demand for Waldorf schools, for example, was still about three to five times as great as the capacity of these schools to accommodate that demand (Mattern, 1979: 199). Since then, the number of Waldorf schools has almost doubled. The fact that fewer new schools are now being founded suggests that a balance is gradually being reached between supply and demand. In the denominational schools, too, the demographic decrease in pupil numbers has meanwhile made itself felt, albeit to a lesser extent than in comparable state schools. On the basis of estimates made by the school-providing bodies, we can assume that these schools have experienced a decline in enrolments of about 5 per cent. A clear drop has been recorded in the number of private boarding school pupils, where there has been an overall decrease of approximately 20 per cent to 25 per cent in the past few years, so that both denominational and independent private boarding schools have in some cases been forced to close down. It is demand for those private schools which have developed their own particular (pedagogical) profile which has remained most constant.

The fact that demographic changes have not yet affected these schools and have only slightly affected other private schools suggests that it might be necessary to consider other possible interpretations for differences in the development of enrolments in the private and state school systems. If one regards this development as an indication of a general increase in interest in private education, then it would seem obvious to seek a possible explanation for this in societal changes and contemporary developments in the public educational system. To a certain extent this has already been mentioned in connection with the discussion of the functions of private schools.

The following could be listed as societal changes which may potentially influence parental decisions when choosing schools: changes in the structure of the value system, which are evident, for example, in the growing importance of 'post-material' value orientations and (in connection with this) the emergence of 'alternative' lifestyles; the general 'legitimacy crisis' of state institutions, which has also affected the state-school system, and the improved material and non-material resources of (now smaller) families, which are reflected in increased pedagogical interest and involvement on the part of the parents (pedagogisation of the family).

As far as internal developments within the educational system itself are concerned, the most important include the negative side-effects of educational expansion which have already been mentioned ('mammoth' schools, increasing proliferation of legal regulations, the loss of the broader educational dimension, etc.) and the results of the educational reform, which - for differing reasons - were a disappointment to many. Above all, the absence in the state schools of the stable values and unambiguous value orientations sought by many parents and the increasing lack of consensus as regards the educational goals of the schools (as a consequence of the greater pluralism of values) have probably influenced parental decisions in favour of private educational institutions when choosing schools. The development in enrolments suggests that those private schools which are more strongly orientated towards values related to 'self-fulfilment' (such as, for example, Waldorf schools) have benefited from this, as have to a degree the private church schools, which uphold more traditional values. The church school associations confirm that consensus between home and school on fundamental educational principles, together with parental confidence in the orientation of church schools to values which they consider important, are often of greater relevance for the choice of a denominational school than membership of a particular religion or the pedagogical concept of the school.

In a recent written survey of 2,700 parents, whose children attend private boarding schools (see Becker, 1988), 90 per cent stated that the prime reason for their choice of school was the anticipated stability of values. Other results of this survey deserve attention too, especially since there have been no parental surveys of this sort in the FRG with comparably revealing results and equally topical relevance. Almost 90 per cent of the parents questioned claim to have been dissatisfied with the state school previously attended by their child; for 50 per cent this had been due to the impersonal nature of the teaching, 44 per cent found the quality of the instruction doubtful, and 43 per cent complained about the lack of commitment of state-school teachers owing to their civil-servant status. In contrast, difficulties at school or social problems in the pupil's former school class play a far smaller role in the choice of a boarding school. Family reasons, such as inability to supervise adequately and take care of the children (due to one-parent families, or the mother's job, or external commitments) had only been of any significance in the choice of school for 28 per cent of families. Of thirty-six possible alternative reasons for the choice of school, the social background of the other pupils also ranked only in twenty-ninth position. It was even explicitly stated by 31 per cent of the parents that, for them, the exclusive nature of boarding schools (owing to the social homogeneity of the student body) had had little or no bearing on their choice of school. Furthermore, the 'mental climate' which prevails at boarding school and the internal consistency of the school character seem to be important. Finally, 80 per cent of the parents would choose a boarding school education for their child again and 87 per cent would even choose the school currently being attended once again (Becker, 1988).

The results of this survey are, however, only representative of a relatively small private school clientele (i.e. the parents of boarding school pupils). It is not possible to use them to draw similar conclusions about the motives of parents who have chosen other private schools. It is also doubtful whether such written surveys are a reliable means of detecting all the important motives for the choice of school. At times the correlation between certain developments in the state-school system and the demand for private schools is so obvious that this seems to offer a more reliable indicator for the (actual) motives for the choice of school. A particularly striking example of the problems of putting into practice state-initiated innovations, requiring the support of the majority of the population, has been provided by the comprehensive schools. A further explanation for the increased interest in a greater privatization of the educational system may possibly be that it became evident in the course of educational reform that changes in the educational system can be better achieved with less conflict by applying decentralized strategies at grass-root level (i.e. by leaving the introduction of innovation to the initiative of private groups and individuals).

There can, for example, be no question that the disagreements about reform measures, which have sometimes assumed almost the dimensions of a cultural holy war (in particular, the establishment of comprehensive schools) have triggered off a sort of flight reaction from the state school sector. Gellert and Ritter (1985: 341) quote in this context a representative of the Working Group of Free Schools: 'We can assume that everywhere where comprehensive schools are forcefully brought about by the government, there occurs a certain amount of transfer from the state schools to us.'

In order to avoid the negative consequences of the early assignment of pupils at the end of the fourth grade to one of the three types of secondary school, some Länder decided to establish a comprehensively organized 'orientation level' comprising grades 5 and 6. The proclaimed intention of the governing coalition of the Social Democratic Party and the Green Party to impose the 'orientation level' throughout the whole country gave rise to a reaction recently in Hesse, causing applications for admission to private schools to rocket. However, the result of the state elections in spring 1987, which brought to power a new Conservative/Liberal coalition between the Union of Christian Democrats and the Free Democratic Party, meant that this plan failed and numerous applications to private schools were withdrawn.

Working conditions at primary (Grundschule) and secondary modern (Hauptschule) schools have become more difficult (especially in the densely populated urban areas because of the relatively high proportion of foreign pupils) and have led to a rise in the number of applications to private schools, at which children from ethnic minorities are extremely under-represented. This can be concluded from the statistics for the city-states, where there is an above average proportion of foreign pupils: while in 1986 on average only 1.3 per cent of pupils at primary and secondary modern schools in the FRG attended private institutions, 7 per cent did so in Hamburg, 5.8 per cent in Bremen and 5 per cent in Berlin. (In 1986 almost 700,000 foreign pupils attended general schools, i.e. every tenth pupil belonged to a minority family. Nearly half of them came from Turkey.)

The legal situation and government policy towards private schools and their financing

Article 7, 4 of the Federal Constitution guarantees the right to establish and run private schools as independent institutions parallel and with equal rights to the state schools. However, in its legal capacity as the supervisory and authorizing agency for the private schools, the state has retained responsibility for the schools in order to protect the public against inadequate educational institutions. We may distinguish between 'substitute' and 'supplementary' private schools. Those private schools which are of a type which also exists in the state educational sector are defined as substitute schools. While they must correspond to the state schools in structure and goals, they are free to determine their learning objectives and contents and their teaching methods. Supplementary schools, on the other hand, do not replace any form of state school, but supplement the educational system by supplying types of school not provided for in the state school system. Thus they cover a demand only inadequately served by the state school system, if at all.

The division of private schools into substitute and supplementary schools (for details, see Figure 7.1) has manifold and far-reaching consequences, especially for the financing of the schools. Supplementary schools which have no counterpart in the public school system are not obliged to have a licence, but must give formal notice of their establishment. These schools are to be found almost exclusively in the vocational education sector. Substitute schools, however, are subject to a licensing procedure in which the authorities ensure that it is not inferior to state schools in terms of its educational aims, facilities, and staff qualifications, and that it does not promote discrimination of pupils on the basis of parental income. The constitution requires the fulfilment of additional conditions for the

Private Schools

Substitute schools	Supplementary schools
Establishment subject to state recognition (prerequisite for this is equivalence to a state school)	Establishment subject to registration only, not to recognition
Compulsory state school attendance requirements can be fulfilled	Compulsory state school attendance requirements cannot be fulfilled
Licensed to award state qualifications when approved (often)	Not licensed to award state qualifications (exceptions seldom)
Legal right to state financial aid.	No right to state financial aid.

Figure 7.1   Division of private schools into substitute and supplementary schools

establishment of private primary schools (this explains the minimal quantitative importance of this type of school). The main motive for this restriction is the interest of the state in pupils from all sectors of the population receiving a common basic education.

The state is legally obliged to officially recognize the substitute school if it meets the criterion of equivalence. This state recognition does not, however, automatically imply that substitute schools are entitled to award certificates and qualifications (e.g. the right to university entrance) like state schools. They are only entitled to do this if they are state-approved, for which the precondition is usually that private and state school should be identical. This is one of the fundamental reasons for the lack of pluralism mentioned above. As Vogel (1979: 137) states:

The aim of every substitute school must be to acquire state approval, and they do this at the price of almost total conformism with state schools. Accordingly a state approved substitute school will take care not to

169

risk its privileges by deviating too greatly in its syllabus and method.

Until a ruling of the Federal Administrative Court confirmed in 1966 the legal right of the substitute schools to state financial aid, the Länder agreed that no claims for the support of private schools from public funds could be derived from Article 7 of the Federal Constitution. Nevertheless, all the Länder eventually granted certain private educational institutions the right to financial assistance.

The reason given by the Federal Administrative Court for its decision was that the guarantee of establishment laid down in the Constitution implies a right to financial support, since the conditions for authorization in accordance with Article 7, 4 of the Constitution (equivalence, no selection of pupils on the basis of parental means, safeguarding of the economic and legal position of the teachers) can only be fulfilled with the financial support of the state. The obligation of the state to secure the existence of the substitute school system and to support it so that the requirements for state approval laid down in Article 7, 4 of the Federal Constitution can always be fulfilled, also forms the core of a ruling passed by the Federal Constitutional Court in 1987. It is important to point out that, according to a ruling of the Federal Administrative Court in 1984, the state is not legally bound either to provide complete alimentation or to safeguard the existence of a particular substitute school, but only that of the private school system.

As to the level of legal entitlement to financial aid, the Federal Administrative Court only conceded financial support for the maintenance of the schools, not for their establishment. According to this, only the recurrent school costs must be subsidized: investment costs (i.e. the cost of establishing the school) are counted as appropriate and acceptable private contributions to be borne by the providing body of a private school. The Federal Constitutional Court has also confirmed this interpretation, arguing that if the private schools were granted subsidies which covered their total costs they would be exempted from entrepreneurial risk and competition with other state and private schools. Most affected by this are the non-denominational schools which are not supported by financially well-situated providing bodies.

Detailed legal regulations for the private school system, including its financing, are to be found in the relevant laws of the individual Länder, which are according to the Federal Constitution (Article 20, 1) responsible for the educational system (for details, see Vogel, 1984). The differences in private school legislature which have resulted (for historically and politically understandable reasons) from this responsibility of the Länder are manifested in the regulations pertaining to both state approval and financing, which are sometimes incompatible with the Federal Constitution (e.g. Vogel, 1984; Eiselt, 1987). Considerable differences exist, especially with regard to the regulation of state financial assistance, such as the stipulations governing the eligibility of schools for official support, specification of the purpose for which the money is to be used, and the amount of financial assistance.

The lack of uniformity in the Länder regulations has been criticized again and again by the private schools, as have some of the financing stipulations specific to certain Länder, some of which have been made the object of suits of law. The most recent ruling of the Federal Constitutional Court has clarified and corrected, in some points, the constitutional limits of the Länder legislature, without this substantially restricting the scope of the Länder for autonomous decision-making. In this ruling, the Länder are explicitly allowed to retain their freedom to decide the form in which they will fulfil their duty to protect the substitute school system: through direct financial support or provision of staff and/or material aid. We may assume that the Länder will in future take greater advantage of the second option in view of the staff and material resources 'released' by the decrease in enrolments and the precarious budget situation: this will probably still further reinforce the alignment of the substitute schools to the state schools which is already fostered by a corresponding differentiation of the preconditions for financial assistance. Especially serious effects are anticipated from the possible deputation of state teachers to private schools.

> Precisely the private schools with their philosophical or ideological orientation have always relied on the commitment of their teachers to these ideals. If they have teachers more or less imposed upon them by the state by means of short term deputisation they will have not entirely unfounded cause to fear a change in the school climate.
> (Berkemann 1987: 400; see also Hardorp 1988)

In the case of financial support, the Federal Constitutional

Court has indeed limited the possibility of differentiation by referring to the equality clause in the Federal Constitution (Article 3, 1), ruling that when it comes to the basic allocation of aid, all substitute schools are to be treated equally. This allocation is based on a subsistence minimum which is not specified more closely; however, beyond this minimum the legislators of the Länder can differentiate as regards the type and extent of financial aid. This means that they retain scope to implement their own educational preferences and school policies.

Sources of financing

The most important sources of finance for private institutions, the quantitative significance of which may vary according to the type of school ('substitute' or 'supplementary', primary or secondary, providing body, etc.) comprise four categories: school fees; public subsidies; grants from the providing bodies; and donations. In a wider sense, services that are performed free of charge have to be added (e.g. free instruction by members of religious orders at denominational schools).

The vast majority of private schools depend on school fees. According to an investigation by one of the authors in 1985 (see Weiss, 1988), Lutheran Protestant schools with residences for pupils charge on average DM 850 per month for accommodation. The relatively high school fees for boarding schools are determined by the lack of state subsidization of school residences. Schools without residences charge either no fees or only a small amount (DM 30-50 per month). A similar system is reported for Roman Catholic schools. Catholic boarding schools charge an average monthly rate of DM 500-600. The Association of German Private Schools (non-denominational schools) quotes a monthly rate of DM 170-280 for substitute schools. The fees for private (non-denominational) boarding schools are considerably higher (DM 1,500-2,000 per month). At the Waldorf schools, the amount of school fees is fixed by the parents themselves on the basis of their financial capacity and willingness to pay. Tables of standards provide a means of orientation. In 1986, the standing contribution of parents amounted to an average of DM 176, including donations, per pupil per month.

Grants from the providing bodies of private schools are particularly important for the denominational schools. Since they usually receive state aid at the same time, these schools either charge no school fees or only a small amount. Representative figures on the support of church providing bodies are not yet available. The same applies to private donations.

Public financial aid is given in different ways (Vogel, 1984: 126ff):

(1) as regular financial aid in the form of contributions to the recurrent costs differentiated according to types of school;

(2) as subsidies (in some Länder), e.g. as old-age pensions for teachers, building costs, expenses for teaching materials;

(3) as reimbursement of school fees (in Bavaria only) and costs for student conveyance (in some Länder);

(4) as leave granted to teachers of state schools to perform educational services at private schools, partly with continued payment of wages, which is then set off against the financial aid, and partly without continued payment but with a pension contribution.

Two basic types of subsidy can be distinguished in order to assess the amount of regular state financial aid:

Deficit financing
Applicable to Bavaria, Berlin, North Rhine-Westphalia, Rheinland Palatinate and Sarrland. Here the private school must have its budgetary needs (i.e. its expenses) scrutinized and qualified by the Land for support; a certain fixed percentage of the recognized expenses is granted as a subsidy, which is usually based on the previous year's expenses of a corresponding state school. It is related to actual expenses and involves considerable administrative work and allows the relevant state authorities a great deal of scope for exercising control and influence.

Lump sum payment
Applicable to Baden-Württemberg, Bavaria, Bremen, Hamburg, Hesse, Lower Saxony, Schleswig-Holstein. Here a flat-rate fixed contribution, regardless of the actual expenses of the substitute school, determines the level of state financial aid. The assessment is guided by the staff costs for a comparable state school pupil based on the average state school class size. This flat-rate sum is not orientated to the specific financial needs of the substitute school, but the school retains complete freedom as regards the utilization of the aid.

In all, state financial aid covers about two-thirds of the

costs (including the investment costs) of the substitute schools (Mattern, 1986: 319ff). On average DM 4,578 were spent per private pupil (general and vocational schools) by the Länder in 1983. The amount per pupil ranged from DM 2,915 in Lower Saxony to DM 5,610 in Baden-Württemberg (Holtappels and Rösner, 1986: 232). In addition, there are also the varying levels of financial aid from the municipal and local authorities, which is usually granted in the form of investment aid, rent subsidies and payment of school transportation costs.

The basic principle is that the subsidies for substitute schools may never exceed the costs for comparable state schools, even if special pedagogical necessities legitimate the excess. The state school system thus represents the norm and the criterion by which financial assistance for private schools is given. In particular, criticism has been levelled at the way in which state financial aid is based on 'unit costs', which has only been possible to assess inadequately from the official statistics available (see Hardorp and Vogel, 1984: 30ff; Mattern, 1986: 310ff). However, even the most meticulous calculations of unit costs cannot prevent the amount of state financial aid granted ultimately remaining a political decision - within the legally prescribed framework. The argument continually put forward by the representatives of the private schools - that the charging of school fees necessitated by the inadequate state financial aid leads to social divisiveness (which Article 7, 4 of the Federal Constitution forbids) - does not offer a viable basis for demands for higher state subsidies. The charging of school fees is considered compatible with this ban on social segregation if the private schools grant needy pupils a reduction or exemption. Moreover, the extent of actual social segregation attributable to the financial participation of the parents is not known. The scant empirical evidence concerning the social composition of the pupil body at private schools (e.g. Lemper and Graf von Westfalen, 1982: 215) does suggest that selective inequality of opportunity based on class differences, which continues to be endemic in state grammar schools, applies even more to private grammar schools. The lower classes did benefit from the increase in educational participation at the grammar school level. However, this did not lead to a noticeable reduction in class-determined differences in participation, since the other social groups have also been able to increase their share: even now only 11 out of every 100 working-class children attend grammar school, in contrast to 40 per cent of children of white-collar workers and 50 per cent of children of civil servants (Klemm, 1987: 831). Yet a connection with the financial participation of the parents is improbable, as the private schools included in this study are church schools which generally charge little or no school fees. Thus it is necessary to consider other factors for the relatively higher social selectivity at these schools (see also Weiss, 1988).

Summary and Perspectives

In the FRG today, in tune with the 'Zeitgeist', priority is given to preserving and extending 'consumer sovereignty' in the educational system. The school is no longer considered the 'agent of society', as in the reform phase of the 1960s and 1970s, but has become the 'agent of the family'. This fundamental change in ideological attitude as regards the function of school is also manifested in the most recent court rulings (e.g. with regard to licences to establish private primary schools in the form of free schools). However, demographic changes are increasingly creating limits to the provision of a wide and varied educational supply conforming to the (more differentiated) educational preferences of the parents. The maintenance of a sufficiently differentiated state supply (in three separate school types) at the secondary level is proving increasingly difficult.

The Federal Constitutional Court has also recognized this problem. In its ruling on private school financing, it explicitly mentioned that the legislator may respond to decreases in pupil numbers at state schools and is not obliged to support the private substitute system without taking this into consideration. In future this could lead to an even more fraught relationship between politicians, the majority of whom pay at least lip-service to the ideal of securing the establishment of private schools, despite decreasing pupil numbers and school administrations being confronted with the problem of securing a differentiated supply of state secondary schools. There are already signs of a more restrictive practice as regards licensing and financing private schools. Some Länder, for example, only grant newly established schools financial aid after a certain 'probationary period', while others try to delay the licensing procedures, and thus the start of claims to financial aid, through bureaucracy and red tape. But complaints have even been heard from established private schools that the state school administration (through demands for information, stipulations and recommendations) is trying to intervene and regulate the freedom of private schools. Confronted with tight budgets and falling pupil numbers, various private schools - especially those run by parents' organizations - are using new and imaginative forms of financing in an attempt to counter increasingly restrictive financing policies, such as covenanting, pooling savings, or establishing groups to meet short-term cash-flow problems (Mattern, 1984: 84ff).

Whether the proportion of pupils will continue in the future to shift in favour of the private sector as it has done in the past 10 years depends on various factors whose relative influence is difficult to assess at the present time. For example, strategies adopted by the state schools to respond within the framework of their possibilities to the changed demographic situation will play a role. It is certain that in the competition for a shrinking clientele they will be increasingly forced to develop 'marketing strategies'. We may also assume that, in order to preserve existing numbers, the higher ranking types of secondary schools will show an increasing willingness to accept and keep pupils. In addition, the competitive position of state schools will improve with the disappearance of some of the negative side-effects of the period of educational expansion mentioned above, which were part of the reason why parents sent their children to private schools. The decreasing problems on the labour market and the normalization of the situation at the universities (dropping the numerus clausus) will probably have a similar effect. In the long term this could cause recruiting problems for private schools.

However, the private schools are also striving to expand, or at least to preserve, their share of the market. The boarding schools, for example, have been able, despite the enormous drop in the number of boarding school pupils, to maintain their overall enrolments by admitting 'extended day' pupils. In contrast to the regular day pupils, who attend the boarding schools only during the school hours, these pupils participate in the life of the boarding school until the evening, when they return to their homes. The provision of such 'extended day' places at boarding schools has met demand from pedagogically interested but employed parents who seek the advantages of a boarding school education for their children without the disadvantage of their absence from the family community at home. Private schools with a special pedagogical concept, whose 'treatment' of their pupils represents a genuine alternative to what the state schools have to offer, probably need have no fear for their existence.

References

Arbeitsgemeinschaft freier Schulen (1984) Handbuch Freie Schulen, Reinbek b. Hamburg: Rowohlt.

Becker, G. (1988) 'Elternerwartungen - Elternhoffnungen, Eine empirische Untersuchung aus deutschen Landerziehungsheimen', Neue Sammlung 4.

Berkemann, J. (1987) 'Schutzpflicht des Staates gegenüber Ersatzschulen', Recht der Jugend und des Bildungswesens, 386-402.

Eiselt, G. (1987) 'Zur Privatschulsubventionierung', Die öffentliche Verwaltung 40, (13), 557-68.

Gellert, C. and Ritter, R. (1985) 'The private school system of the Federal Republic of Germany', European Journal of Education 20 (4), 330-40.

Hardorp, B. (1988) 'Neue Masstäbe in der staatlichen Finanzhilfe für freie Schulen?', in Müller, F. (ed.) Zukunftsperspektiven freier Schulen, Berlin: Duncker und Humblot.

Hardorp, B. and Vogel, J.P. (1984) 'Wieviel kostet ein Schüler?' Schulmanagement 1, 30ff.

Heckel, H. and Seipp, P. (1969), Schulrechtskunde 4, Aufl Neuwied/Berlin: Luchterhand.

Holtappels, H.G. and Rösner, E. (1986) 'Privatschulen: Expansion auf Staatskosten?' in H.-G. Rolff, K. Klemm, and K.-J. Tillmann (eds) Jahrbuch der Schulentwicklung, 211-35 Weinheim/Basel: Beltz.

Klemm, K. (1987) 'Bildungsexpansion und ökonomische Krise', Zeitschrift für Pädagogik 6, 823-39.

Lemper, L.T. and Graf von Westphalen, R. (1982) Privatschulen im öffentlichen Schulwesen, Melle: Knoth. (Forschungsbericht 18 der Konrad-Adenauer-Stiftung.)

Mason, P. (1986) 'Patterns of independent education -factors which determine the degree of elitism; illustrated especially from Germany, Denmark and the UK', paper presented at the 1986 AERA Conference, San Francisco (unpublished manuscript).

Mattern, C. (1979) 'Zur Situation der in Verbänden organisierten privaten Schulen. Einige quantitative Aspekte', in D. Goldschmidt and P.M. Roeder (eds) Alternative Schulen?, 197-211 Stuggart: Klett-Cotta.

——— (1984) 'Private Bildungsfinanzierung und Theorie der öffentlichen Güter', Zeitschrift für erziehungs - und sozialwissenschaftliche Forschung 1, 69-94.

——— (1986) 'Schulvielfalt: Okonomisch', Recht der Jugend und des Bildungswesens 34 (3), 307-30.

Preuss-Lausitz, U. and Zimmermann, P. (1984) 'Alternativschulen und grüne Bildungspolitik', in H.-G. Rolff et al. (eds) Jahrbuch der Schulentwicklung, 204-24, Weinheim/Basel: Beltz.

Richter, I. (1984) 'Privatschulrecht', in D. Lenzen (ed.) Enzyklopädie Erziehungswissenschaft, Bd. 5., 536-9 Stuggart: Klett-Cotta.

Roeder, P.M. (1979) 'Einleitung', in D. Goldschmidt and P.M. Roeder (eds) Alternative Schulen?, 11-35, Stuggart: Klett-Cotta.

Vogel, J.P. (1979) 'Goldener Käfig oder Förderung freier Initiativen? Die staatliche Finanzhilfe für Privatschulen', in D. Goldschmidt and P.M. Roeder (eds) Alternative Schulen? 131-48, Stuggart: Kletta-Cotta.

——— (1983) 'Verfassungswille und Verfassungswirklichkeit im Privatschulrecht', Recht der Jugend und des Bildungswesens 31 (3), 170-84.

——— (1984) Das Recht der Schulen und Heime in freier Trägerschaft, Neuwied/Darmstadt: Luchterhand.

Weiss, M. (1987) Educational Expansion and Reform in the Federal Republic of Germany: Outcomes and Implications for Future Policy, Frankfurt: Deutsches Institut für Internationale Pädagogische Forschung.

——— (1988) 'Financing private schools. The West German case', in W.L. Boyd and J. G. Cibulka (eds) Private Schools and Public Policy: International Perspectives, London: Falmer Press.

CHAPTER 8

THE NETHERLANDS: BENEFITS AND COSTS OF PRIVATIZED PUBLIC SERVICES - LESSONS FROM THE DUTCH EDUCATIONAL SYSTEM

Estelle James

Historical origins of the Dutch system

The evolution of the Dutch system of primary and secondary education is unique in the western world. (The best historical summary is presented in Lijphart, 1968.) From a relatively secular public monopoly at the beginning of the nineteenth century a shift is seen to a highly pluralistic private religious-based system by the end. While secular public school systems were clearly in ascendancy in the rest of the western world, the Dutch system was moving in the opposite direction and has remained there to the present day.

At the turn of the nineteenth century, Catholics constituted a large minority (about 35 per cent) of the Dutch population. Their right to practice their religion, as well as to establish schools, had been severely restricted between the time of The Netherlands' War of Independence from Spain in the sixteenth century, and the French Revolution at the end of the eighteenth century. However, after the Napoleonic invasion, Dutch Catholics began to enjoy greater religious freedom. In 1848, the situation was further liberalized and private groups were given the right to establish their own schools - using their own revenues. The state no longer had a monopoly, but did have advantageous access to resources. Nevertheless, we begin to see the appearance of separate Catholic schools, financed by voluntary contributions and the free teaching services of monks and nuns, as soon as they became legal.

At the same time, another religious group was developing in size and political power in The Netherlands - the Dutch Reformed Church of Calvinists. These were orthodox Protestant sects that grew during the period of religious revivalism, dissatisfied with the secularism and liberalism of the Dutch Reformed Church. In addition to their purely religious functions, the Calvinists formed their own Anti-Revolutionary Party and became a potent political force. Thus, instead of one dominant and one subordinate group, by the mid-nineteenth century Dutch society was split three ways, leaving room for the formation of coalitions and new policies.

Regarding the issue of education, each group had a different 'first preference', the Dutch Reformed preferring a relatively secularized system of public education for everyone, the Calvinists preferring a public school system with a strong fundamentalist theology, and the Catholics preferring separate public and private systems, both with state support. Given the size and strength of the Catholics and liberal Protestants, however, it was clear that the Calvinists would not be able to achieve their first-best goal. Thus, they formed a political alliance with the Catholics to achieve their second-best goal: complete state subsidy of private schools, in which each group could teach its own religious philosophy. The Catholic-Calvinist coalition, with this educational programme as its major issue, now had a small majority over the Dutch Reformed-dominated Liberal Party, came to power in 1889 and successfully obtained limited state support for private schools.

Power see-sawed back and forth between the Christian and Liberal parties over the next 25 years, with state support to private schools gradually increasing but still not complete. Concomitantly, still another political group was developing - the Socialists. Thus, in the 1913 election neither the Christian nor the Liberal Parties could gain a clear majority, since the Socialists held the balance of power. This electoral crisis was resolved by a 'log-rolling' arrangement in which each group got what it wanted most, giving in on the other issues: while the Liberal Party formed the basis for the new government, the Socialists got universal manhood suffrage and the Christians got full financial parity for their private religious schools. Moreover, this principle was accepted as a long-term rather than a short-term decision, and was embodied in the new Constitution of 1917.

'Separate but equal school systems' became a central component in a society which was sharply segmented along religious lines during the first half of the twentieth century. This system is now so deeply entrenched that it is not raised as an issue even when far-reaching socio-economic changes are made in Dutch society. For example, when the (relatively modest) shift toward comprehensive secondary education occurred in 1968, the principle of separate subsidized denominational schools was not put on the agenda, and during the budget cuts of the 1980s, public and private schools and universities were treated alike. Thus, privatization is non-controversial and virtually never analysed, or even questioned, in Holland today.

Indeed, not only education, but also most other collective activities, such as health care, social services, media, political parties and trade unions, are provided separately by and for each religious group, in a process known as 'verzuiling' (columnization or pillarization) of society. Many of these activities were funded privately, often on a voluntary basis, initially; but even when financing was taken over by the state, religious-based organizations continued to provide the service. In the following pages I examine with particular care how the separation of financing from service delivery worked in the field of education.

Entrepreneurship and the supply response

Most private schools in Holland, the US, and the UK are formally non-profit organizations (i.e. organizations that are not permitted to distribute a monetary residual), therefore a major issue is: how do such organizations get started? In the absence of a profit motive, who will provide the entrepreneurship – the leadership and the venture capital for starting new enterprises or, in the case of education, new schools? Will the private sector respond rapidly to increases in demand? If government policy encourages privatization in order more fully to satisfy consumer preferences, the incentives and conditions for entry are obviously crucial. The Dutch system throws some light on how these mechanisms might work. Most notable is the key role of religious organizations in providing the entrepreneurial function – also a common observation in other countries I have studied. In this respect, the Dutch situation is the norm, rather than a special case. Religion seems to be the major source of differentiated demand for education and private non-profit supply.

The 1920 Law on Education, which implemented the 1917 Constitution, 'solved' the entry problem by enabling relatively small groups of parents to start their own schools and by requiring the government to provide almost all initial capital costs as well as ongoing current expenses. The law provided that if a specified number of parents got together in a formal non-profit organization (a 'foundation' or an 'association') and requested an elementary school with a particular religious or pedagogical philosophy, the municipality had to provide them with a building and miscellaneous inputs, while the central government would pay teacher salaries. The requisite number of parents varied by size of municipality: 125, 100, 75 or 50 for municipalities with residents of more than 100,000, 50,000-100,000, 25,000-50,000, or less than 25,000, respectively. Thus, only a minimum amount of organizational and political skills were needed to set up a private elementary school. (For the best single source on financing primary education in Holland, see van Gendt, 1979).

It is noteworthy, then, that most of this entrepreneurship came from the church; in general, unrelated groups of parents did not come together to form secular private schools nor did secular organizers unite them. Instead, the parents involved already knew each other and leadership was provided by their priest or minister. The few neutral schools that exist are concentrated in large cities and are small in number (i.e. the private primary sector in Holland is 95 per cent church-related).

In the case of secondary schools, where more capital resources are involved, the entry procedure is somewhat less automatic. Here, the Minister of Education is required to set forth an annual 'plan', which specifies that state, municipal and private schools be supported in each area for the next 3 years. Negotiation and discretion, in which each group tries to convince the Minister of the need for 'its' own school, thus play a more important role. One mechanism used by private groups in the past was to self-finance for the first few years, to demonstrate that a demand existed (obviously some financial support from the church was particularly helpful here). However, in the end, the public-private configuration at the secondary level was very much like the elementary.

Given the ease of entry, the provision of entrepreneurship by organized religion, and the provision of capital and other costs by the government, the huge supply response of private school places is not surprising. Public schools were also provided directly by municipalities. Data on the public-private responsibility for education from 1850-1980 is provided in Table 8.1, which shows the dramatic shift that occurred when government subsidies became available in 1920, at the primary and secondary levels.

Table 8.1 Public and private enrolment shares, 1850-1985

			Primary School			
Year	Total	Public	Total Private	Protestant	Catholic	Other
1850	100	77	23			
1900	100	69	31			
1910	100	62	38			
1920	100	55	45			
1930	100	38	62	25	36	2
1938	100	31	69	26	41	2
1950	100	27	73	28	43	2
1960	100	27	73	27	44	2
1970	100	28	72	27	43	2
1980	100	32	68	28	37	3
1985	100	31	69	29	36	4

			Secondary School*			
Year	Total	Public	Total Private	Protestant	Catholic	Other
1850	100	100				
1900	100	91	9			
1910	100	87	13			
1920	100	75	25			
1930	100	61	39	13	18	8
1938	100	53	47	17	22	8
1950	100	43	57	19	29	9
1960	100	35	65	22	35	7
1970	100	28	72	27	41	4
1980	100	28	72	27	39	6
1985	100	28	72	27	37	8

Sources:
1850-1960: de ontwikkeling van het onderwijs in nederlands, editie 1966, 65, 66, 119, 120, 148 The Hague: Central Bureau of Statistics.
1970-1985: Statistiek van het gewoon lager onderwijs, 1966-7, 1971-2, 1976-7, 1980-1, 1985-6, The Hague: Central Bureau of Statistics.
1970-1985: Statistiek van VWO, HAVO en MAVO, 1966-7, 1971-2, 1976-7, 1980-1, 1985-6, The Hague: Central Bureau of Statistics.
* Data shown for 1850-1960 are for grammar schools; for 1970-80 (after an educational reorganization), for general secondary schools.

How schools are financed: tied public and private budgets

One concern of many educators is that if the private school system expands, financial support for public schools might decline. For example, if a community's public school budget is determined by the median voter, and if the median voter sends a child to a private school, he or she may opt for a very low public school budget, quality level, and tax rate. In Holland this danger is avoided simply by tying private school budgets to public school budgets and by limiting their power to charge tuition. In effect, each family gets a voucher equivalent to the per capita cost in the local public school which must be spent on education (see Pocketbook of Educational Statistics, 1985: 123). In 1982 this voucher was approximately 3,600 guilders at primary level and 5,400 guilders at secondary level (roughly equivalent, at 1982 exchange rates, to about $1,200 or £900 for primary, and $1,800 or £1,350 for secondary. The school which receives the voucher is then entitled to funding that will cover specified amounts of teacher salaries and other expenses. Private schools can and do supplement this voucher by charging ancillary fees; however, this right is severely limited, as discussed below. Municipal public schools collect similar vouchers from parents, but may not charge additional fees during the 10 years (ages 6-16) of compulsory schooling.

The actual process by which private school costs are covered is more complicated and has three fundamental characteristics: the central government has most of the taxing power and pays most of the costs; a limited degree of local government discretion is allowed; and substantial restrictions are imposed on the ability of private schools to raise and spend funds as they please.

First of all, the central government pays all teacher salaries directly, both for public and private schools. These salaries are based on fixed scales that take into account education and experience. Schools are not permitted to supplement the salaries (e.g. to try to attract better teachers by paying higher salaries). The number of teachers to which a school is entitled depends on its number of students, according to a schedule which embodies a student/faculty ratio of approximately 31 : 1. Since 80 per cent to 90 per cent of all current school expenditures are for teacher salaries, this immediately places the bulk of budgetary decisions in the hands of the central government.

As noted above, the buildings for both public and private primary schools are provided by the municipality - but with reimbursement by the central government for interest plus depreciation, or for rent. There remains a small fund for operating expenses, which the school may allocate at its discretion among activities such as maintenance, cleaning, heating, libraries, and teaching aids. This sum is determined separately by each municipality, which must then give all public and private schools the same per capita amount (in 1980, usually about $200).

The financing procedure is somewhat different at the secondary level. Here, there are state as well as municipal and private schools. Once again, all teacher salaries and building costs are covered directly by the central government. In addition, municipal and private secondary general schools which are included in the Minister of Education's 3-year plan get the same discretionary fund per capita as do comparable state schools.

Private fees are only a minor source of financing. As noted above, the first 10 years of public schooling are legally free, while small fees may be charged by higher secondary schools and universities. At all age levels, however, private schools are allowed to impose their own fees - ostensibly for 'educational facilities' (e.g. libraries and swimming pools) rather than for 'education' per se. Information about private fees is not relayed to the government and is jealously guarded, so I could not secure precise data. However, parents and school authorities indicated that they ranged between $100 and $200 per year at most primary schools in 1980, slightly higher at secondary level - a very modest sum by American and British standards.

Why have the fees remained so low? Since 'education' itself is supposed to be free, many schools fear that an excessively large fee might disqualify them from receiving the large government subsidy - a risk they do not want to take. If the government subsidy were small, a larger number of schools might have opted out of the system, charging fees and retaining their autonomy. Thus, a voucher with low values may lead to a much more differentiated system than a high-valued voucher.

In addition, market competition keeps fees generally low, particularly in view of the easy entry conditions mandated by law. Even these low fees are not obligatory. In the past, in many schools, if a family could not afford the

185

fee it would usually be waived. If the school had some excess capacity, its revenue per student from the state would far exceed its marginal cost, so it was better off practising downward price discrimination and accepting the child even if the parents paid nothing. More recently, this economically motivated rationale has been reinforced by the state under a law, passed in the early 1980s, which provides that failure to pay a school fee does not constitute legally acceptable grounds for excluding a child from a private school. Other reasons why elite selective schools, opting out of the publicly-financed system and charging high fees, have not developed in The Netherlands (as they have in other countries) will be discussed later in this chapter.

Thus, from the budgetary point of view, every voter in a community is in the same school system. The voter must support the public schools at the same time as he or she supports the private school. While the Dutch system avoids the danger of a gross deterioration in the public schools, due to opting out and social choice on school budgets, this comes at the cost of restricting the ability of the private schools to make their own spending decisions and the ability of parents to spend much more than average on the education of their children. Furthermore, since this arrangement requires that the voucher be set high enough to cover almost all educational costs, the tax burden of providing a given quality of education is greater than in a system where private schools are privately financed. These are the routes to and costs of financial educational equality, which the Dutch have accepted, and which others would have to consider, in moving toward greater public funding of private schools.

Governmental regulation

A major issue when privatized education is discussed, concerns the relationship between government funding and government regulation. Does more of the former imply more of the latter? The argument here is that the subsidies create a rent whose distribution politicians can control via regulations in ways which maximize their political benefit. In the case of the educational system in Holland, there is indeed a considerable amount of both funding and regulation, consistent with (but certainly not proving) a positive correlation between the two.

The government controls could obviate some of the advantages (and disadvantages) of the private sector, which stem from its independence, flexibility and differentiated product. Both society (in choosing its system) and private schools (in choosing where they fit into the system) would then face a trade-off between more autonomy and more funds. In this trade-off, the Dutch private schools have clearly chosen the latter, so long as they can retain their specific denominational or pedagogical identity. A very small number of schools, that teach a foreign curriculum in a foreign language and serve a primarily foreign clientele (such as the American and British schools), remain independent of government funding and controls.

Significantly, many of the regulations in the Dutch system apply to inputs rather than outputs. One rationale is that inputs are easier to measure and control than outputs. In addition, this observation is consistent with the well-known hypothesis that government financing is often a response to producer as well as (or instead of) consumer interests, and the regulations are designed in large part to protect the producers.

I have already noted some of the controls over inputs. Historically, teacher costs were the first inputs to be government financed and regulated. Teacher numbers (based on student/faculty ratios) and salaries, as well as required teacher credentials, are centrally determined, as are hours and other conditions of work. We also find rigid restrictions on the school's ability to fire teachers. The building cost is also separately determined, as is the small fund from the municipality for meeting other current expenditures.

While these regulations are justified as an attempt to achieve equality, they give the private school very limited discretion to choose the preferred point on its production function. It has no incentive, for example, to economize on building costs in order to buy more books. Nor can it hire three young teachers instead of two with more seniority, even though these alternatives might cost the same. If one argument in favour of decentralization and privatization is that the schools know more about their own teaching technology than does a central government official, then the Dutch arrangement does not allow them to exploit this potential advantage, since the schools cannot freely vary their relative use of different inputs to minimize the costs of producing a given quantity and quality of education.

Direct controls over outputs also exist. All schools must

follow a uniform curriculum, which specifies the number of hours to be spent on each required subject each year. All students must take a uniform national exam at the end of elementary school, and in major subjects at the end of secondary school; these exams, which help determine admissibility to further education, serve as an important control mechanism, since all teaching must be geared to helping the student perform well. In addition, central inspectors periodically check on the activities of each school, to assure that all input and output regulations are being followed.

Controls extend, too, over the distribution of service and the criteria for selecting students. For example, as noted earlier, the government places de facto limits on the fees that schools can charge and on their right to exclude students who do not pay.

However, subject to these broad restrictions, educational institutions at all levels are permitted to teach in the manner they please. They can choose their own texts and their own teachers, including the possibility of using religion and lifestyle as a criterion for hiring. Each denomination runs its own government-financed teacher-training colleges, which are empowered to grant certification, providing the required curriculum is followed. Teachers can choose their own day-to-day classroom delivery. Certain subjects, such as history, have been taught in very different ways in different denominational schools (see, for example, Lijphart, 1968:53; Gadourek, 1961:544-7). Gadourek quotes from texts used by each of the groups on sensitive subjects such as the Reformation and the War of Independence from Spain; the contrasts are striking.

Other school characteristics have also varied by religious group. Historically, for example, Catholic schools were more likely to be single-sex rather than co-educational, and to employ a high proportion of female teachers, probably nuns. However, these differences appear to be declining, with the secularization of society. (de ontwikkeling..., 1966:69). In this connection, it is interesting to note that a recent attempt by a controversial, conservative bishop to reassert the authority of the Catholic hierarchy and to re-establish the distinctiveness of the Catholic schools in his jurisdiction led to widespread opposition from the parents and teachers involved (see numerous articles appearing in de Volkskrant and NRC Handelsblad, June and July, 1987).

Cost and efficiency

The evaluation of the Dutch system, and the desirability of providing public finance for private schools in other countries, depends partially on its efficiency. The chief benefit of the system is that it provides product variety and gives consumers a choice - thereby enabling preferences about school characteristics to be satisfied. The corresponding costs of variety and privatization depend on a number of factors, including the relative cost-effectiveness of public and private schools, the existence of scale economies, transportation costs, the expenses of regulation, and the responsiveness of the system to disequilibrium and innovation. The last four factors are dealt with at length in an earlier version of this paper (see James, 1984). Briefly, I show there that teacher costs and costs of buildings and other substantial, specialized, educational facilities in The Netherlands are probably 10 per cent to 20 per cent higher than they would be in a more monolithic efficiency-oriented system. This is the main price paid for product variety, and it is exacerbated in the present unstable, declining environment - although some mechanisms are being developed to mitigate these effects. Higher transportation expenses are also implied, but are largely taken into account by private cost-benefit calculations. Costs of regulation exist, but may not be greater than in any other publicly-funded system. Ironically, while the Dutch system encourages diversity among schools, and innovation in individual schools, it makes overall structural change very difficult to achieve, and for people who oppose the social stratification inherent in the present system this is one of its costs.

Here I compare the relative cost-effectiveness of public and private management. Small schools may be less efficient than large; however, if private management is more efficient than public, the advantage of the latter may outweigh the disadvantage of the former. Unfortunately, given the method of funding in Holland, it is difficult to make this comparison by the methods usually employed in econometric analyses. As described above, private schools are given the same government funds per capita and similar factor combinations as public schools in their own community; they spend it all, plus the small additional fee received from parents. Thus, private schools are slightly more costly than public schools, and to analyse their relative efficiency we would have to compare outputs, rather than inputs. What is the 'value added' by the two school types, controlling for any differences in the entering-student raw material? A recent analysis of longitudinal data suggests that, at the secondary level, private schools have a small edge over public schools with respect to academic achievement, although this effect only holds for certain subgroups in the population, e.g. for males more than females (see van Laarhaven et al, 1987). One problem here is that student inputs cannot be completely controlled once they are, by definition, differentiated along religious lines. For example historically, relatively few Catholics have gone to university. Is this due to a Catholic school effect or an effect stemming from the student's cultural background?

We can, however, use a more direct market-based test to examine public-private differences in school quality and efficiency in The Netherlands. Since people have a choice, we can simply observe their actions to make inferences about perceived benefits and costs. The fact that 70 per cent of all parents choose to send their children to private schools, which charge a specified fee, suggests that they believe they are getting more for their money there. Given the smallness of the fee, this cannot be interpreted as a preference for 'more' education (which may be inefficiently provided), nor as a device for socio-economic class segmentation. Instead, it appears that most parents believe that, for approximately the same cost, private schools provide a 'better' mix of school characteristics.

Part of this preference, of course, comes from religious identification, and from the desire for religious segmentation. However, since the proportion attending private schools has not declined with the increasing secularization of Dutch society, other forces must also be at work. Many people with whom I discussed this issue believe that the private schools are more personal and responsive to consumer wishes, more careful about how they spend their funds than public schools. Private schools are considered more flexible, less bureaucratic, and effectively overseen by a board of directors specifically concerned about the welfare of the school, rather than by a generalized municipal administration. An OECD study of pre-primary education in Holland suggested that private nurseries were less expensive and more efficient than public nurseries (see van Gendt, 1979:29; Tweede Interimadvies van de Interdepartementale Werkgroep Regeling, 1981). However, the full evidence on this issue is as yet unavailable.

Selectivity and elitism

One of the strongest arguments against privatization is that the rich and middle classes would vote for low-cost, low-quality public schools, thereby saving on taxes, and would send their own children to high-quality private schools. We would therefore get a segmentation of education along class lines, and perpetuation of class differentials. Has this occurred in Holland?

It is true that certain 'problem' and 'special' groups, such as the children of the guest workers from Turkey and Morocco, are heavily concentrated in the public schools (see Statistiek van het gewoon lager onderwijs, 1980:19). However, for most communities, and for the country as a whole, the entire class spectrum is represented in both the public and private sectors of the educational system. Moreover, at the elementary level, selective or exclusive schools seem rare.

Data on current class breakdowns of various schools is difficult to secure. However, some historical data is available. For example, during the 1950s in the public junior secondary schools there were 6 per cent upper-class, 51 per cent middle-class, and 43 per cent lower-class enrolments, while in the private sector these numbers were 5 per cent, 55 per cent and 40 per cent respectively. In public secondary grammar schools there were 27 per cent upper-class, 50 per cent middle-class, and 23 per cent lower-class enrolments, compared with 21 per cent, 54 per cent, and 25 per cent in the private sector. These numbers suggest a slight tendency for the upper classes to attend public schools, the middle classes private schools. However, the aggregated data does not allow us to test whether these small differences were statistically significant (see de ontwikkeling..., 1966:46).

Why has the private school system not become the elite school system, attracting the upper classes into higher quality more expensive institutions? Part of the answer lies in specific restrictions imposed by the government for schools which accept its subsidy. For example, there are longstanding regulations forbidding such schools to charge for education per se; they may charge only for 'educational facilities' and, more recently, they have not been able to exclude students for non-payment. Therefore, price

191

rationing as a method of achieving educational differentiation by class is legally limited. Neither are schools able to attract better teachers by paying them higher wages, since salary scales are determined by the central government. These kinds of rules could be replicated in other countries such as the United States and Great Britain. If we moved toward public funding of private schools we would probably find that some private schools would be willing to accept the rules together with the funds, while others would prefer to forego both and retain their autonomy. We would probably also find that, even if these rules were imposed, class segmentation would result if private schools were permitted to select their own students. Thus, we need a more fundamental explanation for the absence of elite private schools in Holland, and I believe the explanation lies in the overall structure of the educational system as well as the relationship between education and society.

In the early part of this chapter I discussed the religious basis for most private schools, which tends to make them 'inconclusive' rather than 'exclusive'. In particular, in small communities where only one primary school from each denomination may exist, it cannot be selective along class or ability lines.

Further insight is obtained if we examine the internal structure of the educational system, i.e. the high degree of 'streaming' or 'tracking' within the public as well as the private sectors and the inter-relationship between the higher and lower levels of education. Education in Holland is still characterized by a low proportion of university attendance and a streaming system which determines at an early age who will occupy those places - a system which gives an advantage to students coming from high socio-economic backgrounds and which most other European countries have gradually abandoned during the period after the Second World War.

Although the 'Mammoth Law' of 1968 brought about a more integrated secondary educational system than existed previously, it remains the case that at the age of 12 or 13, upon leaving primary school, most Dutch children make choices that determine their future access to further education. Approximately one-third (30 per cent in 1979) go into 'junior vocational training' (preparation for occupations such as agriculture, domestic service, and retail trade). The remaining 70 per cent go into secondary general education

(Pocketbook of Educational Statistics, 1985:42-3). However, a multiplicity of tracks exist at this level, including a junior secondary track known as MAVO, which primarily prepares students for senior vocational training; HAVO, which prepares them mainly for higher technical training; and VWO - the major pre-university route. Most general secondary students opt for MAVO. In 1983 only 11 per cent of students at the lower secondary stage were enrolled in VWO and only 5 per cent of all 19-year-olds were attending university (Pocketbook of Educational Statistics, 1985: 44, 52). It is true that another 9 per cent attended various technical colleges and a still larger group attended senior vocational training (which is roughly equivalent to community college in the US), so that the proportion receiving some kind of higher education is not very different from that in the US. Nevertheless, the fact remains that different secondary school tracks led to each of these higher educational institutions and occupations, with the basic choice made at a very early age.

Moreover, these choices are highly correlated with the family's socio-economic status, both historically and currently. For example, in 1954, the ratios of lower- to upper-class students enrolled in junior secondary schools, secondary grammar schools, and universities were 8:1, 1:1, and 1:5 respectively (see de ontwikkeling, 1966: 46). More recent data is somewhat less exaggerated but still consistent with this pattern.

Although the final choice of secondary-school type is made by parents, it is heavily influenced by the advice of the primary school's headmaster, which in turn depends partially on the student's score in the sixth-grade national exam. In the past, students coming from upper-class backgrounds were more likely to receive higher test scores and, for any given score, their headmaster was more likely to recommend a higher-track secondary school. However, analysis of recent data has shown that a teacher's advice no longer has a direct class bias but still has an indirect class bias, due to the higher academic achievement of middle-and upper-class students (see Vrooman and Dronkers, 1986; Faasse et al., 1987). In addition, upper-class parents are more likely to send their children to VWO, despite negative headmaster advice. The net result is a heavy bias in the class distribution of pre-university students. For example, in 1979, over half of all high-salaried employees sent their children to a school offering VWO, or VWO plus HAVO, and only 7 per cent went into junior vocational training while, for the working class, these numbers were 16 per cent and 43 per cent respectively (Pocketbook of Educational Statistics, 1981). These percentages probably have not changed greatly over the last decade.

Thus, Dutch upper class families need not look for elite private schools if they want their children to associate with other achievement-oriented students from similar backgrounds; they can accomplish the same thing simply by utilizing the highly selective pre-university track which is found in both the public and private sectors. Along similar lines, a study of science achievement in twenty-nine countries, based on data collected in the early 1970s, showed that the proportion of the variance in student performance that was explained by family background and school track was much higher in The Netherlands than in most other countries, while the proportion explained by school 'quality' variables (i.e. school inputs and organization) was among the lowest (Heyneman and Loxley, 1983).

This conclusion is further reinforced by a variety of procedures within the educational system which have the consequence of minimizing the importance of the particular school attended. As noted above, universities (even the private ones) do not select their own students. Instead, students are centrally assigned, with a lottery used in cases of excess demand, and without taking identity of secondary school into account. Elite universities have not developed, in part because academic selectivity by institution has been ruled out, and in part because they are divided along religious lines and total enrolments are not large enough to support more and less prestigious institutions within each 'pillar'. Similarly, labour market recruitment has depended more on religious networks than on old school networks (see Dronkers, 1985). Consequently, some of the economic motives that exist for attending elite private schools in other countries do not exist in the Netherlands.

In the United States and Great Britain there is concern that privatization will increase class segmentation in education. The Dutch experience suggests that this need not happen, under certain circumstances. Some of these circumstances, including restrictions on tuition and salaries, could be transferred to the American and British scenes (although many private schools would by unhappy about such a development). Other conditions could not easily be replicated, since they involve a complex set of interrelationships among the various parts of the educational system, and its broader role within society. Two such conditions are particularly important: the existence of a highly selective secondary educational system (which itself segregates along class lines at an early age); and a university system and labour market equally accessible to all those who have passed through the pre-university screening in both the public and private sectors. Privatization does not necessarily contribute to class segregation in education. However, it would be dangerous to extrapolate from the Dutch to the American or British scenes without taking this complex confluence of regulatory and broader societal factors into account.

Conclusion

In summary, I have described the Dutch system of publicly-funded private education as an alternative mode of delivering quasi-public services (i.e. services which provide private as well as collective benefits). This analysis suggests that private organizations and local governments are in competition to provide quasi-public goods. Privatization may have a comparative advantage in cases where product variety is possible, tastes are differentiated, and economies of scale are relatively small. In other words, diverse organizations may be better able than government to offer a heterogeneous product mix and enable people to make separate choices about different services, rather than tying together a bundle of public goods, as is done through local governmental provision.

In The Netherlands, where people's choices about schools, hospitals, social services, trade unions and many other 'collective' activities were traditionally church-related, the latter potential advantage was not realized. In effect, membership of a church community had many of the same economic implications as membership of a geographic community has in other systems; in other words, each person had to utilize the services offered by his (or her) group, rather than making an individual choice. However, as secul-arization proceeds, people may be able to make separate decisions about different quasi-public goods, independent of their choices about residence and religious affiliation.

Another potential advantage of private-service provision is that this often permits some reliance on voluntary payments, thereby revealing people's intensity of preferences and reducing the necessary amount of taxation and tax-induced disincentive effects. The corresponding disadvantage is the free rider problem, leading to underprovision, unless the private benefit component is very large. In the Dutch system we find little scope for this advantage or disadvantage, since most costs of both private and public schools are covered by the central government. Choice exists with respect to the philosophy of education, but only slightly with respect to funding or quality components which are dependent on funding.

I have used the Dutch system as a laboratory to invest-igate the impact of a policy favouring private schools on important educational characteristics (such as supply of schools and school places, cost efficiency, political support for school budgets, and social segmentation along religious, class, or other lines). The supply response to government funding was clearly very positive in The Netherlands, with the entry problem solved mainly by religious organizations. The cost efficiencies of the system depend largely on the existence and size of scale-economies and the relative effectiveness of public and private schools. Some scale-economies can be, and have been, realized by sharing sub-stantial specialized facilities across schools. However, current data suggest that many schools have excess capacity with respect to teacher costs and space, as a result of the privatization policy, so that substantial savings could be realized if entry and variety were reduced. Moreover, be-cause a privatized system is rather cumbersome and slow to adapt to change, these inefficiencies will probably grow in the near future as a consequence of the demographic decline.

The extensive reliance on private schools in Holland has reinforced the religious segmentation within society. If all groups prefer such segmentation, it is pareto-efficient; but a social dilemma exists if one group prefers segmentation while another group prefers integration. Then, a choice between the two policies also implies a choice about the distribution of utility between the two groups. In Holland, the separatists won a clear victory in this struggle.

The separatist-integrationist division did not, however, correspond to a class division, nor has the private school system contributed to class segmentation. This is partially because specific mechanisms, such as restrictions on tuition charges and teacher salaries, have been adopted to maintain equality and partially because class segmentation is, instead, provided by other structures within the educational system. Relatedly, the Dutch system has probably strengthened rather than weakened the political willingness to support public education, since private-school budgets are directly tied to public-school budgets and non-governmental financing sources are limited. This suggests that privatization does not necessarily contribute to elitism, perpetuation of class differences and weak public schools - but elaborate structural differences between the Dutch, American, and British educational systems and their role in society preclude easy transferability of this result.

We have seen that private schools in The Netherlands are heavily regulated by government with respect to inputs. Also, but to a lesser extent, we find regulations over output characteristics (e.g. curriculum, examinations and degree requirements) and service distribution (e.g. tuition and exclusion criteria). These are partially designed to achieve equality, but they come at the expense of the choice which the system was designed to ensure. The concern over democracy and social control has led, furthermore, to recent regulation of the decision-making structure in schools. These rules are consistent with the expectation that government financing can easily lead to government control, that there is a trade-off between more autonomy and more funds.

In my broader international study it appears that cultural heterogeneity often generates a demand for private schools to satisfy these heterogeneous tastes, and for government subsidies to help cover the costs of these privatized services. The subsidies enable the private sector to grow but they also enable the government to extract concessions in return, in the form of regulations over inputs, outputs, and other behavioural characteristics, which satisfy diverse political constituencies (James, 1987b and 1987d). Thus, the very factors that originally created the demand for a differentiated private service also set in motion forces making the private sector quasi-governmental; as the private sector grows, through governmental subsidies, it becomes more like the public sector. Any evaluation of a voucher or grant system or other moves toward privatized education in the United States or Great Britain must take this possible dynamic process into account.

Acknowledgements

This chapter is based on published material, collected

statistical data, and interviews held with numerous government officials, educators, and scholars, during a research visit to The Netherlands in 1981-2. I wish to thank all of these people, in addition to the many staff members at the Central Bureau of Statistics, who were so generous with their time. My research assistant, James Sinclair, was very helpful in assembling the tables and performing related calculations. I also appreciate the financial assistance from the Social Science Research Council and the Exxon Education Foundation for this trip and the facilities provided by the Netherlands Institute for Advanced Study during my stay in Holland. Support has been received from the National Endowment for the Humanities, the Program on Nonprofit Organizations at Yale University, the Exxon Education Foundation, The Netherlands Institute for Advanced Study, the Spencer Foundation, the US Office of Educational Research and the Research Foundation, SUNY, on broader aspects of this project. An earlier version of this paper was written while I was a Fellow at the Woodrow Wilson International Center for Scholars, Washington, D.C. This chapter is an updated version of a paper originally published in Comparative Education Review, vol. 28, 1984, 605-24. Copyright University of Chicago Press. All rights reserved. Reprinted by permission.

References

Cohn, E. (1975) The Economics of Education, Cambridge, Mass.: Ballinger.

de ontwikkeling van het onderwijs in nederland (1966) The Hague: Central Bureau of Statistics.

Department of Education and Science (1985) Statistics of Education, vol. 1, London: HMSO.

Dronkers, J. (1985) 'The recruitment of directors of the largest Dutch firms: a special case?', Research in Social Stratification and Mobility 4, 197-216.

Faasse, J.H., Bakker, B., Dronkers, J., and Shiff, H. (1987) 'The impact of educational reform: empirical evidence from two Dutch generations', Comparative Education 23, 261-77.

Gadourek, E. (1961) A Dutch Community, Groningen: Walters.

Hanushek, E. (1981) 'Throwing money at schools', Journal of Policy Analysis and Management 1, 19-41.

Heyneman, S.P. and Loxley, W.A. (1983) 'The effect of

primary school quality on academic achievement across twenty-nine high and low income countries', American Journal of Sociology 88, 1162-94.

James, E. (1984) 'Benefits and costs of privatized public services: Lessons from the Dutch educational system', Comparative Education Review, 28, 605-24.

——— (1987a) 'The public/private division of responsibility for education: an international comparison', Economics of Education Review 6,(1), 1-14.

——— (1987b) 'The nonprofit sector in comparative perspective', in W. Powell (ed.) The Nonprofit Sector: A Research Handbook, New Haven: Yale University Press.

——— (1987c) 'Public versus private provision of quasi-public goods: the case of education', Conference on Institutional Choice.

——— (1987d) Public Policies Towards Private Education, World Bank Discussion Paper no. EDT 91.

Lijphart, A. (1968) The Politics of Accommodation: Pluralism and Democracy in the Netherlands, Berkeley: University of California Press.

O'Donoghue, M. (1971) Economic Dimensions in Education, Chicago: Aldine.

Pocketbook of Educational Statistics (1981, 1985) The Hague: Central Bureau of Statistics.

Social and Cultural Report (1981) Rijwijk: Social and Cultural Planning Office.

Statistiek van het gewoon lager onderwijs (1970-1985) The Hague: Central Bureau of Statistics.

Tweede Interimadvies van de Interdepartementale Werkgroep Regeling (1981), Rijksuitkeringen Kleuter-En Lager Onderwijs (Werkgroep LONDO), The Hague: Ministry of Education.

van Gendt, R. (1979) 'Netherlands', in Educational Financing and Policy Goals for Primary Schools, vol. III, Paris: OECD, CERI.

van Laarhaven, P., Bakker, B., Dronkers, J., and Schiff, H. (1987) 'Achievement in public and private secondary education in The Netherlands', paper delivered at the International Conference on Nonprofit Organizations in the Modern Welfare State.

Voortgezet Onderwijs en verzuiling c.g. Ontzuiling in Nederland 1953-78 (1981), KASKI, rapport no. 366, The Hague.

Vrooman, J.C. and Dronkers, J. (1986) 'Changing educational attainment processes: some evidence from the Netherlands', Sociology of Education 59, 69-78.

CHAPTER 9

JAPAN: PRIVATE EDUCATION

Brian Holmes

Japanese parents are so committed to the education of their children that they are prepared to pay for it. The term 'education-mad mothers' is frequently used to describe parents who are determined that their children should receive the best possible education. The national system is consequently more nearly a mass system than that of any comparable industrial country apart from the USA. In 1985, 63.7 per cent of 5-year-olds were enrolled in kindergartens. Virtually all compulsory school age children (99.9 per cent) were attending elementary and lower secondary schools. An average of 94.1 per cent of all pupils finishing compulsory schooling were going on to upper secondary schools in that year with a slightly higher percentage of girls than boys. Over the years, the percentage of the age cohort going on to higher education has risen phenomenally from 10.1 per cent (4.6 per cent female) in 1954 to 37.6 per cent (34.5 per cent female) in 1985. In 1983, more than fifteen and a half billion yens (representing 18.7 per cent of the national budget) were spend on education. Parents make a contribution to the costs of educating their children in publicly maintained schools. Annual fees per pupil run to Y49,000 (£216) in elementary schools, Y99,000 (£436) for lower secondary schools and Y218,000 (£960) for upper secondary schools. Compared with these modest sums, fees for private schools are higher. Local authorities and the ministry provide subsidies (which might be quite generous) for each pupil to private schools.

In this mass system of national, prefectural, local, and private schools, the percentage of pupils who attend private schools varies. More than twice as many children go to private kindergartens than to public kindergartens. More than 58 per cent of kindergartens are private and enrol more than 72 per cent of the two million children attending these pre-schools. By contrast, enrolments in private-elementary, lower-secondary and special schools for the handicapped are very small, i.e. less than 1 per cent in elementary schools (0.5 per cent) and special schools (0.8 per cent). The percentage of pupils enrolled in private lower secondary schools is 2.9 per cent and 7 per cent in technical schools (1984). Private universities enrolled more than 73 per cent of the almost two million students in universities in that year. In 1983, of the 458 universities 328 were private. Between these extremes, of the 5,427 upper-secondary schools in Japan more than 23 per cent are private and 28 per cent of senior high school students attend private schools.

It would hardly be true to say that Japanese education is a private system supported by national and local schools, but there can be no doubt that after the age of compulsory attendance this becomes increasingly the case. It is unlikely that without the large number of private upper-secondary schools, junior colleges, colleges and universities, the impressive figures at these stages of education might have been difficult, if not impossible, to achieve in such a relatively short period of time.

Reasons for private education

The strength of private education in Japan lies in the extent to which, in a family-based social structure, educational success unlocks the door to worthwhile occupations, political power, and status. The ad hoc National Council on Educational Reform in Japan commented on this by stating that:

> In Japan, however, there is a tendency for the value of an individual to be evaluated not from a variety of angles, as it should be, but mainly in terms of the formal school background gained at an early stage of one's life. This tendency has caused fierce competition among people for a better educational background, and has produced a great many students who are unable to keep up with their classroom lessons.
>
> (National Council on Education Reform, First Report, June 26 1985: 21)

Competition finds expression in the 'examination hell', to which frequent reference is made in the literature about education, and was condemned not only by the Council on

Educational Reform, but also in the entrance examinations held by most employers.

Since Japan's social structure is based not on class but on family, unacceptable levels of nepotism are ameliorated by entrance examinations on which the whole future of pupils and students depend. Parents still want their children to attend the same school and university as they did. Big corporations like to recruit new employees from universities with which they have long and close ties. Once in a particular firm, employees tend to remain there, working their way up the promotion and salary ladders by virtue of length of devoted service. This traditional system is now criticized by some younger men and women, although defended by older people. The ad hoc Council recognized the situation but, in its proposals on recurrent (or life-long) education, did not advocate radical changes which would make the re-training of personnel necessary. There is no doubt that examinations are the key to personal success. Recruitment to industry and commerce from among university graduates depends much less on the skills which have been acquired or the knowledge which has been learned than on the status of the university to which, on the basis of very competitive examinations, admission has been gained. Labour market training is undertaken largely by industry and commerce.

In this system, private universities play an important role. Some national and private universities are more than 100 years old. Many others were established by upgrading existing institutions such as training colleges in 1949, and more have been created since then. Among the 458 universities, the national universities and some of the older private universities like Waseda, Keio, Doshisha, Chou, and Rikkyo enjoy the greatest prestige. Tokyo University graduates have traditionally entered government as senior civil servants or as members of parliament. Over the years, by far the single largest group of persons listed in Japan's Who's Who graduated from Tokyo National University. A long way behind are graduates from Kyoto National University and from Waseda, Keio and Chuo. The private universities have supplied leading figures in the commercial and industrial worlds. However, the present (1988) Prime Minister, N. Takeshita, is a graduate of Waseda - a distinction which faculty members of the university consider reflects much credit on an institution from which very many of they themselves graduated. The role of the top universities in Japan in producing members of the governing and non-governing elites is similar to that of the universities of Oxford and Cambridge in Great Britain. Among these top universities are private institutions, many of which have associated with them upper-secondary and sometimes lower-secondary schools. Parents want their children to get into one of these family-like systems and enter a top university at all costs.

Many upper secondary schools have close links with top universities. The private Waseda University in Tokyo has two affiliated senior high schools. Students who have successfully completed 3 years in either of these schools are admitted to the university without having to pass the highly competitive entrance examination taken (in 1988) by more than 34,000 applicants, of whom about 25 per cent were offered places. Other universities, some with a similar status to Waseda and others with much less prestige, have similar senior high schools from which graduates are granted similar admission privileges. The result is that admission to these senior high schools is very competitive. Entrance to them virtually guarantees admission to a high-status university. The many senior high schools which are part of a private high school/university organization, in which the university has less status and prestige than nearby national universities, cannot attract the same number of high-quality applicants for places.

Competition is still fierce. The private Nakamura University and its associated lower- and upper-secondary schools for boys and its senior high school for girls is a case in point. The National University of Kyushu in the same city of Fukuoka has more prestige and status. The public upper-secondary schools enjoy high reputations and prepare students to enter Kyushu University. As a result, those who run private upper-secondary schools recognize that they are likely to admit on the results of their entrance examinations less able pupils than the public high schools. Nevertheless, as many as 3,000 candidates take the entrance examination for the girls' high school (which can admit 650 pupils). It grants admission to 1,000 candidates on the confident assumption that, of these, some 350 will have passed the entrance examination to a more highly desired upper-secondary school. This pattern is repeated in some private vocationally orientated upper-secondary schools in Fukuoka. For example, the principals of the Fukuoka Minami Girls High School and the Chikushi Technical High School concede that they accept students who have failed to get into upper-secondary schools with more demanding entrance examinations. Nevertheless, both schools are very popular and possess an ethos based on service to the community which is quite remarkable.

Bunri High School, located in a new suburb on the outskirts of Tokyo, has a similar enviable number of applicants for places. Between 4,000 and 5,000 candidates take the entrance examination (out of which only 650 can be accepted). While not officially regulating the number of pupils who can be admitted, an application to increase the number of pupils in the school has to be made to the Ministry of Education. The special attention paid in this school to children who have returned to Japan after a period of education abroad means that a new scheme introduced in July 1988 allows 'returnees' to take a special entrance examination rather than, as in the past, expecting them to compete alongside pupils who have not been educated overseas. This policy is in line with a recommendation made by the Reform Council. At the moment (1988) returnees have to reach the same standard in Japanese as other candidates. It remains to be seen whether special entrance tests will affect standards.

In some parts of the country, private upper-secondary schools are becoming more popular than some of the previously outstanding public senior high schools like Hibiya. In Tokyo, socialist council policies transformed some academically very distinguished senior high schools (entrance to which was on the basis of highly competitive entrance examinations) into 'neighbourhood' schools, admission to which was on place of residence. Their popularity with 'education-mad mothers' declined and the popularity of private schools grew. The demand for private education is closely related to the success that private senior high schools have in preparing students successfully for admission to a well-known university. The fierce competition is reflected in the large number of private preparatory, or 'cram' schools (juku) and private tutors who coach pupils specifically for admission to the next stage of education. They charge high fees to prepare students for upper-secondary school and university entrance examinations. It is even reported that juku prepare children for admission to good kindergartens and private primary schools, of which there are very few indeed. These coaching activities are big business in Japan, because even those pupils who drop out of upper secondary schools before the end of the 3-year course have to take a national certificate examination if they wish to enter for university entrance examinations. It could be said, therefore, that the private sector, including juku, provides opportunties for parents to make sure that their children are able to compete successfully for status-conferring educational institutions within a mass system.

There are, of course, other reasons why parents choose to send their children to private schools. Deeply held family traditions, to which reference has been made, persuade parents that their children should go to their family's school or university. This reason for seeking admission to a particular university cannot be divorced from the reasons for seeking admission to private and public high schools. Among students in universities, top of the list of reasons given by them for attending their present university was that they had failed to get in to another university. The fact that the university had a special character and spirit came next in order of the reasons given, probably reflects the grounds on which the popularity of upper-secondary schools is based. The special ethos provided by private schools provides variety in a system in which the guidelines laid down by the Ministry of Education (Monbusho) reduces it. The Chikushi Technical High School in Dazaifu, a small town outside Fukoaka, in which a famous shrine attracts visitors from all over Japan and indeed the world, trains automobile technicians, many of whom enter Honda after passing that firm's entrance examination. The school buildings are modern and situated on a hill which commands an impressive view of the surrounding countryside. The Ministry's curriculum guidelines make it possible for students to complete thirty credit hours out of the eighty minimum required to receive a high-school diploma, in vocational subjects. Much of the work in an automated car factory is programmed by computers. In Chikushi Technical School most of the laboratories and classrooms are lavishly equipped with computers on which students learn to program sophisticated industrial robots. Such a machine was used to train young technicians. However, evidence of more traditional skills and creativeness was shown in the workshop in which roadworthy test machines enabled students to learn how to test the brakes, steering, lights, wheel bearings, transmission, tyres, chassis and overall road worthiness of used cars. Nearby this sophisticated equipment was a car assembled from parts taken from old cars whose back wheels as well as front wheels helped to steer the vehicle. Many wrecks were being repaired to high standards.

Impressive though the technical aspects of their training are, it is the spirit and ethos of Chikushi Technical High School which make it so well known and popular. The emphasis placed on the building of character is exemplified by the motto of the school: 'Perseverance, creativity, and fellowship'. Great emphasis is placed on group spirit or identity, working together for the benefit of the group, together with well-known virtues such as cheerfulness, kindness, courtesy, thoughtfulness, and gentleness. These virtues are combined with ambition, 'guts', and toughness. Major ways in which character is developed are through an emphasis on polite behaviour and through incentives given for punctuality and regular attendance. One of the difficulties identified by the Reform Council was in the high levels of absenteeism or truancy among Japanese children. Chikushi places great emphasis on the regular attendance of individuals and groups. In recent years on three occasions (1980, 1981, and 1987) no member of one class had been absent on any occasion during the school year. Prizes are given to individuals as well as to classes who are never absent. This, together with an insistence that pupils greet each other politely ('good morning', 'thank you', 'excuse me but I must be going now', and 'I'm sorry'), are examples of what is expected of all pupils.

If an assessment is to be made of the success of a school which members of the staff concede enrols many pupils whose levels of educational achievement are low, it must lie in the extent to which it develops among potential workers, group spirit, diligence, obedience, ambition, and perseverance. The technical skills, though important, contribute less to the efficiency of the automobile industry than the kind of spirit which is well developed in this well-equipped private technical school.

The ambition of the principal of the Fukuoka Minami Girls High School, who set up the school more than thirty years ago having worked with persons who had been gaoled, is to do more than provide her relatively less able girls with business skills largely through the use of computers. Her major aim is to develop their personalities in such a way that they become good mothers. The aim is traditional but it demonstrates that academic achievement is not the sole aim of some private schools in Japan. The Minami Girls High School offers something different in a well-designed and well-equipped school building which is certainly well up to the standard of most public schools.

In the Nakamura high schools, affiliated to the Nakamura University under the son of the inspired female founder, the aim is the development of character. A willingness to serve the community is exemplified by insisting that students clean their own classrooms regularly. While providing courses within Ministry regulations, great emphasis is placed on the 'moral' education of high-school pupils and college students. Character development is seen as promoted by the integration of theory, practice, and reality. The boys' high school is housed in a magnificent building in spacious grounds on the outskirts of the city. It combines on the same campus a lower- and an upper-secondary school. Opportunities for extra-curriculum activities re-enforce the special emphasis placed on 'moral' education by these private schools.

The emphasis given to all work done by students in Bunri High School, opened eight years ago in a new and affluent suburb of Tokyo, is international education. Monbusho regulations allow the school to provide three somewhat specialized courses. The balance of credit hours taken in the General Course between humanities, the social sciences and the natural sciences does not allow for specialization and a majority of pupils enrol on this course. Students on the mathematics and science course can, in the second and third years, take more credit hours in these subjects than they would in a general course. On the third course - English - students take more 'credits' in English than is expected of students on the general course. The academic aim of the school is to prepare students for admission to well-known universities, although since it is relatively new it has not yet developed close links with any one university. It hopes that some of its graduates will return to teach in the school when they have studied in a university and received a certificate to teach.

A good many special programmes emphasize the unique purpose of the school. Students from the school visit foreign countries such as Hawaii and Thailand. Exchanges are made and some students spend the summer months in private homes in Canada. In addition, Bunri High School admits several pupils who have returned with their parents to Japan after having received part of their school education overseas. Such pupils constitute a serious problem for Japanese educators, because 'returnees' find difficulty in re-entering Japanese society and its school system. Their skill in writing Japanese frequently declines when abroad. Some private schools seek to help well-placed Japanese diplomats and business people to ensure that their 'disadvantaged children' do not fail to enter the university of their choice (frequently the one attended by one of their parents).

It should be said that many private schools in Japan, like some private schools in England, were founded by far-sighted determined idealists who wished, through education, to help individuals and benefit society. Each of these schools in its own way possesses an ethos which is different from that found in the majority of public schools, whose purpose has been, since the end of the Second World War, very much geared to preparing young people for the next stage of education and a good job. Some private schools are religious foundations. The Japanese are very tolerant in religious matters and it is relatively easy for them to attend Shinto, Buddhist, and Christian ceremonies. Private Christian and Buddhist schools exist in Japan. The influence of Christians and Christian schools on the ethos of private education is probably far greater then their small numbers would suggest. Universities like Sophia and the International Christian University, which has its own affiliated high school, exemplify this longstanding tradition.

Many Japanese parents also consider that single-sex schools offer a more acceptable education for their girls than the co-educational schools, which were introduced as a result of American pressure after the Second World War to democratize Japan and its educational system. Members of the American Mission, which visited Japan during the early days of the Occupation, considered that single-sex schools placed girls at a disadvantage and they helped to persuade the Japanese authorities to include in the 1947 Fundamental Law of Education a clause stating Article 5, that 'men and women shall esteem and co-operate with each other. Co-education therefore shall be recognised in education'. It has to be said that this represents an American view of how men and women co-operate based on US history. It went very much against the deeply held view of many Japanese parents, whose attitudes on appropriate relationships between the sexes need to be seen in the context of Japanese cultural traditions which accorded women a special place in the family.

Consequently there remain in Japan many parents who would prefer their girls to attend single-sex schools. Evidence from England in terms of academic interests and achievement suggests that they are not entirely mistaken in believing that in single-sex schools girls are less likely than in co-educational schools to be relegated to the non-masculine subjects and compete among themselves success-fully on the basis of greater equality. In any case, private schools are free to offer parents, as in England, an opportunity to ensure that their children are educated in accordance with their wishes in single-sex schools. In Japan, girls dominate enrolments in private junior colleges. These institutions are regarded as part of higher education, since entrants to them have completed upper-secondary school. In two-year courses many women are trained as kindergarten and elementary school teachers. Many of them take domestic science courses in needlework, cooking, home management, and the very traditional aesthetic skills associated with flower arranging and performance of the tea ceremony.

Private schools are attractive. Another reason why they are popular is because not all is well with the public schools. The National Council on the Reform of Education in Japan reported that in view of the fierce competition to enter universities, bullying and violence in schools, juvenile deliquency, and truancy, 'parents are losing respect for and confidence in their schools and teachers' (National Council on Educational Reform, 1988: 6). Conditions in public schools may well convince parents that the discipline in a private school will contribute to the all-round development of their children. Certainly the emphasis placed on polite behaviour and service to the community suggests that private schools in Japan provide a type of education which combines respect for Japanese traditions, an acceptable ethos and an awareness that examination success is extremely important to parents and children. The decline in some of these features in public senior high schools helps to promote the demand for private education which offers something different from the normal public school and is able to conduct its affairs in a disciplined atmosphere.

In many respects, private schools in Japan exemplify the well-known comment 'Western technology, Japanese spirit' by offering technological sophistication within a conservative ethos. Minami Girls High School, Chikushi Technical High School, the Nakamura Boys High School and

Private education in ten countries

Bunri High School are all housed in very modern, extremely well equipped buildings. Computers are in evidence everywhere and are being used. The extra-curricular activities which are stressed in these schools are well catered for in vast gymnasiums and outside sporting facilities. The buildings are immaculate. Slippers have to be worn at all times inside the school and uniforms are worn. These private schools, at least exude an atmosphere of prosperity which is evidenced by the new buildings which are being erected to accommodate another level of education (e.g. a junior college at Bunri), or new activities.

Private education and family obligation

The 'spirit of Japan' finds its most authentic expression in family obligations. After the Meiji Restoration in 1868, tremendous efforts were made to create a national family inspired by National Shintoism under the divine leadership of the Emperor. Post-war changes in the position of the Emperor have modified the Japanese social structure, but distinguished Japanese sociologists maintain that it should not be analysed in terms of social class as is often done by foreign observers. Hence the kind of analysis made in Britain and the USA of the inequalities perpetuated by private education is inappropriate. Private education in Japan is a family not a social class affair. Members of the family (often grandchildren) of the men and women who founded them still own many private schools. Founder's day in private universities is linked with the scholar who set up and impressed his educational ideals on the new institution. Parents wish their children to attend the same high school and university as they attended. Even big corporations, until recently, were family concerns in which an employee had life-long security. Such corporations still recruit graduates from 'family' high schools and universities, regardless of what their new employees have studied. Once in the firm they are trained for the job. Assessment in terms of educational achievement is based on examination success rather than on the content of high school and university courses studied.

Consequently, education perpetuates family traditions and familial inequalities in status, power and wealth. However, the expansion of educational provision since 1946 and the dramatic growth in the Japanese economy make wealth a less important criterion than status and power on which to identify inequalities. These criteria are much more difficult to quantify than income but clearly private education has contributed greatly to the expansion of educational provision and opened up opportunities for individuals who previously might have been denied them.

Undoubtedly, the former Imperial Universities (now national universities) continue to attract the most able students from well known families. A majority of them are designated to become members of the political or non-governmental elites. The fact that the present (1988) Prime Minister, N. Takeshita, is a graduate of Waseda suggests that the monopoly of Tokyo University graduates on positions of political power and status is likely to be broken. It is evident that graduates from the national universities have never, in terms of Who's Who entries, dominated industry and commerce.

As changes take place in wage and salary structures (employees can no longer expect to receive annual increments throughout their working life in the same firm) and 'head hunting' by smaller expanding companies becomes more common, the previously closely knit family structures will change. It seems likely that the expansion of private education and the flexibility it introduces into the system will play a role in accelerating changes in a system in which both public and private institutions have competed success-fully to promote their graduates to positions of status, power and wealth.

Content in the school and university curriculum in Japan

The freedom of teachers in Japan to teach what they think fit is more restricted than that enjoyed by teachers in English private schools. In Japan, curriculum standards are laid down for each level of education. Among the principles stated by the Ministry of Education, Science and Culture for kindergartens are the harmonious mental and physical development of children, the building of desirable living habits and social attitudes which will foster their interest in society, nature and moral behaviour. A minimum of 220 days, each of 4 hours, constitutes the kindergarten year. The content is prescribed in a way which allows considerable flexibility. Activities related to health (twenty-seven affairs), social life (twenty-seven affairs), nature (twenty-one affairs), language (twenty-two affairs), music and rhythm (twenty-six affairs), and art and craft (seventeen affairs) are prescribed, covering altogether what are called in translation 'affairs'. These are intended to provide an educational environment in which the body and mind of children between the ages of 3 and 5 can be developed. Marginally more attention is devoted to health and social life but the programme is broadly based. Curricula in private kindergartens must follow this national pattern. It is said that in some elite private kindergartens in urban areas attention is paid to reading, writing, and some number work. This contrasts with public kindergartens in which officially no attention is paid to the development of academic skills. Nevertheless, there are private juku which help pre-school age children to enter prestigious kindergartens and private elementary schools (of which there are very few).

Curriculum standards in elementary and lower-secondary schools are laid down in the Course of Study issued by the Ministry (Mombusho), based on recommendations made by the Curriculum Council - one of the twelve permanent councils (1982) attached to the Ministry. Compulsory subjects in all six grades which constitute the elementary school are Japanese language, social studies, arithmetic, science, music, art and handicraft, and physical education. Home-making is required in the fifth and sixth grades. Private elementary schools can substitute religious education for part of the school time required in the national curriculum for 'moral' education which occupies one lesson a week. Special activities for class assemblies, club activities, and classroom guidance allow private elementary schools some freedom to introduce special activities in their programmes.

A similar pattern is laid down for lower-secondary schools. The time allocated to special activities is twice that in elementary schools, and industrial arts and elective subjects are included in a way which allows each school to organize its curriculum in the light of actual conditions in its local community and the development of the individual characteristics of its pupils. Thus, for the few private lower-secondary schools which exist, there is a measure of flexibility.

Upper secondary-school curricula are based on the Course of Study for Upper Secondary Schools which was revised in 1978 and put into effect in 1982. Certain subjects must be studied by all students following either a general or a specialized vocational course. These subjects are Japanese, modern society, mathematics, science, health and physical education, music, and (in the subject area of the arts) either music, fine arts, handicraft, or calligraphy. A minimum of eighty credit hours (thirty-five school hours of fifty minutes yields one credit) must be completed over the 3-year course to 'graduate' from high school. Students on a specialized vocational course (as at Chikusho) take not less than thirty credits in the field and girls must gain credits in home-making. Not less than one lesson a week is set aside for home-room and club activities and some of the subjects in the five main areas - Japanese, social studies, mathematics, the natural sciences, and arts - plus English (as a foreign language), are required. The national university entrance examination consists of papers in these five areas. Some courses in each area are optional and make it possible as at Bunri High School for specialized programmes to be established within the 134 standard 'credits' authorized by the Ministry of Education, Science and Culture. Private schools similar to those referred to earlier take advantage of these regulations to offer special high school programmes.

Private universities work within the national system in which a 4-year course leads to a bachelor's degree. A minimum of 124 credits must be completed if a student is to obtain a degree. Private universities frequently expect students to take more than the minimum number of credits and are free to adjust courses to meet the Ministry's requirements if teachers in training are to obtain a teaching certificate and their own academic principles. Most universities are required to offer thirty-five credits of general education, including credits in the natural sciences, the social sciences, and humanities. A recently established national university - Tsuba - has been allowed to grant to its undergraduates a free choice of subjects to be studied.

Since 1949, when a number of institutions were upgraded to universities, many new universities have been established. Many of them are private and are run in the light of principles which are somewhat different from those on which traditional universities operate. Dokkyo University on the outskirts of Tokyo is such an institution. It was founded in 1964 by a renowned scholar of German philosophy. He envisioned his university as 'the place for the development of personalities through studies'. It has several campuses and concentrates in its various faculties on the promotion of an international perspective. Special attention is given to foreign language studies and in economics on relationships between computers and society. Foreign nationals and Japanese students returning from abroad are able to take special admission tests. Dokkyo's entrance examination system allows 'returnees' to take examinations in Japanese as a foreign language, Japanese composition, and an interview in Japanese. Many returnees have entered the university under this scheme. All students, no matter what their major field of study, are required not only to gain practical ability in foreign languages but also to develop a philosophy of their own through the study of the liberal arts. The campus in the city of Soka is spacious. Its buildings are elegant and superbly equipped with the newest technology. Its unique humanistic curriculum is widely known and respected.

Kanagawa University was founded in 1928 and became a university in 1949. It is committed to the ideals of international community and to an education combining the best aspects of the old and the new. It prepares young men and women for a world in which they will strive to create a prosperous, peaceful, and happy world by demanding the highest academic standards. It has an extensive campus on which laboratories, library, gymnasium, university hall and other facilities are modern and lavishly equipped. It has basketball courts, a boxing gym, a swimming pool, and baseball and athletic facilities. Its library holds 620,000 volumes and seats over 1,100 readers in beautifully designed reading rooms, each with its own colour scheme to prevent large-scale monotony. On the campus are several research institutes, a graduate division, and a very well equipped information processing centre. As well as a programme of international exchanges with the Republic of China and Aston University in England, it has a long established University Night School which meets the needs of young working men and women who wish to gain higher education awards. It offers degrees in the same range of departments as can be obtained in the regular 4-year course.

These two universities are examples of the many private universities which, while not having the same prestige as Waseda, Keio, Chuo, Doshiba and Rikkyo, nevertheless serve the various needs of people who place education high on their list of priorities.

Teachers

Many private schools are 'family' affairs. Well-known names are associated with the founding of many of the famous private universities and their affiliated high schools. Since 1945, many schools and universities have been established by idealists whose children and grandchildren continue the tradition by taking an active part in running the institution. Reitaku University and the closely associated Institute of Moralogy is an excellent example of a private educational foundation which had its origins in the work of Chikuro Hiroike who, through a detailed study of the writings of the great religious leaders and philosophers, like Christ, Buddha, Confucius and Mohammad, induced some general moral principles wich form the basis of a world-wide system of morals. The Institute of Moralogy is devoted (under the father's grandson) to the scientific study of morals - moralogy - and the development of international under-standing. The university itself is small and offers foreign language courses. The Institute of Moralogy, however, has associations throughout the country to which many members belong. They hold conferences and meetings at the place where Hiroike did much of this work in the peaceful Japanese countryside. In the absence of a major unifying religion and with the rejection of the divinity of the Emperor after the Second World War many Japanese educators are extremely interested in the moral bases of education and their work finds expression in many private schools.

In general, teachers in private schools do not differ greatly from those in public schools. All teachers must possess a certificate issued by the prefecture in order to teach in either a public or private school. Certificates are level and subject specific. Teachers are awarded certificates to teach either in elementary, lower-secondary, or upper-secondary schools. The subjects they are allowed to teach are stated on their certificates which, although issued by a prefecture, are valid throughout the country. In this respect, private-school teachers are fully qualified members of a group of people who, in spite of the statement made in the Reform Council's Report, still appear to command a great deal of respect. 'Sensei' - teacher - is still used to describe a person with a high status.

Salaries vary somewhat. In one school, the vice principal said that in his private school, teachers' salaries were somewhat higher than those of teachers in public school. Private school teachers enjoy other advantages. They appreciate the greater freedom they have in a private school and welcome the possibility of staying in one school for as long as they wish. Teachers in public schools can be, and are, moved from school to school by the administration. Consequently, private school teaching staffs are likely to be very stable and made up of devoted teachers whose ideals go beyond simply preparing pupils for competitive examinations.

Retirement ages seem to vary in universities. It is obvious, however, that many public servants after retiring from their jobs in public universities or schools take up important posts in the private sector. Many professors in the national universities become presidents of private universities after retirement. They bring to the leadership of these institutions, knowledge of the standards of scholarship expected in the national universities which are very high, although variable, as in most countries. Since university academics once appointed enjoy security of tenure, self motivation determines how much work they do beyond the minimum. In a similar way teachers who have served in the public sector may well, on retirement, be invited to join a private school and are able to bring a wealth of experience to the management of an institution which might well wish to preserve a special ethos associated with its founder.

The constraints on teachers in private schools are not vastly different from those which operate in the public sector of education. The greatest of these constraints is the emphasis placed on examinations within the system and at the point of entry to the labour market. In this respect the Japanese system differs from other universal systems of education only in the intensity of the competition which informs it. Teachers in private schools seem well able to accept and cope with this competition. It would be unwise to draw very sharp distinctions between the two sets of teachers but some of the most imaginative and creative teachers in the system are undoubtedly to be found in prestige private universities and upper-secondary schools.

Usually the attention of foreign observers is concentrated on the national universities and the public schools whose achievements are considerable. Private education in Japan provides alternatives for which teachers are responsible. The prestige and status of many private institutions make them leaders in an endeavour which has the support of the parents of Japan.

References

Asian Cultural Centre for UNESCO (1987) Outline of Education in Japan 1987, Tokyo: Ministry of Education, Science and Culture.

Dore, R. (1973) British Factory - Japanese Factory, London: Allen and Unwin.

Duke, B. (1973) Japan's Militant Teachers, Honolulu: University Press of Hawaii.

International Society for Educational Information (1986) The Life of a Senior High School Student, Tokyo: ISEI.

Japan Association of Private Colleges and Universities (1987) Japan's Private Colleges and Universities, Tokyo: Japan Association of Private Colleges and Universities.

Ministry of Education, Science and Culture (1982) Education in Japan 1982, Tokyo: Research and Statistics Division, Ministry of Education, Science and Culture.

Monbusho, A. (1986) Education in Japan, A Brief Outline, Tokyo: Ministry of Education, Science and Culture.

Nakane, C. (1984) Japanese Society, Harmondsworth: Penguin.

National Council on Educational Reform (1985) First Report, Tokyo: Government of Japan.

—— (1988) Reports on Educational Reform, Tokyo: Government of Japan.

National Institute for Educational Research in Japan (1986) New Upper School Education in Japan, NIER Occasional Paper 02/86, Tokyo: NIER.

Rohlen, T.P. (1983) Japan's High Schools, Los Angeles: University of California Press.

White, M. (1987) The Japanese Educational Challenge, New York: Free Press.

CONCLUSION

Geoffrey Walford

In this book the extent and nature of private schooling in ten industrial countries has been described. The accounts that have been provided make it immediately obvious that there is considerable diversity in the ways in which different societies finance and provide education for those of compulsory school age. The most obvious difference is in the size of the private sector in relation to the state sector where, in the countries discussed in this book, the range is from 4 per cent in Scotland (less than 3 per cent in Wales) to about 70 per cent in The Netherlands. Such an enormous variation in the proportion of private-sector schools makes it clear that there is nothing inevitable about the nature of the organizational structure which any particular society has chosen. The current temporary balance between the different forms of provision is the result of a series of historical compromises, achieved over the last century or more, between the state and the various other secular and religious providers. The balance is subject to modification as the result of changing social, economic, and political pressures.

The various chapters of this book illustrate that the balance achieved within any particular country can only be understood through a consideration of the history of that educational system. The most important element is usually the way in which the religious schools developed in relation to the state sector. In England and Wales, for example, most of the Catholic and Church of England schools were integrated into the state system in 1945. They became voluntary-aided or assisted schools, where recurrent costs are fully covered by the state and, although they are still officially owned by the church and controlled by semi-independent governing bodies, there are very tight regulations and restrictions on what those schools and governors can do. The result is that the private sector which remained after 1945 was small, and parents now tend to choose the private sector because of its associations with privilege and elitism, rather than for any religious emphasis.

In contrast, in the United States, the constitution ensures a separation of church and state and the religious schools have remained outside the state sector. Most private schools thus have religious origins and affiliations, and about 12 per cent of the school population is in private education. Included within this total is a small elite school group which has a somewhat similar function to the British public (i.e. elite private) schools. It is important to note that, even though there is a constitutional guarantee of separation in the United States, most of the church and private schools do, in fact, receive financial aid from the government. Those schools which are organized on a non-profit basis pay few taxes of any sort, and are also able to receive financial gifts from individuals and other charitable trusts without payment of tax on transfer. In some states, the main example being Minnesota, tax deductions are even available for personal educational expenditure whether that be in relation to state or private schools.

State support for private schools is, in fact, one of the aspects which the countries considered in this book have in common. In all of them, the government gives either direct or indirect financial support to the private schools, but the degree of support differs markedly. However, one of the most notable general trends to be seen in these countries is that, over the last few years, there has been a gradual increase in the proportion of pupils attending private schools and, at the same time, a growth in the level of support from government to the private sector.

The growth in the proportion of pupils in private schools is part of a much larger movement towards the privatization of welfare services that has occurred in many of these countries. Various governments have gradually privatized many industries and services formerly in state ownership, state provision of welfare has been less well funded than previously, and there has been a shift towards private provision. The growth of private health care and private pensions are just two examples of the trend. This belief in the logic of free-market capitalism has been extended to education, where it has become much more generally acceptable to advance the ideas of choice and consumer sovereignty, moderated only by the ability to pay. In several countries, the growth in government support for private schools has led, rather than followed, the growth in student numbers. Government finance has been channelled towards the private schools and has made it easier for parents to choose private provision.

Where the level of support is already high, of course, there is less possibility for increase. The Netherlands provides a good example of a contrast to the United States or Great Britain. In The Netherlands, the state first gave direct financial support to private schools in 1889. Full financial parity for state and private schools was achieved as a result of compromise between the various political and religious parties, and was incorporated into the 1917 Constitution. Since 1920, relatively small groups of parents have been able to start their own schools, with the government providing almost all of the capital costs and all of the recurrent expenditure. Various religious groups, or groups with particular educational or social beliefs, have thus been able to establish their own schools, such that about 70 per cent of pupils are now in private schools. What is of particular interest about private schools in The Netherlands is that the degree of freedom which the schools have to act independently is severely curtailed. In return for full financial support from government, the private schools are subject to a high degree of regulation. For example, the government pays salaries directly to all teachers, whether they are in public or private schools, and private schools are not allowed to supplement them. Neither are they able to pay for additional teachers, for their numbers are set by government according to a set staff/pupil ratio. The first 10 years of schooling are legally free, so private schools are only able to charge fees for 'educational facilities'. Even these fees are not obligatory, and the schools must keep them small or risk losing their right to funding from the state.

The Dutch case illustrates that there is no necessary connection between the existence of private schools and elitism. With the small 'facilities fees' now legally optional, no child can be excluded from a private school for lack of ability to pay. In return for financial support equal to that of the state schools, the private schools are heavily regulated and their freedom of action is greatly proscribed, including being open to scrutiny by state inspectors and having to follow a set core curriculum for practically all of the school day. This means that, although on the whole state schools are less highly esteemed than private schools, in terms of curriculum and facilities, there is little real difference between them. There are no elite schools where facilities and teaching provision are vastly superior to the majority of state schools and where access is dependent upon ability to pay. Some would argue that this means that the possibility of 'superior schools', which by definition can only be available for some, has been sacrificed in order to provide a more egalitarian system for all. The Dutch would argue that their system ensures high quality schooling for all rather than just for some, and regulation has been designed to promote equality within a limited diversity of schooling provision. Private schools thrive, but they are less differentiated, less flexible and have less autonomy than in most other countries.

This does not mean, however, that The Netherlands has an egalitarian system. There is a high degree of streaming within both the private and state sectors and, after primary school, choices are made which allocate children to one of four main tracks. Only one of these is seen as a clear route to university and thus to the highly paid and prestigious occupations which require a degree. These choices are heavily influenced by parental social class. Affluent Dutch parents have no need to establish a separate elite private system of schools, since the selectivity which operates within the combined state-financed system has already ensured that their children are likely to have privileged access to higher education and the advantages which that bestows.

Australia provides an interesting case-study of an educational system with a more varied private sector. The Australian private sector is dominated by the Catholic schools (which educate some 18 per cent of the school population), but there is also an elite sector of schools providing for about 6 per cent, and a growing number of schools run by evangelical sects and other minority groups. Here, as in several other countries, the public funding of private schools has been a major political issue. By 1969, class sizes in Catholic schools were far higher than in public schools and the financial burden on the church was becoming overwhelming. The government was forced to act to support a private system on the verge of collapse, and, rather than just target the Catholic schools, authorized funding to be given to all non-government schools. The most recent

221

changes are such that private schools are allocated funding from the Commonwealth according to a twelve-category assessment of need. The elite schools receive a small grant, while substantial help is given to the poorest schools. Additional finance is provided by the individual states. The elite schools have thus been able to benefit from an alliance with the poorer Catholic schools and present themselves as part of a wider, and quite diverse, private sector. Concerns about inequality were originally masked within general support for the private sector and only fairly recently has the system been reorganized to make support more selective.

Throughout the whole of the Australian private sector, although financial support is high (amounting to about 55 per cent on average), the degree of accountability and regulation is relatively low, even though it may not always be perceived in this way by the schools. In practice, private schools still have high autonomy. In particular, they can choose students as they wish, such that the elite schools are selective both socially and academically. This is a rather strange position for a Labour government to support, even one as pragmatic as the present Australian government, and there is a growing interest in extending the accountability of the schools and the degree of regulation under which they operate.

In these ten industrial countries it has been shown that not only is there considerable variation in the size of the private sector, but also that there are major differences in the degree to which the private sector is regulated by the state. In terms of the extent to which particular schools act to reproduce patterns of inequality and privilege in a society, it can be seen that it is the degree of government regulation which is important rather than whether or not the particular schools are private or public. For example, it is quite possible to have a mixed system of private and public provision, both financed by the state, where the private schools do not necessarily have better facilities or are not more likely to lead to academic and occupational success. In this respect, a focus of debate on private schools in isolation might be regarded as misdirected. In many educational systems there are ways by which specific state schools are able to perform a similar function to elite private schools, and to concentrate attention on the private schools obscures the importance of somewhat similar schools within the state sector. For example, where parents are able to give voluntary gifts to individual state schools, which over the years lead to substantial differences in facilities and support staff, the house prices near those schools rise above the general level. Affluent parents are thus able to 'buy' a place at a well-supported state school by taking up residence within the school's catchment area. These schools can be more socially and academically exclusive than some private schools, being largely homogeneous in terms of class and ethnic group. Similar inequalities can occur where there is selection for different types of school or strict streaming within single schools, as middle class parents are generally better able to negotiate these decision-making points, such that their children benefit disproportionately.

In terms of equity and social mixing, the extent of the private sector, and the degree to which the state supports the private sector, are of only partial importance. A larger private sector could be more egalitarian than a smaller one. Greater government funding without any change in regulation would lead to greater inequality and social class differentiation, but greater support linked to tighter regulation could have the opposite effect.

However, while the introduction of increased regulation is logically possible, policy-makers do not have a free hand. They are tied by the political, economic and social relationships and understandings that have developed historically. Further, it is evident that solutions to problems developed in one country are not necessarily directly transferable to another. All of the countries considered in this book have a mixed educational system of private and public schools, with the private schools being supported either directly or indirectly by the state to differing degrees. If a society wishes education to become more egalitarian it is necessary to make changes in both forms of provision - one cannot be changed without the other - since concentrating attention on private provision alone may mean that more important sources of inequality within the state sector are ignored.

INDEX

Index